PLASTIC-BODIED LOCOS
TIM SHACKLETON

CONTENTS

WILD SWAN PUBLICATIONS LTD.

BACKGROUND READING

This list is far from definitive, but it does faithfully record the major sources that I drew on in building the engines featured in this book.

4F

R J Essery and D Jenkinson, *An Illustrated Review of Midland Locomotives,* Vol. 4 (Wild Swan 1989). Excellent — but stops short of the LMS-built engines.

R J Essery, 'The Class 4s in their final condition' in *Midland Record* No. 2 (1995) pp69–80. Continues the story into LMS days, with GA drawing and detail photos.

R J Essery and G Toms, 'The Midland Big Goods and LMS Standard Class 4Fs' in *British Railway Journal* No. 19 (1987) pp428–35. Handy general resumé.

County

R Guy Williams, *The 4mm Engine: A Scratchbuilder's Guide* (Wild Swan 1988). Step-by-step guide to building a Hall — with much that is directly relevant to a County.

John Hayes, 'A 4mm Hall' in *Model Railway Journal* No. 55 (1991). A wealth of constructive ideas.

J S Whiteley and G W Morrison (eds), *The Great Western Remembered* (OPC 1985). Five pages of useful photographs.

R Guy Williams, *More 4mm Engines* (Wild Swan 1988). Too late for me, but his scratchbuilt County will be an inspiration to many. Includes GA drawing.

Terrier

Tom Middlemass, *Stroudley and His Terriers* (Pendragon 1995). Highly desirable — large, clear photographs of all the Terriers at every stage of their careers.

C Hamilton Ellis, *The London, Brighton and South Coast Railway* (Ian Allan 1960). As entertaining (and informative) as ever.

Gordon Gravett, 'Brighton Works' in *Model Railway Journal* No. 63 (1993) pp139–47. The construction of a 7mm masterpiece, with many details to copy and ideas to steal, plus GA drawing (but no prototype pictures).

B1

Locomotives of the LNER Part 2B, Tender engines B1 to B17. The definitive factual guide.

P W Swinger, *The Power of the B1s* (OPC 1988). Lots of pictures but not too clever on fine detail.

Chris Pendlenton, 'Hal O'The Wynd' in *Model Railway Journal* Nos 28/9 (1989). This legendary A1

influenced Dave Bradwell's B1 chassis design and these articles present a very useful background to its mechanical rationale.

Bulleid

Tony Fairclough and Alan Wills (eds), *Southern Steam Locomotive Survey: Bulleid Light Pacifics* (Bradford Barton nd). Knowledgeable and informative.

Stanley Creer and Brian Morrison *The Power of the Bulleid Pacifics* (OPC 1983). Illustrates most of the permutations.

Chris Pendlenton 'Hal O'The Wynd' in *Model Railway Journal* Nos 28/9 (1989). The application of Dyna Drive to model steam locomotives.

9F

Locomotives Illustrated No. 75 (Ian Allan 1991). Concise general survey.

John Scott Morgan, *The 9Fs: BR's Heavy Freight Lomotives* (Ian Allan 1994). Weak on points of detail; primarily useful as a guide to weathering ideas.

G Weekes (ed), *BR Standard Class 9F* (Bradford Barton 1975). Big close-up pictures of details the others miss. Excellent.

© Wild Swan Publications Ltd. & Tim Shackleton 1999

ISBN 1 874103 52 6

Designed by Paul Karau

Printed by Amadeus Press, Huddersfield

FOR IAIN who showed the way

34043

Published by

WILD SWAN PUBLICATIONS LTD.

1-3 Hagbourne Road, Didcot, Oxon, OX11 8DP

INTRODUCTION

A very well-known and highly regarded modeller was poking around my workroom not so very long ago, looking at the various bits and bobs that, as usual, littered every available surface. The shelves around my workbench were host, among other things, to an Impetus industrial still in bare brass, an almost complete AC Cars railbus made from an indifferent whitemetal kit, and a newly finished Gibson J15.

Each locomotive was studied intently. Perceptive and very knowledgeable comments were made, a murmur of approval here, a gentle word of criticism there. I sat at my desk and was reminded of the sixth form, as the week's essays were handed back.

Finally, the magisterial eye fell on a BR Standard 2–6–2T, painted black but not yet lined and lettered and looking, I felt, still very raw. He studied it for quite some while, then nodded. He ran his finger affectionately along the line of the boiler.

"You can't beat the old Kemilway kit, can you?" he said. "I don't think DJH quite got it right, somehow."

I'd been waiting for someone to make a remark like that for ten years and more.

"Actually it's the old Triang model," I said, as calmly and nonchalantly as I could.

The reaction was wonderful, a real kneejerker of a doubletake. Not believing what I'd just told him, my visitor took the body off — it was only fitted loosely to the chassis — and looked inside. There, for all the world to see, was the evidence of the cuts and joins by which I had condensed an overscale plastic toy into a dimensionally accurate replica that I was extremely pleased with, sitting on a reworked chassis taken from something else entirely.

"What about the tanks and cab sides?" he said.

"Overlays of five-thou plastic," I said. "It's easy to do the rivets."

"How d'you do the chimney and things?" I don't have a lathe, you see.

"A few bought-in bits. The plumbing's from fuse wire, mostly. Even with the wheels, the whole lot cost about £30."

"Hmmm," he said and then, suitably chastened, had a go at me for not getting the smokebox door on the J15 quite right.

Quite a lot of my model locomotives began life in this fashion as RTR mouldings, although they may no longer be recognisable as such. One thing that has struck me is that, while quite a bit of the stock on display in the magazines and on exhibition layouts seems also to have its origins in RTR models, there's not much evidence that people have worked on their locomotives much beyond changing the handrail knobs for something more plausible and giving the loco a coat of overall grime. Even in EM and P4, where something obviously has to be done about the running gear, six-inch-thick plastic cabsides are still the norm up top, even though the 'works' down below may be state-of-the-art Portescap and Ultrascale.

I find this state of affairs rather surprising, since there have been many, many magazine articles and several books on upgrading RTR locos. I've learned a lot from them. I've even written some of them myself. There are a lot of commercially available upgrading kits and bits as well, some good, others bad,

mostly rather middling. But I find, when chatting to other modellers, that while they may have read those pieces and know about the add-ons, they are, by and large, content to leave things pretty well as they are as far as their own work is concerned. "RTR is so good these days," they say, half apologetically. Well it is in some ways, compared with the Hornby tinplate with which I began my modelling career, but it could be a darn sight better.

For these past several years there has even been an award at Scaleforum for RTR conversions. I had sometimes thought of entering one of my locos but the trouble was, I couldn't be sure what an RTR conversion was — would my monumental rehashing of that old Triang 2–6–2T come under this category, because it used a few sections of plastic boiler and the cab roof? I had a vague sense that, in finescale circles at least, there was something non-dig about the whole concept, but eventually I did enter the competition, with the reworked 'Terrier' that features in these pages. It not only took the prize but also the MRJ Chalice which, as the plaque on the plinth records is 'for excellence in 4mm scale modelling'. I can imagine no more effective way of saying that there's nothing second-best about models based on revamped RTR equipment. However, I think my approach has always been fundamentally different to that adopted by many modellers, not so much in matters of technique but more in terms of attitude of mind. I don't think of what I do as 'detailing' or 'improving' or whatever. I think of every project as building a model of a locomotive, whether I'm using a cheap proprietary moulding or a Brassmasters kit as the basis. Where I start from is almost beside the point.

Usually, if I want a model of a particular class of locomotive, I will want to build the very best representation that I am capable of. It will always be of a specific engine at a specific period in time. I will look around to see what's available in kits and RTR and pick what seems to be the best starting point. If I wanted to build a Castle, then I'd unquestionably go for the Mitchell kit and leave my beloved three-rail *Bristol Castle* to enjoy its old age in peace. But there have been several cases when a modicum of research has suggested that an RTR body may well represent a better beginning than the equivalent kit — always assuming one exists — in terms of cost, accuracy, and suitability for purpose.

And then, paradoxically, there are cases where I've found myself with a plastic body to hand — a Hornby Jinty, perhaps, or an ancient Kitmaster 08 — and I've thought what the hell, let's see what kind of a fist I can make out of this. That was how the 2–6–2T came about. The starting point may not always have been the ideal one, given a free choice, but it's fun to see what happens.

I don't like dogmatism in any shape or form and my approach to modelling is essentially a catholic one (no pun intended). I have certain preferences, but I don't have a system. I enjoy working with brass as much as with plastic, and I quite like building the odd whitemetal loco kit. Often I mix these materials, using whatever seems best suited for the purpose. My Clan, for instance, has a whitemetal boiler, a plastic footplate and tender body and everything else is brass and nickel silver. How can you categorise something like that? The answer, of course, is

This Ivatt Duchess was one of my early efforts at producing a finescale model from proprietary mouldings. It retains its Hornby tender drive, while the loco chassis is from a Comet kit. I must do something about those Romford drivers.

not to bother trying to put things into pigeon holes but to enjoy them for what they are.

We've been talking, of course, about cosmetics. The other prime considerations where RTR models are concerned relate to the chassis. With one or two exceptions, I find RTR models run very poorly at anything less than a scale 20mph or so, although, for a 'parade of trains' type layout on the lines of 'Dunwich' or 'Copenhagen Fields', it doesn't really make a heck of a lot of difference if the express sweeping by at sixty miles an hour is powered by a big can motor or a ringfield block. Quite a few of my engines, for this very reason, still have their factory mechanisms, even though the upper works may have been heavily reworked and the wheels and motion revamped. But if you're doing things like starts and stops and shunts and reversals and you have an eye for the way a real loco moves, then something new is called for unless you are lucky enough to get one of those rare RTR mechs that bed in beautifully and just get better with age and slop and wear. Mine just get worse. It's not mandatory, but for some years past, building a decent chassis has been an integral part of my modelling philosophy, however mongrel the loco's origins may have been. I have scratchbuilt a number of chassis but for the most part — because I'm not an engineer and because most of my prototypes are from the more commonplace classes — I prefer to rely on kits. This will be my approach here. I have been heavily influenced in some areas by Iain Rice's *Locomotive Kit Chassis Construction* (Wild Swan 1992) and while much of my writing here may represent a distillation of Iain's work and ideas, I feel I should do the decent thing and refer the reader to source for elucidation rather than take my word for it. He knows more about it than I do, for a start.

This book is based around a number of loco-building projects. I've chosen them to give a balance — big engines and little engines, simple conversions and more complex ones, beam-compensated systems and sprung chassis, Eastern, Midland, Southern, Western, BR Standard, and so on and so on. Paul Karau and I gave a lot of thought to the models I would build for this book. Each of us produced long lists of possibilities before we finally selected the half-dozen that would best suit our purpose. All of them are different and individual but the approaches that I demonstrate will, I hope, have a measure of

universality. My way of building a 4F is not unique to a 4F but could be applied to a number of classes; a 22xx, perhaps, or a J39. This hands-on, highly focused approach is deliberate. My own modelling history has been one of incremental gains, the slow build-up of experience punctuated by the occasional disaster and/or giant step forward (the two come together surprisingly often, since every mistake is an opportunity to learn something). I've always absorbed the theory of things through its exposition in practice, not the other way round. So there's not much of an introductory chapter here that details the kind of tools I use — it's better, I think, that we just pick them up (literally) as we go along. Nor will there be anything more than a brief general mention of techniques and broad philosophies, since these are integral to the projects. Pretty well everything that I think needs saying is covered within the context of specific modelling applications. If it can't be demonstrated in practice, what's the point of mentioning it in the first place?

Who, therefore, am I writing for? The finescale modeller, quite definitely, but even this is an impossibly broad church. As has often been remarked, finescale is an attitude of mind as much as it is about dimensions and tolerances. I work in P4 and also in OO but apart from the obvious measurable differences of gauge and wheel profile, the engineering and aesthetic considerations that inspire me are exactly the same. I would expect the person who has the most to gain from reading this book is someone who is starting to move beyond the tacit acceptance of proprietary and kit-based products, and who is ready to start experimenting with some new ideas. I think of the kind of modeller I was fourteen or fifteen years back, when MRJ No. 0 first came out and I felt the earth move. I doubt if anything in this book will have that kind of effect but I would hope, at the same time, that even the most refined of kit- and scratch-builders might take a look at what can be achieved in this area and, at the very least, consider the possibilities. I guess we are all of us moving down the same road — some of us way up ahead, some who have barely begun, the majority of us bumbling along somewhere in the middle, much as always. I trust this book gives some reasonable sense of direction to my fellow travellers.

Tim Shackleton
Suffolk

CHAPTER ONE

ATTITUDES AND APPROACHES

THE last time I counted, there had been at least seventy 4mm scale plastic-bodied RTR steam loco-motives for the British market. These days some of them — like the old Triang Princess or Hornby's ill-fated King Arthur — are probably of interest only to collectors. But out of what remains, some surprisingly accurate models can be made. As they come, I feel that few, if any, proprietary mouldings are good enough to be stuck on a scale chassis and put to work without further modification. But with a little bit of effort, it is surprising what can be done.

Sitting in front of me as a write is an old Mainline J72 body. I bought it years ago for a couple of quid because it was there and because I fancied a model of one of these interesting old tank engines. To my knowledge, there's only ever been one kit for a J72 — a rough old thing from K's of Shepherds Bush — and this cheap plastic moulding knocks it into a cocked hat. It's dimensionally accurate, it has some lovely fine detail — especially around the tank tops and the smokebox — and it's made from a material that anyone who's ever stuck an Airfix kit together can work with. Sure, it has its faults — there's a big cut-out

in the boiler where the chassis used to go, the chimney's a bit clumsy and the cab side sheets look much too thick — but, for the price, it's a smashing little model. You would need to be a very fine scratch-builder indeed to come near this quality.

To my eye, this scruffy, secondhand plastic body is just loaded with potential. I can build a decent chassis for it, I can put the errors to rights, I can add a lot of extra detail, I can customise it to represent one particular locomotive, I can turn it into a pre-group version, a BR-built J72 or even a J71, and I can repaint it in any livery I like. This is going to call for some effort on my part but, if I hadn't got the body to hand, I don't think I would ever have got round to building a J72. By the time I've finished with it, I hope it will be a model that will stand comparison with any kit- or scratchbuilt equivalent.

One of the nicest things about modelling locomotives from proprietary mouldings is that you can take things just as far as you like. At the most rudimentary level, you can add vacuum pipes and some new handrails, coal-up the bunker, stick a crew in the cab and away you go. Probably this

is how most people start — I certainly did. Then, at the next stage of development, you can fit a more accurate chimney (or one of a different pattern), or model a few detail modifications, or even turn the loco into something else entirely — the most spectacular transformation I've ever effected was to turn a loathsome plastic approx-imation of an Ivatt 2–6–0 into the same designer's rather natty 2–6–2T. It all depends on what you feel happy with and how far you wish to push your own abili-ties and expectations. It's possible, at almost any stage, to say "stop — that's enough." You can't do this with most loco kits. Once you've started, you have to carry on, otherwise you'll end up with a cupboard full of half-built engines.

This book is all about building 4mm scale model steam locomotives using, as the starting point, a proprietary plastic moulding. I'm sure some people may see differently, but it isn't about 'super-detailing' (whatever that is) or 'improving' RTR models. Instead, it's about one par-ticular way in which I build locomotives. I work in brass and nickel silver, too, and in

Given a free hand, I'm not sure I'd automatically go for a Hornby 'Jinty' as the starting point but it offers possibilities – and the spare bodies are dirt cheap. This model represents one of the first LMS batch, which differed from the rest of the class in a number of ways – they lack, for instance, the distinctive 'keyhole'. The boiler fittings are Riceworks lost-wax castings and the engine has one of the early Perseverance chassis.

A selection of injection-moulded bodies, all bought cheaply as spares. The best value comes from 'part-finished' bodies such as the A4 seen on the left – it lacks handrails, buffers and other details which we would probably want to get rid of anyway.

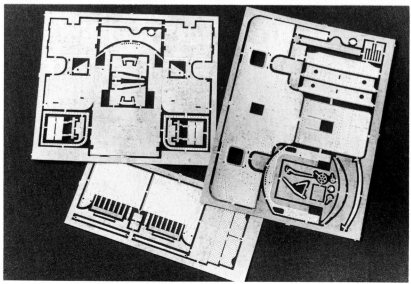

Above left: *My composite approach to loco-building is all about making the best use of what's available. Perfectly formed boilers and nice, level footplates do not always come easily in etched brass or white-metal.* Above right: *We are only interested in the good bits of the RTR moulding. Anything that doesn't pass muster can go – it is a lot easier to be ruthless about these things with a cheap plastic body than an expensive kit. The cab sides and steps of this Mainline model are unconvincing and, like the crude handrails, need remedial attention. I would far rather focus my attention on that nicely shaped firebox and the well-defined cab roof.* Left: *Plastic represents solid objects very well but its major shortcoming is its inability to suggest thin metal edges. While mouldings can be filed down, with varying degrees of success, nothing looks more like sheet metal than sheet metal. This Patriot cab from the Jackson Evans range will be mated with a Hornby boiler/footplate moulding. The pack includes useful extra bits such as smoke deflectors, fall plate and two patterns of buffer beam.*

whitemetal, and sometimes in all these different materials simultaneously (as we will see in due course). The plastic RTR body is just one element — and not always the predominant one — in an equation that includes many constants and variables. The most consistent factor is the desire to produce the best possible model, given the circumstances. The most variable one is just what those circumstances are.

When building models, I use the materials and approaches that seem most appropriate, or happen to be to hand, or which I've been able to get cheap or been given or whatever the reason might be for doing things in that particular way. I am certainly not a 'sheet metal man' or a 'Plastikard man' or a 'springing man' or anything remotely like that. Although people say I have 'a way of doing things', I certainly don't know what it is. To be honest, I tend to make things up as I go along.

Nothing, at least on my workbench, is done according to a system — the only linking factor, as I say, is the desire to produce the best possible model, given the prevailing circumstances and my own limitations. The circumstances vary daily, almost hourly. The limitations are a constant source of frustration and anxiety but overcoming them gives me a tremendous sense of fulfilment. It reminds me of who I am and how my attitudes and approaches are constantly evolving.

Sometimes, if I'm lazy, I cut corners and buy in components. At other times I might spend the best part of a day making something that I could have bought for a couple of quid and that would have looked just as good. When I sit down at my workbench, I do what I feel like doing, not what I think I ought to be doing. I guess that's why I get so much gratification and pleasure out of it.

THE PARAMETERS
It will quickly become apparent that, at the sort of level that I would like to encourage people to try and reach, the concept of 'detailed RTR' becomes almost meaningless. Paradoxically, if it were not for the availability of an RTR model, I would never have tackled any of these prototypes — I feel that making a taper boiler or the cab roof of a 'Terrier', certainly in plastic, is way beyond my scratchbuilding skills. A lot of people, I am sure, feel the same way.

What I tend to do is to take the good bits of the RTR moulding and scrap the rest, using my own resources to complete the model. Playing devil's advocate, though, I sometimes find myself wondering if scratchbuilding might not, in the long run, be a simpler option. People seem to assume that RTR conversions and adaptations are a quick and easy way of building a model. They can be, but compromises are inevitable in the cheap 'n' cheerful approach. When you go for broke, it can take just as long — and involve exactly the same skills — as building the more advanced kind of kit. It certainly doesn't have to cost as much, though, and you can always get off the bus a stop or two early, if you seem to be trying to go too far too soon.

But there's another side to the story, as there so often is. The more you chop and change what you're given — RTR moulding, whitemetal kit or whatever — the more the model becomes a personal statement. Because of the near-flawless quality of the finest etched kits, only a fool or a genius would want to deviate very far from the party line. As a result, we get models which look brilliant but which are uncomfortably similar to one another. While a measure of engineering skill is certainly apparent in their construction, little of the individual builder's flair or initiative — rather than that of the designer — is likely to show through, except perhaps in the way the model is finished. Like everyone else, I greatly enjoy building these kits, but I also like to put my own stamp on things, to be creative rather than simply assembling parts according to the instructions, however delightfully reassuring and educational that process may be. Besides, it's nice to think that all those childhood years spent getting polystyrene cement over cockpit canopies have actually led to something worthwhile.

RESEARCH
Before you begin work on any kind of model, it helps to know not just how you are going to build it, but exactly what kind of animal you are looking at. This may not necessarily be what you think it is. Some research is necessary, and I sometimes wonder if I don't enjoy researching my prototypes as much as the actual build.

The prime requirements for any model-building project are a decent drawing of your subject and about a thousand photographs of it, preferably all taken at the same time. You can take very little for granted with many RTR moulded bodies or, for that matter, with chassis kits and other after-market parts. The makers get a lot of things right, often quite brilliantly, but there are things that go wrong as well — strange dimensional meddling, altered wheelbases, missing details, the same part used incorrectly on two different models. It's up to you to find these faults, because the manufacturers sure as hell won't tell you. I learned a long, long time ago never to accept anything at face value.

The one word that has no place whatever in the finescale modeller's dictionary is 'assume'. In fact, I half-considered 'Never Assume Anything' as the sub-title for this book. Never assume, for instance, that the moulded cab is the right width, or that all the engines in the class had vacuum brakes, or that so-and-so's wheels have the right crank throw, or that the tender is the right type, or even that your drawing is correct. Everything must be cross-checked as far as practicable. Of course, this may be a massive deterrent to some people but, being the academic sort, I actually get a lot of pleasure out of it.

Drawings are important, although you can get away without them if you are good at reading things from photographs. Some sources of scale drawings for locomotives are excellent — I can sit down with John Edgson's superb 'Isinglass' series of LNER drawings much as others study Ordnance Survey maps, poring endlessly over the finer points of detail — but others are nowhere near so trustworthy. The main requirement is that the dimensions are given accurately; if you measure direct from the drawing, you need to be sure that it really is reproduced to the scale it says it is and that the draughtsmanship is reliable.

Photographs are a lot easier to come by. Ideally you need ones from lots of different angles showing your chosen loco at the specified period at which you wish to model it. At the drop of a hat, real engines have a nasty habit of acquiring double chimneys, plain-section coupling rods, new safety valves, different arrangements of lamp irons and so on without these things necessarily being recorded in the published texts. It obviously helps if you can see for yourself what was where at which time.

BITS AND PIECES
The next question you need to ask is, just how am I going to make this model of the Turbomotive, or a Crosti-boilered 9F, or a streamlined Castle? Do I just buy an RTR model and a set of detailing parts (assum-

Hundreds of detailing parts and fittings are available from the after-market trade. Some locomotive classes are better catered for than others but the main snag is that quality control is monumentally inconsistent, even within the same range.

Left: *Exquisite castings for the 9F-pattern Giesl ejector (by Steph Dale) and a GWR live steam injector (by Roger Farrant, available from Exactoscale) show what can be done by skilled hands.* Right: *One of the gems from my Black Museum — the injector pipework for a Jubilee, apparently. I can't even tell which way up it's meant to go, let alone work out where the flash ends and the solid 'detail' begins. The whole thing is a hoot . . .*

ing any are available), or is there more to it than that?

Proprietary mouldings and after-market parts give me a leg up but for much of the climb I am on my own, and it takes me quite a while to figure out the route I will take. In the 1980s a considerable trade developed in after-market bits and bobs for model locomotives. Its mushroom growth, like everything else connected with our hobby, has since slowed dramatically, but many of the products are still available, if no longer from the original manufacturer or even under the same name. When I first began reworking RTR locos, I used a lot of these add-on parts. They were an important stepping stone for me in moving from the near-blanket acceptance of the plastic moulding to the creation of original finescale models. These days I don't buy anywhere near so many etched and cast detailing components because I've

come to the conclusion that, on the whole, I'm better off making them myself.

Some things I do buy in — chimneys and domes, for instance — because I do not have the manufacturing capacity or the skills to produce my own. Others I buy because there is no way I could ever make anything anywhere near as good. But it is quite amazing just what can be produced by hand by the individual modeller, with a proportionate reduction in expenditure and increase in satisfaction — and, dare we say it, the model may well look all the better for it. An injector, for instance, can readily be fabricated using a few lengths of wire of various gauges, bits of tube — perhaps sliced off to represent collars and flanges — as well as solid sections that can be judiciously filed to shape. It doesn't take a great deal of effort to produce something that looks far better than the blobby excrescence supplied by some manufacturers.

Not having a lathe need not be a limitation. I can turn up a pretty decent whistle or a set of safety valves by chucking up some brass rod in my mini-drill and working it with needle files. It would be nice, of course, to have a small lathe, and maybe one day I will, but I don't feel the lack of one as acutely as I would not having a compressor for my airbrush, a power drill or some of the other expensive so-called luxuries which I now regard as well-nigh essential.

The main reason for cutting down on the bought-in detail fittings, though, is that, while some are excellent, others are awful. The discrepancy in standards is frequently evident within the same range, so you cannot safely assume that Joe Bloggs's LNER driver's tea-can will be a corker simply because you liked the look of his GWR guard's whistle. Another common phenomenon wheeled out in the name of commercial expediency is the same part masquerading as something else. Is that really a Cleator & Workington sandbox lid, you have to ask yourself, or the Isle of Wight Central version with a different header card?

One has, therefore, to be cautious. An element of pot luck is inevitably involved since, with the closure of so many shops that used to stock these bits, it's not always feasible to see what you're buying. I have no compunction about sending back mail-order items that don't cut the mustard, but it's a pain to have to do it and the phone calls can be expensive. If what you make yourself doesn't come up to scratch, on the other hand, then you just chuck it in the bin and start again. If something takes more than three or four goes, you must be going about it the wrong way.

TOOLS

Few creative hobbies can be as undemanding as loco building in terms of the number, cost and calibre of the tools needed, assuming, that is, that one's sights are set somewhere below the level of professional engineering evident in the work of a Tony Reynalds or Stanley Beeson. Not having a particular item of equipment is, as is well known, a good excuse for not doing anything — I know any number of photographers *manqués* who, despite ambitions to the contrary, don't actually take any decent pictures, because they 'only' have an instamatic and not a Hasselblad — but the restricted scope of the modeller's tool kit is hardly an inhibition. Patience, competence, confidence, vision, imagination — these qualities, as far as loco building is concerned, are infinitely more important than toolboxes bulging with top brand names.

I refuse to believe, therefore, that anyone could be reading this book and not already own and know how to use some kind of drill and the bits to go with it, pliers, cutters, fine-pointed tweezers, ruler and square, a vice, a soldering iron, various sizes of modelling knives or scalpels, piercing saw, razor saw, small screwdrivers, a magnifying glass, a set of fine needle files and perhaps something a bit more muscular for filing down the rough stuff. It doesn't sound like much, but it is with tools such as these that ninety per cent of the work you see in these pages was done. Items not found in everyone's tool kit, perhaps, are a set of tapered cutting broaches or reamers — an infinitely preferable way of opening

These are typical of the conditions in which I choose to work. There's a 9F around here somewhere . . .

out holes to exact diameter, instead of working up through the drill sizes — and an electric mini-drill which, especially when used with a full set of grinding, cutting and slitting tools, is for me the most important and useful item of all the equipment I own. I also possess a resistance soldering unit which, while undoubtedly very useful indeed, isn't quite in the same must-have category.

Almost as important as any posh tools — at least the way I do it — are offcuts of wood which I use to support, hold and generally line up all manner of assemblies. If I've run out of wooden cocktail sticks I get into a panic, because I use them for everything from mixing epoxy and applying paste flux to nudging components into place. I also am a great one for using simple emery-board nail files where feasible, because plastic — and whitemetal and solder too, for that matter — so quickly clogs up good needle files. My best needle files, used exclusively for etched kits, cost me deep in the purse but these things can be bought for pennies at the corner shop.

What else? There are a few interesting things to hand around my workbench, such as a micrometer and a wheel-press and a high-quality headband magnifier, but again these might perhaps be better covered as and when we need them, which not everyone might. I work in an absolute flood of light on a big and extremely cluttered bench but I only actually use an area about the size of a computer mouse mat,

the rest being covered by tools, materials, work in progress, cups of tea, solvent-stained instruction sheets and a gritty coating of filings. I feel at home in this setting, which is just as well, because I spend so much time there.

JOINING THINGS TOGETHER

Where adhesives are concerned, I always feel manufacturers over-stress the alleged strength of their products. I take all reasonable care with cleanliness, drying times and suchlike but I do repeatedly find — especially if I need to dismantle something unexpectedly — how tenuous is the grip of glue on material. As a result, I tend to go for something 'a little stronger'.

For plastic-to-plastic joins, I use Mek-Pak for very small items but for anything that doesn't need to be handled with tweezers, I prefer a much stronger solvent such as Humbrol Liquid Poly, applied with a cheap paintbrush. This will also secure very small metal items by effectively 'melting' them into the plastic but, for any other kind of metal-to-plastic bond, I would normally opt to use a quick-setting two-part epoxy. I much prefer the Bostik or Plastic Padding brands to the five-minute Araldite, which never sets anywhere near as firmly as the blue-label 24 hour variety, which I use for really critical stressed joints.

I don't go much on impact adhesives or superglues, though I do use both of them from time to time. They just don't have the

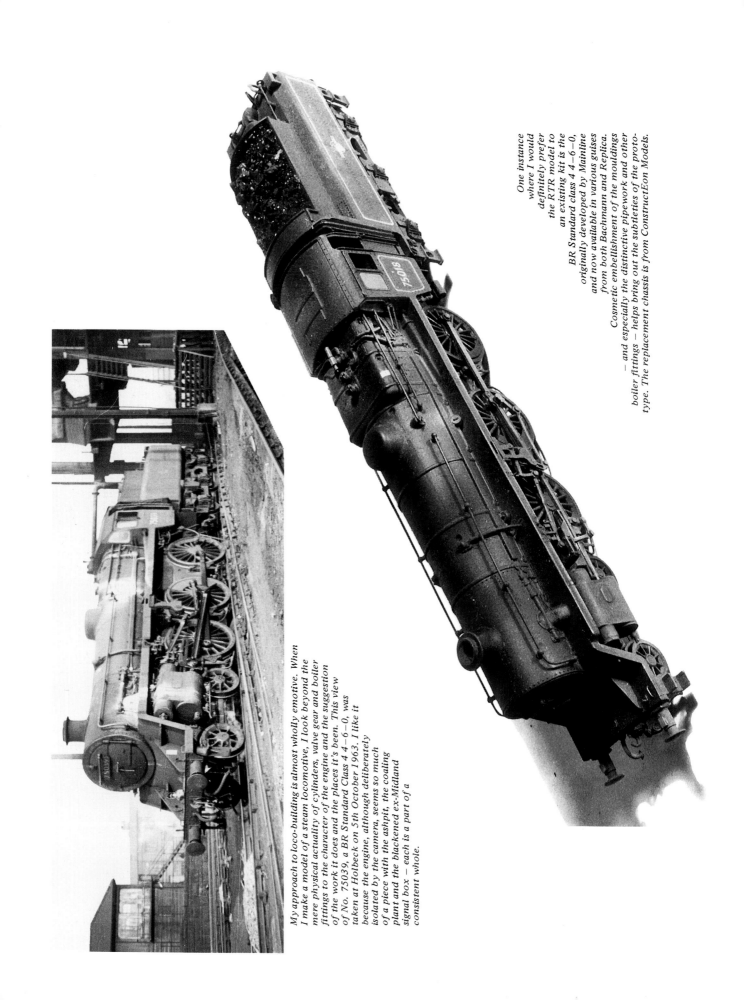

My approach to loco-building is almost wholly emotive. When I make a model of a steam locomotive, I look beyond the mere physical actuality of cylinders, valve gear and boiler fittings to the character of the engine and the suggestion of the work it does and the places it's been. This view of No. 75039, a BR Standard Class 4 4–6–0, was taken at Holbeck on 5th October 1963. I like it because the engine, although deliberately isolated by the camera, seems so much of a piece with the ashpit, the coaling plant and the blackened ex-Midland signal box – each is a part of a consistent whole.

One instance where I would definitely prefer the RTR model to an existing kit is the BR Standard class 4 4–6–0, originally developed by Mainline and now available in various guises from both Bachmann and Replica. Cosmetic embellishment of the mouldings – and especially the distinctive pipework and other boiler fittings – helps bring out the subtleties of the proto- type. The replacement chassis is from ConstructEon Models.

grip I require and they seem to go brittle and weaken with age, causing parts to drop off after a few years and sometimes much sooner. I know there are various 'professional' formulations available and these may very well do the trick, but they cost an arm and a leg and tend to go stale before I've had my money's worth. As a result — apart from the always-useful Loctite 601 for ferric metals — I use stuff I can get at my nearest DIY superstore.

I very much enjoy the art of soldering, and have quite a bit of tackle lying around the bench with which to perform it. Only a small portion of this gear, however, gets used on locos such as the ones I am describing here. Structural items, like loco chassis, I would normally assemble, (in 4mm scale at any rate) with an Antex 25w iron and Carr's 188° solder throughout. Smaller items like valve gear go on with the same iron but this time using 145° solder and a 1mm bit — this last gives me almost but, of course, never quite the control that I can achieve with my resistance soldering unit. I use the two almost interchangeably but the RSU comes into its own when sweating components together (overlays, double-thickness coupling rods and so on) and for heavy metal. I have a big conventional iron of 45w or so but, since I got the RSU, I don't think I've used it once, preferring to whack the output up a notch or two; it is so much cleaner, quicker and neater than waggling about between the frames with a red-hot bit the size of a shovel. With the RSU, incidentally, I normally use Carr's 188° solder paint in tiny quantities but I often pre-tin components and sweat them together by fluxing, which is always Carr's Green Label. This is my preferred general-purpose flux as well, but for electrical work, when soldering near steel and especially when assembling valve gear, I use Fryolux paste flux which isn't so corrosive and can be cleaned off with white spirit or meths.

SOURCES

There are various issues involved in setting out my stall about this kind of modelling and, since they tend to come up not in isolation but in association with other ideas, I'm aware that I may not be treating them in the most logical order. One question that comes most obviously to mind is where do I get the basic proprietary mouldings from? For the kind of surgery I have in mind here, only the fabulously wealthy would buy a complete RTR

model, junk the chassis and use what's left. Wherever practicable I buy spare bodies, either direct from the makers or an authorised supplier, or pick them up at various events on the great model railway circus — swapmeets, exhibitions, open days and so on. Some manufacturers seem more willing than others to oblige, but the supply can be erratic, being often dependent on production over-runs at the factory. Your best bet is probably the 'unfinished' body which is often sold, minus irrelevancies such as handrails and minor detail fittings, for a fiver or less.

Second-hand is another obvious source, although, as the field that's of interest to collectors moves steadily closer to the present, prices are considerably dearer than they used to be. Non-runners are a gift, especially if the bodywork is in good condition — traders seem only too happy to accept whatever you may offer. Older models, however, can be a bit of a liability. While many moulds appear to have been used for generations (Hornby's Bulleid Pacific, for instance, has been in production since 1961), the kind of plastic that was used in the 1960s and 1970s seems to have had a far lower resistance to scuffs and train-set knocks than more modern materials. It doesn't matter one whit if that early-seventies Britannia is lacking one smoke deflector and both its front buffers, but it might also have acquired a patina of fine scratches and a general dulling of detail that can never be put right.

SOME THOUGHTS ON CHASSIS CONSTRUCTION

Irrespective of gauge, I take it as axiomatic that anyone who wants to build a finescale model from proprietary beginnings will want to ditch the RTR chassis. OK, some of them aren't bad in terms of looks and running quality (Dapol's LYR Pug and the J94, for instance) but most fail dismally on both counts. The valve gear of the Replica B1 is often praised as much as the bodywork but I'm not impressed with its behaviour on the track. On the other hand, one of the nicest RTR runners I've ever had was a Hornby 'Patriot' but this had foul stamped-tin motion and impossibly coarse wheels, and that make-believe chassis just had to go.

In the projects that follow, I have used widely available chassis kits as the basis of construction work. My remarks about them are by and large confined to matters that instruction sheets do not cover. Some of them may be plain common sense,

others may already be second nature to you. They are, however, things that it has taken me an unconscionably long time to realise are important, and that I feel need to be spelled out from the off.

The first point is that a chassis kit may not be quite what it seems. I don't mean by this statement that it may not be quite as complete as you may wish since, with some makes, you may need to source your own hornblocks, wire, washers and other fittings as well as the more obvious wheels, gears and motors. This is neither here nor there but what is important to remember is that the kit — in whole or part — may not be strictly accurate for the prototype you are modelling. For reasons of manufacturing and economic expediency, kit components often double up on a one-size-fits-all basis. Fluted coupling rods, as a case in point, are often included where plain would be more correct; or tapered rather than parallel. Bogies and pony trucks are far from universal and the same sideframes may be supplied for locos which, though of broadly similar outline (the smaller Great Western 4–6–0s, for instance) may have differences in wheel diameter and other dimensions which would affect important matters such as wheel pitch and ride height. If we were told this, right from the start, I wouldn't mind so much, but the fact is that usually we are not. It is up to the individual modeller to decide whether these things are worth agonising over and what remedial steps may be necessary.

But the main thing that I would suggest by way of a homily on chassis design is never to stint on the checking procedures and, once again, never to assume anything. Never assume that things are automatically going to be in the right place, the right way round and at the right angle — and to stay there. It is particularly important to bear this in mind when we come to solder up the chassis sideframes with the spacers, and again when we fit the hornblocks, both of which operations should be carried out using the appropriate jigs that are seen in the photographs. A lot of verification is necessary, right the way through the assembly sequence. Much of this can be done by eye — we are, on the whole, pretty good at recognising a right-angle when we see one — but do make liberal use of engineers' squares, micrometers and any other measuring devices that may be to hand. No longer having the vision of a hawk, I frequently use a magnifying glass to supplement the naked eye.

If something looks wrong, don't try and ignore it. Put it right immediately. Problems — many of them unseen — start to arise as soon as we get things out of square or lined up incorrectly. As chassis construction continues, it becomes progressively more and more difficult to make parts fit until you may reach a point when the loco becomes almost unworkable — even unbuildable — without major surgery. As a way of putting things right, I don't go much on tweaking and bending, which tends to cause other distortions and to upset the applecart all over again. The best solution is usually to desolder, clean up if necessary and then start again from the point where you went awry. Errors in loco chassis construction don't go away — they have a knock-on effect and it can be maddening in the extreme to have to remove the pick-ups, desolder the brake gear, take the wheels off, drop out the hornblocks and start the whole assembly sequence all over again just because you got one spacer or a hornguide slightly out and ended up with an irrevocably twisted chassis. I have done this a number of times and I'm still capable of doing it, despite all my precautions. It's often said that flexi-chas, unlike other compensation systems, enables small dimensional errors to be absorbed and accommodated. There may well be something in this but I think it's best to make every component as clean, decent and true as one can, right from the off.

MOTOR AND GEAR CHOICE

As has often been remarked, there is no one motor/gear combination that is suitable for all steam-outline model locomotives. There are some pretty good compromises — the Portescap RG4, for instance — but the size and weight of the loco, the kind of speeds at which it will be run, and the diameter of the driving wheels all need to be borne in mind when choosing a power train, not forgetting the depth or otherwise of the modeller's pocket. There's also the business of concealment — for me, the works must always be totally hidden.

For a while back in the 1980s, I was pretty settled on the RG4 for the big stuff, a D13 open-frame motor with Romford 40:1 gears for lesser main-line engines and the Mashima 1224 with Ultrascale 38:1 gears for smaller prototypes. I don't use any of these so very often nowadays. The Portescap comes ready assembled and for many people, myself included, this can

answer a lot of questions. However, I found through experience that it's not so very difficult to build a high-quality custom drive train using bought-in components. If you can put together a set of Romford gears in an etched mount, then it's not so great a step forward to build something more technically advanced — the gearboxes marketed by Exactoscale and Backwoods Miniatures, for instance, both of which are featured in this book. Moreover, you can then create a power unit that is ideally suited to the kind of loco you are modelling — a tiny shunter that will rarely move much faster than a crawl, for example, or a heavy freight loco that can pull big loads slowly through complex pointwork without faltering.

In each of the builds described in this book, I have tailored the design of the drive train to suit particular requirements. Other alternatives are usually possible. Once again, I think each idea is best expounded as and when it arises, but for elucidation on the general theory of drive train design, I would refer the reader back to *Locomotive Kit Chassis Construction*. This book had a powerful influence on me and while a lot of it still holds true, I've now moved on to ideas and preferences of my own. I don't feel there's a lot of point, however, in my describing hypothetical applications — better, I feel, that I should attempt to teach by example.

MAKING IT GO

Having said all that, a belief still seems to be abroad that, if you shake your credit card at a high-quality motor, all kinds of binds and tight spots and short circuits that may be lying dormant in the chassis will miraculously disappear. Would that it were so, but the point is that the motor is just one factor in a complex equation that includes pick-ups, wheel quartering, hornblock design, weight distribution and any number of other considerations. If your chassis is twisted or the pick-ups are badly designed — making only intermittent contact with the wheels, perhaps, or at the other extreme exerting such pressure on them that they interfere with the compensation — then the running will always be compromised. Even a BMW 7-series runs like a pig with a blocked fuel line and a flat tyre.

I have tried plunger pick-ups and I found they were a nightmare. Splits work fine for some people but mine just got gunged up and led, eventually, to very jerky running. I'm sure I'll go back to both

methods one day but most of the time I use simple wiper pick-ups from Alan Gibson's hard brass wire, sprung out from strips of gapped copperclad or PCB affixed to the chassis. On a very small engine, where there is limited space, I use the 0.33mm variety to gain sufficient flex to make the pick-ups work. On larger engines where the pick-ups might be an inch or more in length, and the 0.33mm wire would be too springy, then I prefer 0.45mm wire. It is all a matter of experiment to see what is most suitable.

I work out well in advance where each pick-up will go, what obstacles such as springs and brake gear it will need to avoid, and then shape it to fit before offering it up. Once the pick-up wire is soldered in place, then I can give it a final tweak with pliers or tweezers before testing it on wander leads from the controller. Very rarely does a pick-up work perfectly first time. The eye may suggest it is making good contact throughout the rotation, but a gap of only a thousandth of an inch or less between wheel and wire will be enough to interrupt the current flow. So it's a matter of prodding and coaxing until it all comes right.

Pick-ups can be easily dislodged, of course, especially during the setting-up process. I follow a specific sequence to avoid this. First of all I solder the motor leads to the nearest PCB strip. Then I add the busbars or connecting wires (usually more 0.45mm brass) that link this strip to the others. Finally I fit the pick-ups, one wheelset at a time and each one tested before moving on to the next. The point is that the pick-up is always the last thing to go on each PCB strip. If you try and fit the motor lead or any other circuitry after the pick-up, then the heat build-up will probably melt the blob of solder securing it and cause the wiper to move, even though this displacement may not be visible. Checking wiring with some form of eyeglass is good practice — it often surprises me how much clearance I actually have or, at the opposite extreme, reveals information that enables me to winkle out potential shorts and poor contacts. Since pick-ups don't stay accurately in place indefinitely (or at least mine don't), then similar checks should be made as part of routine and regular maintenance.

WEIGHTING THE MODEL

This is another important consideration. Plastic bodies do not have much mass but sprung or compensated chassis work much better with a great heavy weight on top of them. Therefore, we need to add weight, usually as much as we can squeeze in without bringing the loco to its knees, smoke pouring from the commutator.

Ideally we should get the same kind of loading on each axle to give an even distribution of weight and thus maximise the adhesion and current pick-up. The optimum weighting of a model locomotive can be calculated mathematically but I rely on trial and error, trundling the bare chassis up and down the test track festooned with various weights and measures until I find the ideal. We are always constrained, of course, by the limitations of size and the available space inside boilers, within tender bodies, underneath chassis spacers and so forth.

I make my weights out of lead roof flashing from my local builders' merchants. I cut it into strips with a hacksaw, bend it, bash it with a hammer and otherwise cajole it into assuming the form that will best fit the space available. With the 4F, as a case in point, once the desired figures had been arrived at, I managed to get a whisper under 6oz of lead inside the boiler with another half-ounce or so at the back of the chassis behind the motor and a further 2½oz in the tender, bearing down on the drawbar. There is another little bit of weight amidships in the tender — it is there to keep the rear wheels on the track. Although details may vary, this is a typical weighting arrangement for the plastic-bodied locos that I build.

FINISHING
Painting, weathering and adding the final touches are, to me, perhaps the most important and exciting stages of all. It is at this juncture that, I hope, the model comes to life. I have no time for 'showcase'-type models, at least in the smaller scales, with their flawless paintwork and shiny handrails. To me they are simply unreal. Many is the time I have looked at one of my own models fresh in new paint, with satin-black smokebox and bright lining, and thought — after perhaps three months' work on it — that it looks nothing like the prototype. Only when I have assaulted it with more paints and powders, dabbed and rubbed and scratched and stroked, looking at pictures of real steam locomotives (and other mechanical things) to trigger my imagination and memories, do I start to think of it as anything more than a half-completed sketch.

Being a Yorkshireman by birth and thus possessed of an inalienable right to plain speaking — in the other counties, I understand, the word 'tactlessness' means much the same thing — I have to say that some of the professional model-painters, to whom one might like to look for guidance, are among the worst offenders in terms of the sheer unreality of their work. I wish, oh how I wish I could spray paint as evenly as they can, that I could emulate the beautiful uniformity of their finishing. But to me, the bland perfection of most professional paintwork just doesn't look anything like the real thing. It's as if model and prototype have parted company, and we have a different set of visual protocols for each. This is what a well-finished model ought to look like, the message reads, and it's handed down to us lesser mortals as if it were an incontrovertible truth. I beg to differ.

All the time I am working on a model — even when fiddling with the mechanism — I have the real thing in mind. This is what I see, and when I get to the last stage I go into a kind of trance and create a three-dimensional picture of the way it looks on the surface. This is quite some distance away from the business of dimensional accuracy, minor detail variation and other matters which have, I would hope, already been accommodated earlier in the building process. It is to do with trying to get the feel of the prototype, the emotions it brings out in me, the sense that this is something warm and animate, a hundred tons of locomotive on the move. This quality might be manifested in paint — a burned smokebox door, perhaps — or in a carefully observed detail such as a cab roof shutter or a sandbox lid left half-open. It is at this stage that we begin to breathe life into our models.

This, however, is a book about building locos, and the definitive text about finishing them off has already been written. Having arrived at very similar conclusions over a comparable time-span (I even used to weather my three-rail stuff) I can add very little to what Martyn Welch says on these matters in *The Art of Weathering*. Such comments as I might offer are best made in the context of the specific loco-building projects in this book. Briefly, my main painting tool is the airbrush, powered by a compressor, and although I have a tin full of expensive and well cared-for sables, I make scant use of conventionally brushed paints. Carr's weathering powders, however, are essential — but only for secondary effects, once the main weathering tones are in place. I am also increasingly becoming interested in the effects of various types of varnishes and finishes, especially the polyacrylic ones produced by Protec Hydrocoatings, in suggesting the different surfaces found on steam locomotives. As Martyn so capably demonstrates, texture is very visible in 7mm work, but my feeling is that it is much less critical in 4mm. I have made many experiments with surface pitting, corrosion and other effects (dribbling on diluted paint stripper gives a brilliant heat-crazed look to ancient firebox paintwork) but found that, on the whole, most of these can be adequately represented by pigment alone in the smaller scale.

VALEDICTUM
Having left various cans of worms lying temptingly open, I don't really want to dwell much further at this stage on the abstractions of tools and techniques, preferring to lead by practical example. I am sorry if this leaves the absolute novice rather out in the cold but, in any case, the basics of cutting, soldering and sticking have already been covered well enough elsewhere in the Wild Swan series. For me to add my two-pennyworth on top would be stretching things for those who've already shelled out enough of their hard-earned on learning and relearning how to drill a hole. Even those rather dire general modelling books you find in public libraries — 'How to make realistic planes, ships and cars by looking at big colourful pictures' — usually make some kind of a fist at putting over the rudiments. So I'll leave it at that for now and get on with the fun stuff.

Moulded loco bodies ready to be turned into finescale models. The total cost of this little lot was less than the cover price of this book.

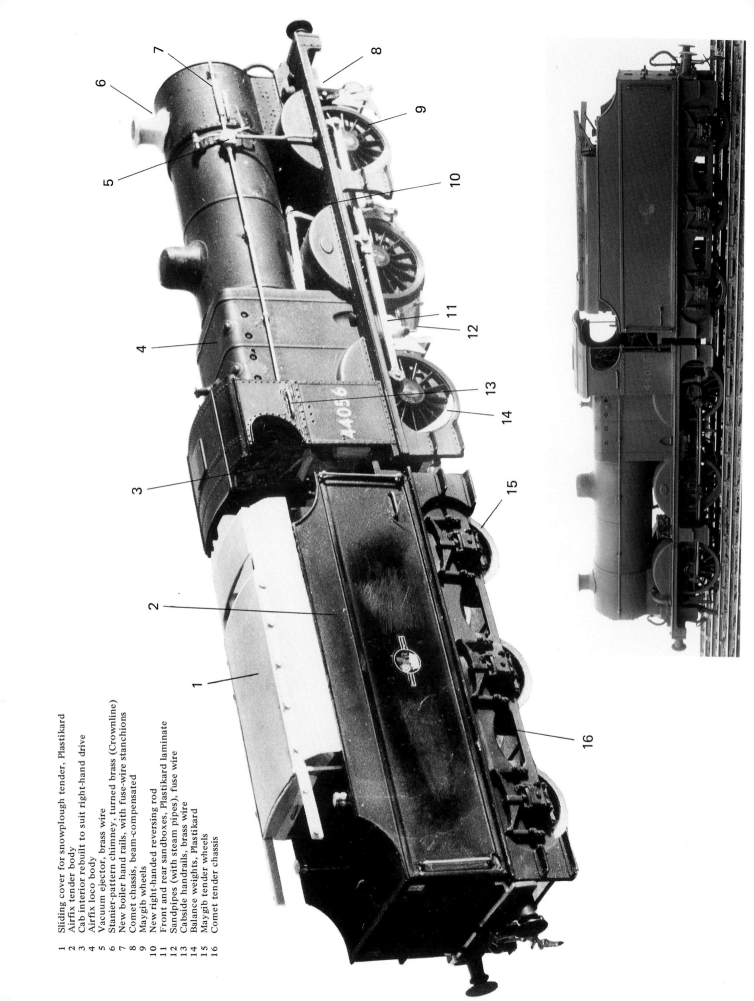

1. Sliding cover for snowplough tender, Plastikard
2. Airfix tender body
3. Cab interior rebuilt to suit right-hand drive
4. Airfix loco body
5. Vacuum ejector, brass wire
6. Stanier-pattern chimney, turned brass (Crownline)
7. New boiler hand rails, with fuse-wire stanchions
8. Comet chassis, beam-compensated
9. Maygib wheels
10. New right-handed reversing rod
11. Front and rear sandboxes, Plastikard laminate
12. Sandpipes (with steam pipes), fuse wire
13. Cabside handrails, brass wire
14. Balance weights, Plastikard
15. Maygib tender wheels
16. Comet tender chassis

CHAPTER TWO

'A SPINSTER AUNT GROWN RATHER STOUT...'

A 4F BASED ON AN AIRFIX BODY AND COMET CHASSIS KIT

No. 44604 of Normanton shed, running through Elland with a Calder Valley freight in the early summer of 1962, was one of a small number of 4Fs which ran with a Stanier 3,500 gallon flat-sided tender. Ten of these were built in 1934 and attached originally to Jubilees Nos. 5607-16. Later they migrated to other classes – the 4Fs, unrebuilt Patriots and a solitary 8F. No. 44604 received this tender (No. 4571) at building and ran with it until withdrawal. Alan Gibson does a 4mm kit to convert a Fowler tender to this high-sided configuration and the instructions include full allocation histories. No. 44604 was the third-from-last 4F built (Derby 1940) and, like all the fifty-odd 4Fs built in the Stanier period, it had plain coupling rods.

HERE'S a nice easy one to begin with. Assuming a reasonably determined rate of progress and not too many distractions, I think this is the kind of project most people could manage in a couple of weeks or so, start to finish.

I thought it might be a good idea, for the first project, to take a fairly run-of-the-mill prototype and try and make something more interesting out of it, but without reaching out to the stratosphere in engineering terms. The magazines of the early 1960s used to be full of heroic conversions such as a Triang Princess to a Black Five or a Dublo A4 to a P2, and only a couple of days before writing these notes I was shown a far from implausible Royal Scot that someone had fashioned years ago from a Kitmaster Duchess. I can't rise to quite so dramatic a transformation here but I hope that this particular reworking might suggest some other possibilities.

The starting point for this 4F is, at least in visual terms, one of the best RTR models ever released in this country. If it didn't have such a dreadful tender-drive system (motors were never Airfix's strong suit) and an irrevocably OO chassis, I would rate it as highly as some of the European RTR paragons from

Fleischmann and Roco. The model is still listed by Dapol, and is widely available on the second-hand market.

It was the Airfix 4F which, as much as anything, drew me back into active railway modelling in the early 1980s after a gap of close on twenty years. At the time I was working for a publishing company just a stone's throw from Cecil Court in the Charing Cross Road which, as modellers of a certain vintage will recall, was where Hamblings had their shop. When no one at work fancied a lunchtime drink, this emporium provided a regular — if expensive — diversion. The attraction was more the books than the models that were Hamblings' prime stock in trade, but one day I happened to see an Airfix 4F in the window marked down to some ridiculous price, a fiver or so.

It seemed light years removed from what I had taken to be the going standard of RTR models, evinced by such nonsenses as the Hornby Hall and the equally dubious Ivatt 2–6–0, and I couldn't resist the temptation. I bought the 4F on its good looks alone, though I didn't even have any track to run it on. The details looked excellent and I can recall how impressed I was by the cab fittings. I did the usual things such as fitting screw coup-

lings, giving the model a new number and adding a sprinkling of coal. I even bought a cheap airbrush to weather it with.

Inevitably, I suppose, I acquired a yard of track and a rudimentary controller. This was all very exciting and soon afterwards I bought, in another Hamblings sale, a K's ROD — one of the kits that, as a teenager, I'd most coveted. In order to build the ROD, I had to buy a vice and a few hand tools. Having gathered this lot together and figured out how to use them — although it would be a good ten years before I finally got that blasted great 2–8–0 to run properly — there didn't seem much point in leaving it at that, and before I knew where I was there were engines all over the place.

It seemed fitting, then, that we might kick off with the same RTR model that I bought all those years ago, but there is a measure of universality here as well, for this is the kind of conversion that has practical applications to many similar engines available in RTR form, such as the Replica Dean goods or Bachmann's J39. The 4Fs, of course, were a truly ubiquitous engine, one that could be found the length and breadth of the country. As well as their usual haunts in the Midlands and the North of England, they turned up in the Scottish

Despite looking unusually clean after a works visit (but note the dusty steps and running plate), No. 44330 – seen here at Ayr shed on 12th May 1958 – is about as typical an LMS-built, left-hand drive 4F as one could imagine.
F. W. SHUTTLEWORTH

No. 44056 running off the Newtown goods branch and on to the main LNWR Manchester–Leeds line at Hillhouse. Shedded at Mirfield for many years, it was a familiar sight in the area on local freight and shunting duties. The unusual sliding roof on the tender was fitted as protection when on snowplough duties. Very few of these were built and they were fitted to engines allocated to areas where there was a risk of heavy snowfall.

Highlands and in the Mendips, in East Anglia (March had a few in the late 1950s) and on LM lines in Wales. They were most familiar on goods duties that ranged from pilot work to heavy slog, but I can recall them on secondary passenger work on occasion.

The 4Fs were based on a long and desperately conservative Derby tradition. For many years they seemed to be just a part of the railway landscape and I don't suppose they ever looked fashionable, or even very interesting; perhaps their character only came out in old age. By 1965 most of the survivors were dumped at sheds like Stourton, Westhouses and Buxton, ousted by snappy two-tone BR/Sulzer Type 2s. I could remember the last of the 'fivers' going a few years earlier and I felt something similar about the 4Fs as they rusted away, chimneys tied up with sacking, numbers bleached white, their simple late-Edwardian lines at odds with the increasingly standardised modernity of their surroundings. It was like looking at a relative or a family friend, someone you have known for a long time, and realising that they are no longer elderly, but old. By the mid-1960s the 4Fs had, like my grandparents, become relics of an almost-vanished era. Among the endless Black 5s and 9Fs, anything small and parallel-boilered just didn't fit in any more.

Their character is difficult to define. Plain but far from utilitarian, they seemed to have a quality of primness about them, like an upright piano or a spinster aunt grown rather stout. There seems little point in recounting their full history here (see the bibliography at the front of the book) although I will say a little about the 4F I chose to model. This is Mirfield's No. 44056, built at Derby in 1925 and a regular for very many years on trip-freight and shunting turns in the Huddersfield area. This was, like all the Midland-built 4Fs and some of the early LMS examples, a right-hand drive engine (there are other detail differences, which we will come on to later) but its most distinctive feature was the sliding wooden cover over the tender coal space. I would see this engine practically every time I went out of my front door but no one could ever tell me what the tender cover was for.

Various explanations were put forward — a self-weighing tender was the most familiar — until I learned that it had been fitted as protection when the engine was on snow-clearance duties. In the wake of the terrible winter of 1947, a large, all-steel design of snowplough (known as a No. 2 plough) was introduced that could be bolted straight on to the front of a 4F, reaching right up to chimney height. Specially modified tenders were produced

to go with them and the engines ran with them all year round. Apart from 44056, the only other snowplough-tender 4Fs that I am aware of were Nos 44172 and 44262 at Rowsley, 44253/4 at Perth, 44255 at Fort William, 44339 at Buxton, 44355 at Uttoxeter and 44510 at Carnforth. There seems to have been considerable variation in detail. Originally the whole of the cab area was sheeted over to protect the crews, but pieces of cladding were removed over the years to make the engines more suitable for everyday work, and at least two tenders (those fitted to Nos. 44172 and 44355) latterly ran without the sliding cover but with the supporting framework still in situ.

THE BASIC CHASSIS

Another good reason for choosing the 4F as a project model is because — like the Mainline/Replica 2251 class 0–6–0 which is another favourite 'prentice piece — it provides an ideal opportunity to learn something about finescale loco construction. In this field there is no substitute for experience — barring a few professional qualifications in electrical and/or mechanical engineering — and we all have to make a start somewhere. I think an engine such as this would be as good as any. It's not too small and it's not too big, it doesn't have any bogies or pony trucks or outside valve gear, but it will — assuming all goes well — demonstrate just how great an improvement can be made to an RTR model in terms of appearance and running quality.

This 4F has a conventional beam-compensated flexichas of the kind whose anatomy and construction have been explained many times in the pages of *Model Railway Journal* (if not in other magazines) and there is nothing very original about my approach. Hopefully the photo-sequence covers everything that is necessary, supplemented by the instructions in the kit chassis and the other bought-in components such as the hornblocks and gearbox. These notes are, as with all the projects in the book, designed to be read in conjunction with the illustrations and especially the captions.

With a measure of confidence, a decent drawing and a modicum of ability with the piercing saw, it's no great shakes to fret out a set of brass frames for a simple 0–6–0. But with so many fundamentally accurate chassis kits available for proprietary models at reasonable cost, I think it's hardly worth the effort. I tend to buy in for preference, and to make my own frames only when necessary.

For the 4F I chose a Comet chassis pack. This provides the frames, oo spacers, brake gear, coupling rods (articulated or rigid can be built from the same fret), axle bushes and wire. I chose Comet out of brand loyalty because I have built several of their chassis kits in the past and found they go together very well, being accurate and consistent in their dimensions. Puffers (née Perseverance) do something very similar and I'm sure theirs would serve just as well.

The etched-brass frames accord well with the drawings I was using for this project and nothing needed correction in dimensional terms. They are designed to be a straight drop-in fit for the Airfix 4F and I was pleased to note that the brake hangers are positioned to be a snug fit in relation to scale wheels. Many kits are designed around Romford wheels which, with their bloated flanges, leave an uncomfortable gap between brake blocks and tyres when using scale wheels.

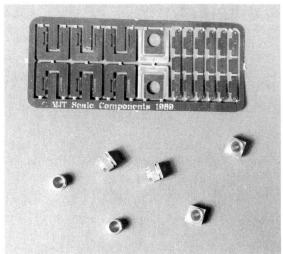 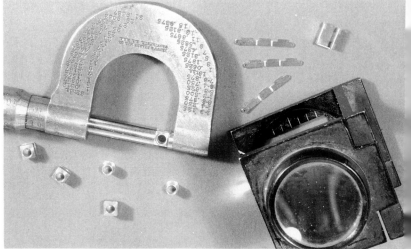

Left: *The constituent parts of the MJT hornblock set. Having the extra pair of guides and backing plates is good insurance in case anything goes wrong. You can buy the bearings separately to use up the spares.* Right: *Systematic checks are vital to chassis assembly, especially for non-engineering types like me. Always ensure that the axles will fit smoothly into the bearings. Never assume that bearings are all the same size externally — there can be enough variation to throw an otherwise perfectly assembled chassis. I always check with a micrometer but this set was spot on. A look at the folded-up hornguides through a linen tester (from a graphic supplies shop) soon reveals if anything is out of true. I do the weathering and things in a creative fury but I try to stay cool when I'm building a chassis.*

Left: *Solder assembly of the hornguides — although epoxy is recommended by MJT. A spot of 188° solder paint suffices. Result — a clean joint with no overrun of solder on to bearing surfaces, which would be inevitable with a liquid flux. No problems thus far with hornguides coming unsoldered at a later stage of assembly.* Right: *Comparison of bearing surfaces before (left) and after polishing with emery. Remember to brush the bearings to get rid of dust and swarf.*

The kit as provided makes no provision for compensation, except that the cut-out outlines for hornblocks (if required) are half-etched into the metal — if you're not going to compensate the chassis, you can ignore them. If you are, then the openings need to be cut out with a piercing saw, preferably before the chassis is assembled.

Something else that should be attended to is to mark the position for the pivoting cross-member for the beam compensation system. Many kits are impossibly vague about this — either they give no guidance at all, or they provide a half-etched dimple but don't bother telling you what thicknesses of rod they have in mind. The way to work out the position of the pivot is first to draw a line through the axle centre holes; this is best done before opening up the cut-outs for hornblocks. Choose a piece of brass rod or tube for the compensation beam — I normally go for ¹⁄₁₆in. The cross-member is a length of telescopic brass tubing (again usually ¹⁄₁₆in) pivoting snugly around a length of rod that corresponds to the inside diameter of the tube. The rod passes through the sideframes where it is soldered in place. The way I figure it, the height of the cross member above the mean axle centre line — which we might call x — needs to be the sum of half the thickness of the axle, the total thickness of the compensating beam and half the thickness of the pivot to which the beam will be soldered. Find the centre point of the two compensated axles and measure up from this by the amount that x represents. With ⅛in axles, then, and ¹⁄₁₆in beam and pivot, the point at which the latter passes through the frames will be ³⁄₃₂in above the axle centre line. If your author, with his shabbily scraped pass in O-level maths, can get this right, anyone can. Make a little scratch at this point with a blunt scalpel blade and then centre-punch it. The hole for the pivot can then be drilled out so the pivot wire will be a tight push-fit (though it should still be soldered in place in case anything shifts around). If it's too sloppy a fit, you will have problems with solder leaching through and locking the pivot up solid.

COUPLING RODS

'It is assumed,' say the instructions, 'that the coupling rods will be furnished from the original model or kit.' This sounds like a legacy from the days when Comet just did the frames on their own, and not as part of a complete chassis kit. This pick 'n' mix

Despite all our precautions, minute dimensional discrepancies will make the hornblocks fit the guides more snugly one way round than t'other. Find the orientation that works best with each one and stick with it. We want a smooth sliding fit without a hint of lateral slop. A bath in Brasso followed by a little gentle up-and-down working of the hornblock in its guide should make everything silky. If you need to file the bearings and/or the guides to achieve this, I would suggest you are using the wrong make. This shot is for Bob Barlow, who shares my enthusiasm for classic packaging designs.

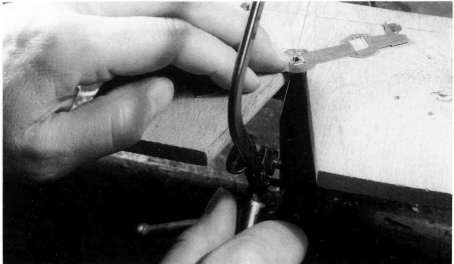

Cutting out the openings for the hornblocks with a piercing saw. You can either saw along the half-etched lines or cut across from corner to corner — as I'm doing here — and snap the waste metal out. It doesn't matter if the cut-outs are slightly oversized.

The completed sideframes, with edges filed smooth. The marks on the rear axle holes tell me not to cut these ones out — I will own up to one or two forgetful incidents in the past.

approach could well be a recipe for disaster — how can you be sure that Airfix's interpretation of the all-important wheel-centre measurements accords with Comet's? Nowadays Comet do their own nickel-silver coupling rods and these are what I used here. Ideally, rods and frames should be etched on the same fret so that measurements can be seen to be consistent. Contrary to what many people assume, etching is not an exact science and errors of several thou are far from uncommon, even between batches from the same photo-tools. If you take the same dimensions (such as coupling rod centres) and etch them at different times on to different materials, there might well be a discrepancy. Here, though, the nickel rods matched the brass frames and all seemed set fair.

The rods are double-thickness and thus need soldering together. Great care needs to be taken when aligning them — I use a couple of drill bits of the same diameter as the etched holes, because solder paint will not (or does not appear to) bond with blackened steel. To the best of my knowledge, all the 4Fs had Fowler-pattern fluted coupling rods when built except for Nos 44562 onwards, which were built in the Stanier era and had the flat-sided pattern. However, it might be the case that one or two earlier engines subsequently acquired plain rods. This it how it appears on a few (admittedly murky) photographs, but I've not seen a clear enough shot to substantiate this. This, however, is a matter of little moment, since the kit enables us to build either variety from the components sup-

plied. I mention it here because one is so often led to assume things which later prove to be false. Never assume anything, in modelling or in life . . .

FRAME SPACERS

I was building this 4F to 16.5mm gauge. The chassis spacers supplied with the kit are a whisper over 10mm which, taken with the 18-thou frames, would give an

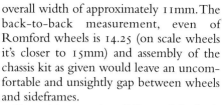

overall width of approximately 11mm. The back-to-back measurement, even of Romford wheels is 14.25 (on scale wheels it's closer to 15mm) and assembly of the chassis kit as given would leave an uncomfortable and unsightly gap between wheels and sideframes.

Few things make OO models look more like OO models than these huge voids, which are unprototypical and yet all

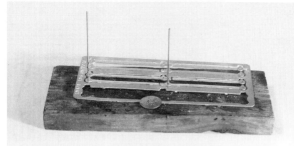

Once the surfaces to be joined have been tinned, the two halves of each section of the coupling rods are aligned using drill bits set into a piece of wood. They can then be sweated together — a resistance soldering unit is ideal for this work. There is a good reason why I do this with one half of the rod still in the fret but I really can't remember it.

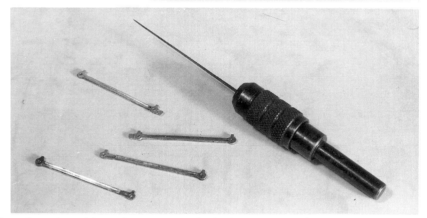

The rods need careful dressing to suggest they're heavy steel forgings, not two thicknesses of nickel silver soldered together. Be careful not to bend them in the process — a gentle tweak usually puts matters right if you err. The holes can then be opened up to accept the crankpins, using a broach.

Left: *After soldering the front spacer to one sideframe and the rear spacer to the other, I rigged up the chassis in my assembly jig, the idea for which was stolen from one of Iain Rice's books. As you can see, I go to considerable lengths to make sure everything is square in each dimension before applying the soldering iron. The blocks are of seasoned oak — metal would soak up too much heat.* Right: *The result is a chassis which is square, strong and true. The centre spacers will form mounts for the PCB strip from which I will run the pick-ups. The holes for the fixing screws are off-centre because I used EM gauge spacers, thinned down a couple of millimetres on one side, but I'll deal with this when the time comes.*

too characteristic of many kit-built locos. One of the things that I find so gratifying about working in P4 is the much-reduced clearance in this area — nothing like the prototype's half-inch, of course, but still a big improvement, even if it can make fitting 'backscratcher' pick-ups a bit of a problem.

My solution is to make my OO frames as wide as possible — a good 13.5mm minimum from outer face to outer face. Even on a long-wheelbase engine, this still gives adequate sideplay where this is necessary (and no engine should really need more than 0.5mm play on any axle). Because the frame thickness of trade products ranges from the customary 18-thou to DJH's bomb-proof 30-thou, no commercial frame spacer is universally suitable and so I normally make my own out of L-section brass, cut to the optimum width

A check to confirm that the motor and gearbox will fit where they are meant to, without further modification. This is all very gratifying, even though everything has been worked out in theory first. With an ordinary 38:1 etched mount, getting the Mashima 1224 into an OO chassis of conventional width usually entails cutting away the sideframes.

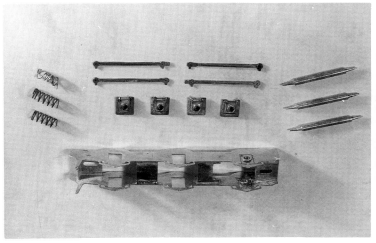

Left: *The essential ingredients for a smooth-running chassis — jointed coupling rods, hornblocks and hornblock assembly jigs.* Right: *The rods slip over the tapered ends of the jigs. Though the springs hold the hornblocks firmly in place, the position of each hornblock can be carefully joggled to get the best alignment.*

from sheet or fret waste. Alternatively, most people will have a few sets of spacers left over from kits and these can be adapted to suit. Here I used EM gauge spacers from an Impetus kit, thinned down to half an inch. This meant that the total chassis width over the rear bearings was around the 14.25mm mark — sailing close to the wind, perhaps, especially since you will need to take into account the presence or otherwise of a moulded boss on the rear face of the wheels. But the snugness of the wheels against the side frames makes a massive difference to the engine's appearance. I think it's well worth the effort.

I always solder frames to spacers in a simple wooden jig — I've tried proprietary 'chassis assembly jigs' but I don't get on with them. Both the jig and the blocks

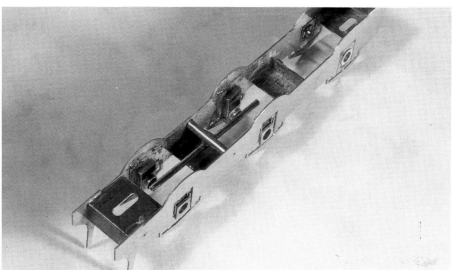

The compensating beam is soldered in place on a pivoting brass tube that is mounted transversely. The bottom of the beam should just touch the two leading axles when their centres are horizontally aligned with the fixed rear axle. Some folks prefer to do this with the wheels temporarily in place.

The bearings are plugged with lengths of pipe cleaner before spraying, to keep the paint out. I love the old-fashioned kind of tobacconist's shop, and buying pipe cleaners and cig papers (to stop flux spreading when soldering valve gear) affords an excellent opportunity for non-smokers like me to sample their special ambience.

of wood I use to hold things in place are dead square, but I still check everything before soldering. I solder the front spacer to one sideframe and the rear spacer to the other and then join them, one side at a time and allowing time for the metal to cool and contract (if you don't, you get a banana-shaped frame). Any other spacers are added one at a time, again soldering first one side and then the other, and once more allowing time for the brass to recover from its ordeal by fire.

WHEELS, GEARS AND MOTOR

All of the major manufacturers make a wheel suitable for a 4F — I used Maygib, merely because I happened to find a set going cheap at an exhibition. Tender wheels came from the same maker.

In anything other than OO, a Mashima 1620 would be a good idea, standing on its head in the firebox. This powerful, slow-revving motor is unfortunately too broad in the beam to fit between OO wheels, let alone frames, and so I opted for the slimmer Mashima 1224, which is smoother but not quite so powerful. I wanted an engine that had good shunting control and a maximum service speed of no more than 30mph, which meant something a little more ambitious than the usual Ultrascale 38:1 gears in an etched mount, although these would be fine for an engine that spends most of its time running on the open road rather than pottering about on obscure shunts.

The gearbox I settled on was the 'Compacto' 54:1 triple-reduction gearbox from Backwoods Miniatures. This uses top-quality moulded gears, made in Germany to a specification far more demanding than those required of the metal gears traditionally used in this

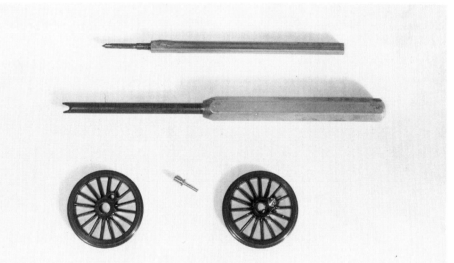

I didn't have enough Kean-Maygib crankpins to hand, so, having tapped the wheel 10BA, I used the Romford design instead — it serves just as well. The shaped end of the special Romford screwdriver fits the notches in the crankpin boss. You could make a similar tool out of tubing or fit the crankpins into a pin chuck, thread outwards, and screw them in that way.

Wheels are pressed on to the axle in a vice and then quartered by hand in the time-honoured tradition. Normally I use the self-quartering George Watts wheel press but this won't take Romford crankpins.

country for model locomotives. It takes a little more care to build a gearbox like this but it's no more difficult than the normal fold-up mount for single-stage gears — it's just that there are more gears involved. The instructions are idiot-proof and there's no need for any further comment here.

TENDER CHASSIS

On most model locomotives, kit-built as well as RTR, the tender just comes along for the ride. On many designs without trailing wheels, however, we may have an adhesion problem caused by the unprototypical distribution of weight around the chassis. The classic British 4–4–0 in etched brass is perhaps the most notorious case but I have encountered major difficulties on the BR Standard classes, irrespective of

Etched brake gear usually look a little thin. I beefed it up with an extra thickness of brake block, using fret waste. The pin is a short stub of brass wire.

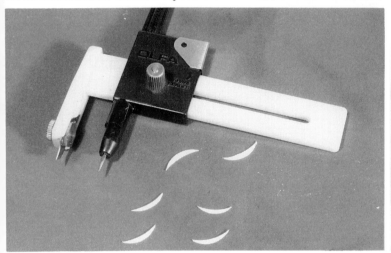

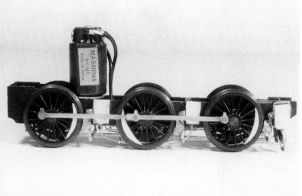

Left: Wheel balance weights are cut out of 10-thou Plastikard with the Olfa compass cutter – a useful tool for the modeller. Right: We take quite a step forward once the wheels are on and quartered. I've added the balance weights and the brake gear, and given the chassis a trial spin with the rods temporarily fitted to see that nothing clouts anything. Steam pipes on the sanding gear may be gilding the lily somewhat, but, if they're visible, they should be there. At some of the less progressive clubs, you can be lynched for suggesting this kind of thing, especially in OO. I sometimes get the impression that OO people think that their locos needn't or can't or even shouldn't have decent underpinnings. Finescale, as has so often been remarked, is about an attitude of mind rather than a set of measurements.

Left: The underside of the chassis, showing the brake pull rods running down the centre of the chassis on a 4F. Right: Weights and measures department — here I am trying to work out the best way of weighting the loco to give optimum adhesion and electrical pick-up. I do it by trial and error, but clever things can be achieved with a decent set of scales.

whether the bodywork was predominantly whitemetal or plastic.

On the typical flexichas 0–6–0, most of the weight is concentrated on the two leading axles and thus the trailing axle (which is normally the driven one) is out of balance. Sometimes we can compensate for this by adding weight over the rear axle but as often as not there is no obvious place to put it. The firebox is full of motor and/or gearbox and the cab is — or should be — packed with interesting detail.

The answer is to hang the front of the tender, once it has been suitably weighted, on the engine's drawbar to give the rear drivers some adhesive bite. The weight of the tender is thus divided between the rear of the loco and the rear set of tender wheels. The two leading pairs of tender wheels play no part in carrying any weight but are merely sprung in some way to stop them derailing. Opting for the weighted-tender system involves little more work than turning the two leading sets of axle holes into slots. On the Comet 6ft 6in tender chassis, this has already been done for us; it can also be built compensated if required. There is an added bonus — this crude form of compensation keeps the rear tender wheels pretty firmly on the track and there is a good case for fitting supplementary pick-ups on this wheelset.

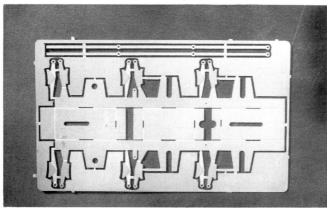

Comet etch for the 6ft 6in tender chassis. I could tell just by looking that, because of under-etching, there was no way the five spacers would bend down between the sideframes. The ends of each one needed mild trimming with a file to get them to fit.

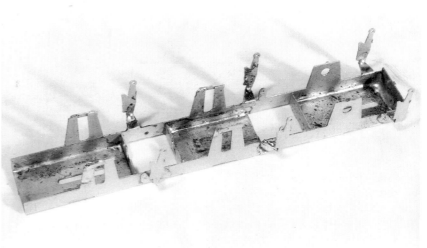

Left: *I always use some kind of a straight edge to make 90° bends in brass.* Right: *Etched tender frames can be a bit fragile and those big blobs of solder are intentional — the brake hangers are folded out from the chassis and need solid reinforcement. I used a 4mm bit on the Antex for this — it doesn't show on the finished model.*

Left: *To add the brake detail — brake blocks and rigging — I switched to my resistance soldering unit. Much neater work results, with no cleaning up. I don't know where I'd be without my blocks of wood.* Right: *The completed tender chassis. The use of 0.7mm wire for the brake cross-shafts looks more prototypical than 0.45mm and makes for a solid job.*

From observation of other people's models, I would suggest that tenders derail more frequently than locomotives and I'm sure this is because their builders don't take nearly so much care with assembling the running gear as they would with a loco. Axles and frames still need to be aligned correctly, however. The brake gear also needs to be soldered up with diligence, since it is very easy to bend those fragile brake hangers and pull rods and induce a short circuit by putting them into contact with the wheels. I belong to the dreadnought school of engineering and make everything as sturdy as possible. I long ago gave up flimsy and undersized 0.45mm wire for the cross-members and use the thickest material I can get away with without compromising scale appearance. Note that on many classes the cross-members were not round-section at all, but formed of flat bar, usually tapered at either end; this can be easily fabricated from fret waste if you are so minded. Tender brake gear arrangements, on the whole, are quite well hidden but the rear set of brakes, directly beneath the buffer beam, is very visible and perhaps some extra detailing should be incorporated here.

THE BODY BEAUTIFUL

If the Airfix 4F had come out recently, I would have thought it was pretty good. It was actually released in, I think, 1975 and by the expectations of the day it was remarkable. The 4Fs were quite well standardised for a class of over seven hundred locomotives and for anyone wanting a run-of-the-mill model, there's very little to be done to the Airfix bodywork. Even the buffers and handrail stanchions, often so wildly inaccurate, would satisfy all but the most demanding modeller. The steam injector on the left-hand smokebox side could use a little refinement and there's a curious cut-out under the boiler that suggests Airfix hadn't always intended a tender-driven model. The position of the front sandbox fillers is open to question and the middle ones are missing altogether. Other than that, it's really the detail variations that need attention.

Considering they were built by eight different workshops over four decades and in two dozen separate batches, there were comparatively few variations among the 4Fs. Since the information is readily available elsewhere, I don't think it's a part of my brief to go into them all here, not least since I think research is one of the most

Tender chassis from the underside, showing the simple springs that keep the two non-loadbearing wheelsets on the track.

The 4F body — in this case a rather tatty pre-cherished specimen — is now stripped for action. It has been broken down into its component assemblies and unwanted details such as the chimney and ejector piping have been removed. The 'Black Hole of Calcutta' beneath my bench is just littered with bits of mauled-about RTR locos. One day I might stick them all back together and see what kind of Frankenstein's monster emerges . . .

I filed the detail off the moulded backhead and then drilled pilot holes for the stay ends which are made from cut-down lacemaker's pins (I am tempted to call them valve-gear pins, since that's what I mostly use them for).

Firehole doors, inner splashers and many of the other cab details are plastic. The Fowler pattern injector was soldered up in minutes from a few lengths of brass. The chimney is a proprietary turning but the steam injector piping (bottom left) is another fabrication from brass wire and pins. The reverser (bottom right) was made from fret waste and the exhaust injector pipe from brass rod, with flanges from a nice little etch by Brassmasters.

interesting parts of any modelling project and I would encourage people to do their own footwork. I have included some guidelines in the bibliography. As ever, a dated photograph of the specific loco you wish to model is an essential starting point. Points to look for when studying photographs of 4Fs are variations of chimney and dome, the more angular cab eaves of the engines built in LMS days, piston tail rod covers that were removed in the mid-1930s (Airfix's LMS-liveried model has them, the BR version doesn't), Ramsbottom safety valves on the Midland-built engines, later replaced by Ross pops, panelled or beaded splashers on Midland engines up to 4011, right- or left-hand drive (the latter the norm except on all Midland and some early LMS engines),

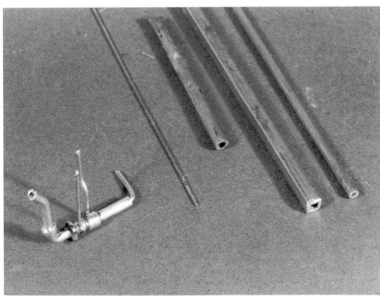

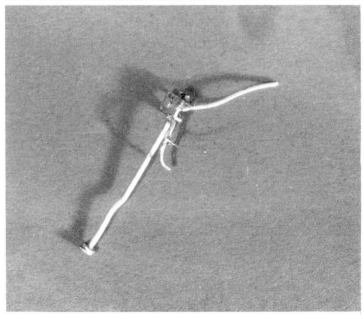

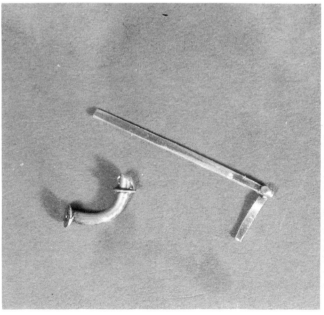

Midland-built, right-hand drive No. 3968 had blanking plates on the buffer beam where its piston tail rods once were. It had acquired an LMS-pattern chimney but retained its original tender.

No. 44363 is another uncharacteristically well-scrubbed 4F. The coal rails on the tender are the only feature of note, and even this was quite commonplace. The everyday familiarity of these engines is a strong part of their appeal in model form

steam ejector/grease separator pipework under the running plate (quite rare and usually — but not always — found on RH drive engines) and the arrangement of the firebox plugs, which had seemingly random variations.

The Midland engines originally had Johnson tenders of various capacities and some of the LMS-built engines also ran with these, either by design or through swapping in works or even at depot level. The vast majority of Fowler tenders attached to 4Fs were flush-riveted; the riveted version is comparatively rare. Quite a few had tender cabs, a feature which I find very attractive on a model, and a handful latterly had high-sided Stanier tenders.

My model of 44056 called for a number of modifications that will not be necessary on the majority of 4Fs. It needed a BR-pattern chimney (Crownline) in place of the Midland pattern supplied. The Airfix dome is also the taller Midland design but this is moulded quite thickly and can be filed down and flattened a little on top to accord better with the 1ft 9in of the LMS version. My prototype also had exhaust ejector piping on the left-hand side, running from the prominent curved pipe at the bottom of the smokebox to the grease separator beneath the footplate at the firebox end. The main work, though,

was conversion to right-hand drive. This involved the total replacement of the cab fittings to suit the new driving position, making a new right-hand steam injector out of various gauges of wire, the switching round of the reversing rod (I made a new one out of brass) and the repositioning of the lubricators. This can all be seen in the photos.

As with the construction of the chassis, the photographs show the incremental way I went about adding detail to the body. The

more general modifications were to refine some of the exposed edges such as the steps, since moulded plastic does not capture the quality of thin sheet metal at all well, and to fill in the gap in the bottom of the boiler with a piece of Plastikard and fit a dummy firebox front. I thought the handrail knobs were really good by proprietary standards but, unfortunately, the 4Fs had particularly inconspicuous stanchions and I created these from 5amp fuse wire. The boiler has shallow depressions for

Airfix cut short the tops of the cab side sheets to accommodate an overscale handrail. The missing bits are easily reinstated in Microstrip.

This shot typifies the level of extra detailing that even the best RTR mouldings can stand. Note the lamp brackets and the resited sandbox filler lids, which have been melted into the plastic. The small moulded handrails on the steam chest covers still need replacing but I opted to leave the buffers as they were — I thought they were very good.

locating the knobs. I filled them with black Plasticine before fitting the new handrails and then glued them in place from the back. There were also the usual bits and bobs to put on like new grab handles, vacuum pipes and lamp irons. All in all, there is enough work to make it interesting and worthwhile but not so much that you begin to wonder that a kit (Alan Gibson does a nice one) might not have been a better starting point. There were very few bought-in components so the cost is pretty reasonable.

SNOWPLOUGH TENDER

There was also the business of the snowplough tender to attend to. The tender itself needs some modification to accommodate the new chassis and the first stage is to break it down into its constituent parts — body, frame, motor unit and weight, the last two being consigned to oblivion. The frame moulding is hacked away until all that remains is the two sideframes, the drawbar and the buffer beam. To stabilise the assembly I fitted sturdy cross-braces of 40-thou Plastikard, allowing clearance for the wheels. This is stuck to the body with Liquid Poly. There is a longitudinal member as well and this will eventually be glued to the tender chassis — screws could be used just as well. Obtaining the correct ride height is a matter of trial and error but there are a couple of ledges running along the top of the tender side frames that give a useful datum point.

The tender body moulding needs little work other than the routine replacement of handrails. Even the steps, so often moulded clumsily on RTR models, just about pass muster. I knew I had some mushroom vents somewhere but, as these things do, they refused to identify themselves when the call came and I turned some up from brass rod instead. I don't own a lathe — I curse myself for failing to buy the lovely little Myford which I saw in Saffron Walden some years back — but it is surprising what can be accomplished in the chuck of a mini-drill.

The major work, obviously, was the sliding cover. I didn't have a drawing but I had some quite reasonable photographs

I built up a Plastikard framework inside the tender body where the new chassis would be seated.

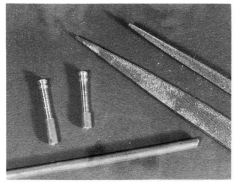

These tender vents were turned from brass rod that I chucked up in my min-drill and worked with good-quality needle files. I don't think I could quite manage a chimney but whistles, safety valves and suchlike are no problem.

The framework for the sliding cover is in place. I've made a start on fitting new handrails of 0.45mm wire — these were carefully melted in with the tip of a soldering iron. I much prefer drilling and glueing but I'd just broken my last suitably sized bit.

and so I was able to work out most of the major dimensions from these and to extrapolate them over the very good Airfix moulding. I was fortunate also in having some video footage of a run-past by the real 44056 and this enabled me to confirm certain important details.

The cover was assembled from Plastikard and Microstrip and calls for little comment — it was just a matter of assembling pre-cut shapes, welded together with solvent. A long time ago I got Alistair Wright of 5522 Models to produce for me an etch of assorted circles, discs and ovals and this is where I found what I needed to produce the little idler wheels or rollers along which the cover slides. They could, I suppose, be cut from brass rod but my method is easier. The sliding cover itself is made from 10-thou Plastikard over formers of 30-thou. I think these tenders usually ran with their covers closed (I've seen only one shot of an engine running with the cover slid all the way back) but I left mine slightly open, for visual interest.

PAINTING AND WEATHERING

All my models are weathered in a consistent way. This isn't to say that they all look the same, merely that the colours, tones and textures that I employ visibly relate to one another. The result is that everything I do — irrespective of whether it's a loco or a wagon, P4 or OO, 4mm or 7mm — is of a piece, and goes together harmoniously.

The tender has been weighted and I've fitted the rollers that support the cover.

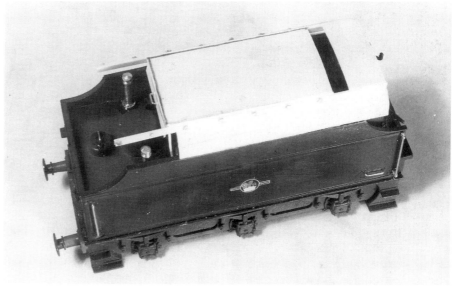

Tender bodywork complete. The covers on No. 44262 had transverse bracing strips and the other snowplough tenders differed in detail to that fitted to my No. 44056.

As weathering projects go, the 4F was straight down the line. Having primed all the metal parts, I mixed up my usual 'underframe' colour from Humbrol matt leather (No. 62) and Metalcote Gunmetal, and airbrushed it on to the whole of the area beneath the running plate, being careful to avoid too even a coverage. I then darkened the mix and sprayed some more — wheel centres and coupling rods, for instance — before moving on to the upper works, gradually building up tones by subtle variations of the basic two-colour mix. No two steam locomotives weathered exactly alike and neither, despite the pre-

ceding paragraph, do my models. I have been interested in weathering for more than thirty years and today I can pretty well do it in my sleep, but all the same, before starting work, I will find some good colour photographs for inspiration. Ideally these should be of a locomotive of the same class so you can see what happens to what. As a typical instance, I might need to consider whether the snifting valves on a 4F were generally rusty, oily, dusty or lime-streaked — a few minutes' study will answer such questions but I do move ideas across from one loco to another providing, and this is the crunch, that they are consis-

tent with the overall effect I am trying to achieve.

With 44056, I wanted the look of a loco that has been in regular, everyday service for a very long time without cleaning. Hence the mottled dark grey/brown of the boiler, a hint of old rust beneath the burned-off paint of the smokebox, a lighter brown (brake-block dust and road dirt) along the tender sides. All this was effected with the airbrush and then I got to work with the Carr's powders.

These, to me, are the secret of effective weathering. I apply them generously with cheap children's paintbrushes, immediately

The major arcana of 4F tenders are seen at Heaton Mersey on 19th July 1963. No. 44220 had acquired one of the Johnson design, latterly fitted with a tender cab. No. 44250 beyond is seen with the standard Fowler pattern.

flicking or blowing the surplus powder away until I have what I want. The exception is when using red and orange tones — these seem to have a very powerful pigment and I use them sparingly. It is easy to add more if the result is not emphatic enough but overstatement is a problem. If I get too glaringly rusted a smokebox door or whatever, I will slosh on a brown-black powder to bring it back down to earth. If this doesn't work, then I'll airbrush out the offending pigment.

Carr's powders can be readily mixed and merged and I really do enjoy dabbing, brushing and rubbing them — it makes a therapeutic change from valve-gear and there is endless scope for improvisation. There is nothing terribly unusual about the way this 4F is weathered but I would point out the variegation of tones of the tender — important, because we have some large flat areas here which could look terribly monotonous if not reworked with a subtle hand — and also the light-coloured patches along the left-hand side where the fire has been thrown out, blowing ash around the steps, cab sides and tender underframe. The oily patches on the coupling rods, wheel bosses, tender axle-boxes and around the mechanical lubricators are represented by Protec's gloss coating, a clear polyacrylic that has many uses in modelling.

I suggest this kind of work is done, wherever possible, out of doors on a bright day. I might well apply basic livery indoors, using pre-mixed proprietary paints, but I'd never do weathering under tungsten or any other form of artificial light. It makes everything turn out very yellow, when viewed in natural light, and while I do occasionally make use of blue 'daylight' bulbs in dire emergency, I much prefer the real thing. It's free, for a start . . .

CONCLUSIONS

I don't hold with the kind of modelling where everything on the layout is a rarity, the sidings brimming with special-purpose vehicles and extraordinary pre-group coaching stock survivors, while every second train on the main line is an express. Sure, I've got a 'Deltic' and a 'Duchess' like everyone else, but most of the time I like to see familiar things and to model the quotidian, those commonplace subjects that say 'this is how it really was'. I think the trick is to introduce just that little bit of variation to make life interesting.

It was so satisfying to recreate the distinctive shape of this locomotive, because 44056 was once an everyday sight for me, snowplough tender and all. And yet I can well understand why other people might regard this particular locomotive as a real one-off which, in a sense, it probably was. All I can say is that it was a familiar enough prototype to me, just as the diminutive Somerset and Dorset Sentinels would have been had I lived in Radstock, or the radial tanks at Lyme Regis.

The other thing that struck me on reflection was just how few hand tools and materials I had used to build 44056. I like to start each new project with a reasonably clear bench but, being untidy by nature, I never put anything away once I've set sail. By the time I was drawing close to home, I could still see the tools of the trade scattered all around me on the decks. There was a 25w soldering iron for the chassis (I used a 1mm bit for the detail work); a pair of side-cutters for snipping wire; a pair of long-nosed pliers for tweaking same; a craft knife with pointed and chisel blades (this last for taking off detail); a mini-drill and a pin-chuck, with drill bits; a piercing saw; a compass cutter; some needle files and emery boards; cocktail sticks for dabbing glue and paste flux; pointed tweezers for positioning parts; solders and adhesives various, and that was about it.

I think this goes to show that you don't need a fully equipped workshop to build this kind of model. You don't need a deep pocket either. Sure, the working parts cost money but the only bought-in components on the body were the chimney and the screw couplings — everything else was made from tube, brass rod, fret waste, Plastikard and Microstrip. The Comet loco and tender chassis left me with more useful bits of scrap brass. All in all, this was a very satisfying project and one that, for once, came in pretty cheap. It's one thing to buy in a load of bits and create much the same loco as a hundred other people have made. It's something else entirely when you use your own resources to build something unique. This is when modelling starts to become a personal statement, even — dare one say it — an art form in its own right.

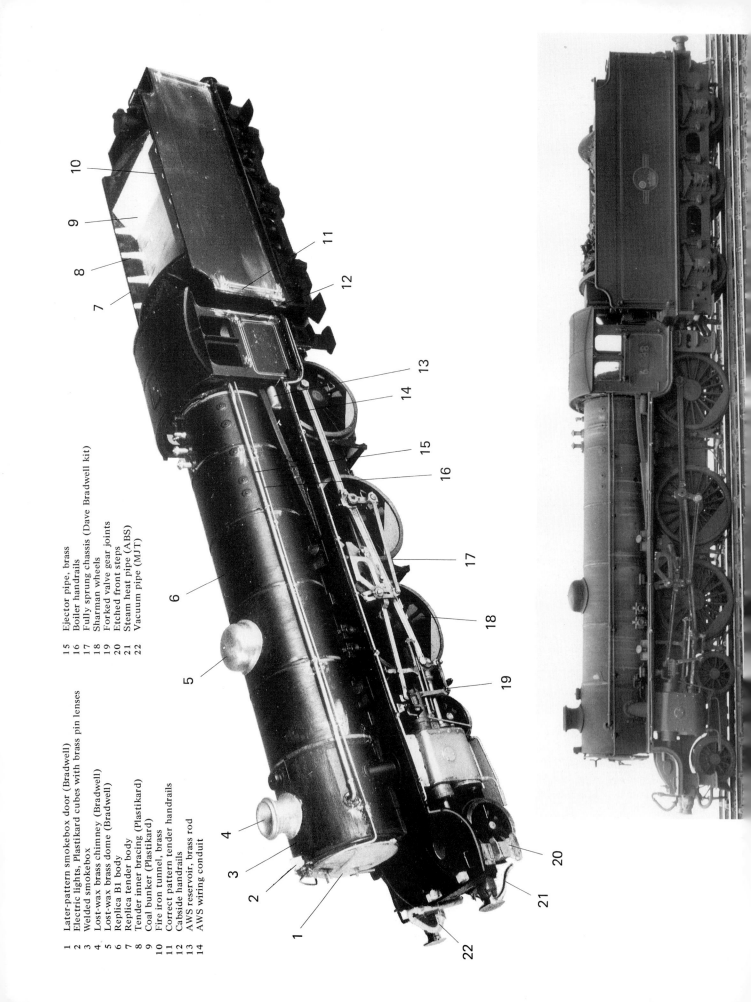

1 Later-pattern smokebox door (Bradwell)
2 Electric lights, Plastikard cubes with brass pin lenses
3 Welded smokebox
4 Lost-wax brass chimney (Bradwell)
5 Lost-wax brass dome (Bradwell)
6 Replica B1 body
7 Replica tender body
8 Tender inner bracing (Plastikard)
9 Coal bunker (Plastikard)
10 Fire iron tunnel, brass
11 Correct pattern tender handrails
12 Cabside handrails
13 AWS reservoir, brass rod
14 AWS wiring conduit
15 Ejector pipe, brass
16 Boiler handrails
17 Fully sprung chassis (Dave Bradwell kit)
18 Sharman wheels
19 Forked valve gear joints
20 Etched front steps
21 Steam heat pipe (ABS)
22 Vacuum pipe (MJT)

CHAPTER THREE
THE UBIQUITOUS B1
A B1 BASED ON A REPLICA BODY AND A DAVE BRADWELL CHASSIS KIT

The first summer of Nationalisation, with brand-new North British-built No. 61128 in British Railways mixed traffic black and No. 61169, not long out of Vulcan Foundry, in the interim apple-green livery.
S. H. FREESE

THE Thompson B1s — how typical they were of the entire British Railways period. Acceptably anonymous, devoid of strong association with any particular part of the country, they rarely excited any comment except when they turned up — as they so often did — miles away from their usual haunts. Ploughing through my back numbers of *Trains Illustrated,* there are regular sightings from such unlikely places as Bath and Eastbourne, as B1s better associated with the humdrum environs of Mexborough or Grimsby came rolling in on troop trains and pigeon specials, football excursions and holiday extras. They were the classic go-anywhere, do-anything design, to the extent that their day-to-day work in Scotland, East Anglia, the Midlands and the North went largely unremarked. Late in 1947, to commemorate the end of its inde-

pendent existence, the LNER bestowed the names of eighteen of its directors on them. The lack of imagination was ironic, coming from the only post-grouping railway to have a clue about the emotive power of locomotive names, but, like good company men, the B1s did what was asked of them, behaved themselves in public, rarely let the side down and made it safely through to retirement. As a result, they became almost invisible.

At heart, I think it is the ubiquity of the B1s that appeals to me. I don't think of them in terms of specific trains or even places — it was just, somehow, that they always seemed to be around. When I was growing up, West Yorkshire was positively heaving with them, not just on the ex-LNER lines around Leeds, Bradford and Wakefield but also on the ex-L&Y route into Lancashire, where they worked many

of the York–Manchester semi-fasts from the late 1950s until the coming of the class 110 'Calder Valley' DMU sets in 1963. The legendary Heaton–Red Bank empty newspaper vans often produced a B1/Black Five combination, but they were probably most familiar on freight — everything from the Hull-Aintree class Cs (on which they really flew) to slow coal plods, often tender-first. Almost any kind of train, in fact, could turn up with a Bl at its head.

It is their commonplace quality that makes the B1s so attractive as models. I like that feeling of sheer ordinariness in a model railway — 16T minerals, DMUs, colour-light signals. The layouts that have made the greatest impression on me are those in which I recognise this quotidian quality — Dunwich, for one, and Borchester, and Wallsea Main, each of

A closer look at No. 61128. Note the North British plate on the smokebox, which has one of the more common patterns of door.

S. H. FREESE

No. 61247 Lord Burghley *with the all-welded flush-sided pattern of Group Standard tender.*   COLLECTION R. S. CARPENTER

which I have watched in operation for hours at a time because they so convincingly replicate everything I used to enjoy, sitting on a lineside fence with a duffel-bag full of Marmite sandwiches. These are all Eastern Region layouts, of course, and inevitably they all feature B1s. If Peter Denny's 'Buckingham branch' could (heaven forbid) be projected forward half a century, I am sure we would find B1s all over the place.

On a purely visual level — which is how I mostly think about railways — I've always felt the B1s were overly conservative in appearance, considering their late arrival on the scene. Set against such uncompromising contemporaries as Bulleid's Q1s or the Ministry of Supply heavy freight locomotives, there was a distinct air of traditionalism about them — a kind of retro styling which some may find more appealing than I do. It seemed to stretch back twenty years and more to the K3s, A3s and other examples of Gresley's

classicism. Compared with the master, Thompson had no pretensions whatever as a locomotive stylist and I would guess that in designing the B1s under his tutelage, Doncaster was largely following form.

MODEL ASSESSMENT

Only a masochist would think of using anything other than a Replica plastic moulding as the basis of a 4mm scale B1. This excellent plastic moulding easily surpasses the whitemetal kit from Nucast, the etched brass kit from Proscale, or the very basic punched components of the Beatles-era Jamieson kit. Better things have, from time to time, been promised by Riceworks and others but nothing has happened and I would guess that Replica will have the field to themselves for the next decade.

The Replica B1 (also available from Bachmann in one of those peculiar Far East tool-leasing arrangements) has been one of the great success stories of the RTR market in recent years. The bodywork is

pretty good by any standards — let alone those of an RTR model. I am particularly impressed by the cab, which is an important part of the character of a B1, and by the delicacy of the various running-plate fittings — it even has the correctly sunken sandbox fillers. In overall length the model scales out to less than a millimetre of the true figure and, most importantly, the proportions are right. This engine looks like a B1 even before any work is done to it. I think it's the best British steam-outline RTR model that has yet been released.

Some details, inevitably, do not satisfy. Three-inch thick cab side sheets (scale is about ⅛in) and plump handrail stanchions are, it would appear, inevitable on an RTR model but are hardly worth cavilling about — one expects to have to do something about these things, and the rectification procedures are familiar. The backhead is excellent but the footplate is too high, while the curved splashers inside the cab — sized and spaced to allow for coarse-scale OO wheelsets — should really be box-shaped. Inaccuracies in the profile of both chimney and dome are, however, less excusable and even less readily rectified. If moulding masters have to be made, why not make them correct instead of miles out?

The buffer heads are the usual chunky RTR variety with oddly domed heads but the shanks give a very good rendition of the LNER Group Standard variety which was universal on B1s, front and rear. The metal lamp irons might be a tad over-long and over-thick but they are nicely shaped and seated very securely; I would be inclined to leave them as they are. The front steps, however, are badly out in terms of thickness and dimension and need to be replaced. The two steps on either side of the smokebox, on the other hand, are really good, which is a blessing because these are not at all the kind of thing we would want to form from scratch. I have never enjoyed making steps, for some reason.

The only other gripe I have about the loco body concerns the finishing. When the model first appeared, I managed by devious means to get hold of a very early sample and it is an infinitely better pro-

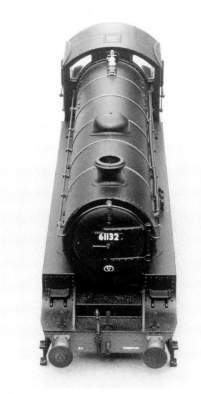

The front end is especially convincing – this really does look like a B1, despite an innacurate smokebox door.

duction than the B1 body and tender that, six or seven years on, I bought as spare parts for this project. Perhaps what I'd really bought was a factory reject, because the cab, a separate unit, was badly seated on the footplate, distorting the latter, and likewise the reverser reach rod was out of position and consequently kinked. Being superglued in place, it was quite an effort to prise them free. The alignment of whistle and safety valves was also off-centre, but this, however, was easily rectified. The single grey line along one footplate edge (there should be a red line as well, of course, and if you want to be really picky a cream one as well) was twice as thick as the one on the other side. The bright red boiler bands were monstrously unprototypical, while the lining was way out of register. The moulding line along the top of the boiler had been smoothed off by some well-meaning soul, which would have been kind of them had they not taken off three or four smokebox rivets into the bargain.

Those riveted smokeboxes, incidentally, were originally found only on the 120 B1s which were built at Darlington, Gorton and Vulcan Foundry. The majority of the

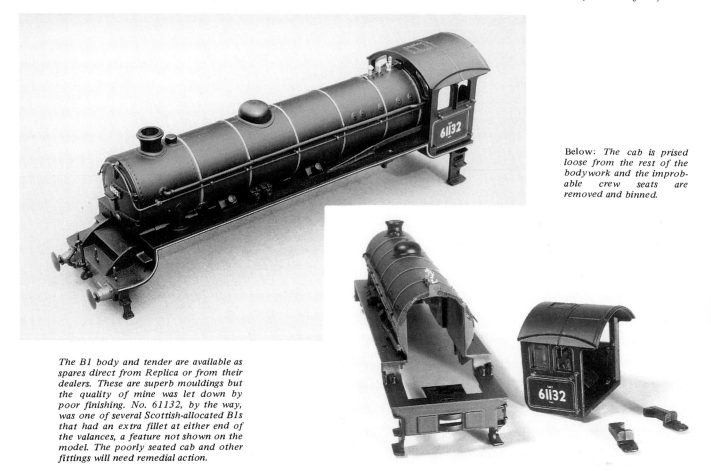

The B1 body and tender are available as spares direct from Replica or from their dealers. These are superb mouldings but the quality of mine was let down by poor finishing. No. 61132, by the way, was one of several Scottish-allocated B1s that had an extra fillet at either end of the valances, a feature not shown on the model. The poorly seated cab and other fittings will need remedial action.

Below: The cab is prised loose from the rest of the bodywork and the improbable crew seats are removed and binned.

class, Nos 1040–1139, 1190–1303, 61304–39/60–99, were built by North British and had welded smokeboxes. Photographic evidence suggests, however, that many engines that were built with riveted smokeboxes later acquired welded ones, and vice versa. Smokebox door types also changed. Some were much more domed than others; the early engines had quite a flat smokebox door but the last fifty or so that were built had a very bulbous design, with closely spaced hinges. Most had something in between although, again, these could change after works visits. Replica's smokebox door, incidentally, doesn't really accord with any style.

While we're talking numbers, we might mention that 1010, 1035–9, 1046, 1190–61399 were fitted with electric lights driven by a Stone's generator on the right-hand smokebox side, a feature missing from the model but, in mitigation, also removed from quite a few prototype engines from the mid-1950s on. In the same period, engines began to acquire AWS equipment and the body moulding has the distinctive step-mounted battery box (but none of the other fittings, although they are easy enough to add). This, by inference, narrows down considerably the prototypes the Replica model can represent without modification. Allowing for the tender variations mentioned below, we would be restricted (in BR numbering) to AWS-fitted engines among Nos 61012–39, 61140–89, 61340–59 and 61400–9, plus any other engine that has lost its generator and electric lighting. Gorton-built Nos 61340–9, however, had a much more angular kind of dome (though not all of them kept them for long) while a feature latterly found on a number of Scottish-based B1s, including several from this list, was a curved strengthening gusset at the front of the footplate valance above the cylinders, with another at the cab end. This made a surprisingly big difference to the appearance of these engines, especially when the footplate-edge lining was visible. As ever, a little research will be necessary before applying the cabside numbers.

TENDER MOULDING

The tender is very good indeed. In fact, Replica have done two versions of it, one which has the rear coal plate straddling the dome (which is the form in which these tenders were built) and the subsequent BR modification with the plate repositioned further forward but leaving correct vesti-

gial marks of the original. Replica models finished in LNER livery have the earlier version, while the BR-liveried locos have the later variant — a nice concern for detail. Bachmann B1s and V2s share the same tender moulding but this appears only to be supplied in the earlier version, whatever the livery.

The LNER Group Standard tender is, of course, anything but standard and you can chalk up six or seven major versions without too much difficulty. Fortunately, at least as far as the B1s are concerned, we

These Group Standard tenders were modified in the 1950s by bringing the rear coal plate forward. Replica have captured very well the vestigial marks this operation left in the region of the water dome. On one of my earlier B1s, I thought this was a flash mark caused by poor mould registration and I trimmed it off...

are supplied with the one we want. Discounting four self-weighing tenders, two V2-type tenders taken from A2/1s and the distinctive pair of tenders sans running plates which were originally built for the booster-fitted Atlantics, the variations were pretty small — a different tender front on the first dozen B1s and square-ended frames on the last seventy (ours has the earlier style). The major visible difference is the coping plates above the tank — on many B1s this was flush but on the others it stands slightly proud and the rear face was riveted.

Fortunately, for all but the first forty B1s (which had different buffing arrangements) the tenders were freely interchangeable, at least in theory, and unless we are really fastidious about these matters we need not get too excited. I suppose the coping, which extends around the rear of the tank, could be got rid of, but life would have been a lot easier if Replica had gone for the flush-sided version in the first place, allowing the zealots among us to improvise the coping out of 5-thou Plastikard. Having said that, I'm more than happy with the tender moulding. The

The tender moulding is again very good. The axleboxes are very crisply moulded and are far better than most castings. The drawhook arrangement shown here would need attention to bring engine and tender closer together – the existing gap could comfortably be halved and the engine would still negotiate train-set curves.

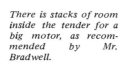

There is stacks of room inside the tender for a big motor, as recommended by Mr. Bradwell.

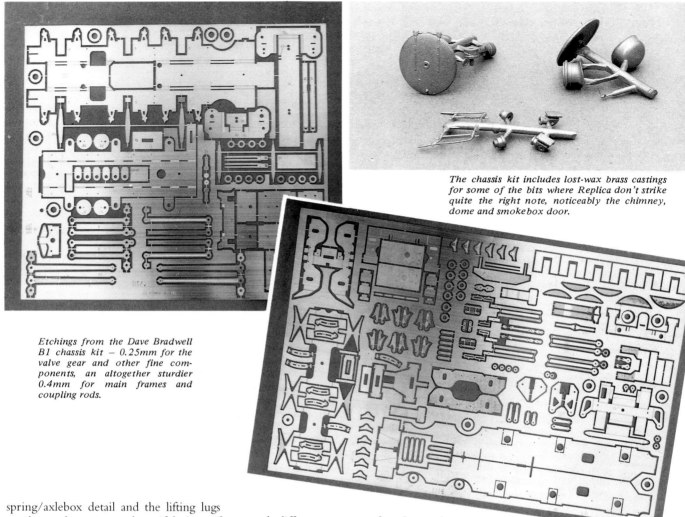

The chassis kit includes lost-wax brass castings for some of the bits where Replica don't strike quite the right note, noticeably the chimney, dome and smokebox door.

Etchings from the Dave Bradwell B1 chassis kit — 0.25mm for the valve gear and other fine components, an altogether sturdier 0.4mm for main frames and coupling rods.

spring/axlebox detail and the lifting lugs on the tender top are a beautiful piece of pattern-making, and so is the tender front. I wish the tool-makers involved with RTR models weren't always anonymous (to me at any rate) as some of them do such wonderfully fine work — this B1, for instance, as well as the Hornby class 25, the Airfix 4F and the later Lima diesels. They deserve our recognition and applause.

CHASSIS

Comet do a B1 loco chassis kit which I would expect is well up to their usual standards. Here, however, I fancied trying something a little more sophisticated. Having decided just by looking at a photograph of a built-up sample that it must be pretty good, I elected to use Dave Bradwell's B1 chassis kit for this project. It covers both loco and tender and, as an added inducement (detail parts for B1s being thin on the ground) comes with a superb set of lost-wax castings for chimney, dome and the two main types of smokebox door. We're also given a replacement set of front and rear steps covering

several different patterns found on the prototype.

This is a pretty thorough and uncompromising kit, designed to be as near as possible to dead scale and featuring sprung suspension, forked valve gear joints and X-rated clearances. And yet, as Dave says in his instructions: "It isn't very difficult to build a basically good model, but it does take a lot of care and patience." I know exactly what he means. I guess it all depends on the different nuances we pick up from terms such as 'difficult' and 'challenging', 'fiddly' and 'intricate'. All too often I've heard people putting down this or that piece of work as though it's the designer's fault they've made a fist of it. Not infrequently it's the builder who isn't up to it but it's a lot easier to run the designer down than to admit one's own limitations. All musicians will know pieces that place tremendous technical demands on them — this doesn't mean they're badly composed, merely that you need to know how many beans make five just to play 'em.

Building a chassis like this can never be as easy as putting together a flat-packed bookshelf from your local DIY store or even assembling a Comet kit — but our Mr B has certainly taken a lot of trouble to help us on our way, not just in the design of his kit but also by the provision of twenty A4 pages of clear, well-written instructions and six more sheets of diagrams. They don't just tell you what to do, they tell you how to do it as well. This thoughtfulness certainly makes the usual single side of A5 look a bit meagre. Because the instructions are so comprehensive, I don't see any point in reiterating them here except where comment is necessary. The pictures will elucidate anything that is unwritten.

You can't rush a kit like this — it simply won't let you — and you need to be in the right frame of mind to begin with. You don't want to be putting fork-jointed valve gear together or fine-tuning the hornblocks if you're in a towering rage or

Left: *The chassis is clamped up with lengths of wood in the vice and folded. I use a heavy steel rule for this operation.* Right: *The second bend is made with another length of wood as a former.*

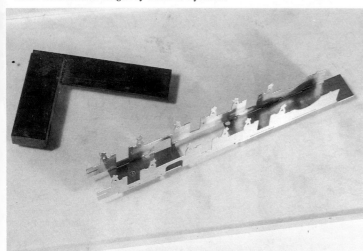 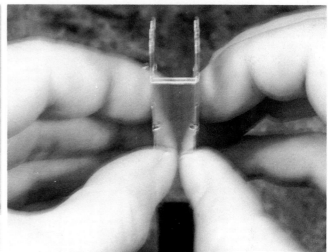

Left: *The chassis is laid on a piece of plate glass and checked for squareness.* Right: *A slight buckling was evident above the centre horns — this is anticipated, I should say, in the instructions. Gentle finger pressure puts things right.*

The outer frame over-lays can be clamped in place with clothes pegs while they are being soldered to the inner chassis. Rods for the brake hangers are temporarily fitted as an aid to alignment. I have seen pieces of contemporary sculpture that look like this, carrying a four-figure price tag.

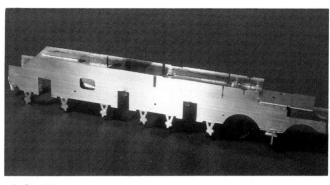

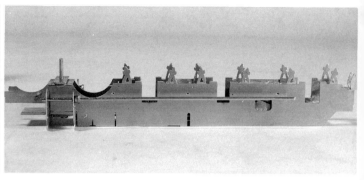

Left: *With the spacers in place we have a nice, strong, healthy chassis.* Right: *The cylinder front and rear are folded up and the assembly is temporarily mounted in the chassis. The correct angle of inclination is divined by making sure a rod passing through the glands aligns with an etched-in mark by the centre hornblock cut-out.*

Left: *The expansion link bracket is a particularly impressive piece of design that is best soldered up on site. To ensure the critical alignments are made, I have jigged it up on temporary wires passing through the frame.* Top right: *The cylinders and motion bracket are designed as an integral assembly that can readily be separated from the chassis. These are the bare bones.* Right inset: *Expansion link bracket complete.*

you've just been doing heavy manual work and your hands are quivering like a convict's after a hard day cracking stones on Dartmoor. But I had a very good feeling about this kit as soon as I felt I'd got sufficient grasp of what was required of me to make a start. Though the kit is designed with the P4 modeller in mind, all reasonable allowances are made for the non-scale gauges — from alternative parts to special notes in the instructions. Again we get a nice, wide, strongly built chassis which will probably get you into trouble if you opt for Romford wheels in EM or OO — but who would want to use Romfords on a top of the line kit like this? At the time of assembling my model, the only suitable driving wheels (6ft 2in, 18 spoke, 13in throw) were from the Sharman range, although Ultrascale have been threatening a V2/B1 wheel for years and Alan Gibson has subsequently produced one of his own.

Building kits of this calibre puts me to the test, but I find them exhilarating. There's a scary element too and I'm not sure that I don't get a kind of masochistic pleasure out of it. I would imagine mountain climbers feel something similar as they study the route ahead. Somehow you seem to become more alert, more conscientious, more determined to get things exactly right. To be honest, reading through the instructions put the fear of God into me — it all seemed so involved, so intricate, so demanding. And yet, once I was under way, my nervousness vanished and I found I was enjoying every minute and, I now realise, pushing myself towards ever higher standards. There may be nearly two hundred parts in this kit but each stage is rarely any more complicated than making a fold or a hole in a piece of nickel and running a piece of wire through it. Broken down into individual steps, it's actually quite

straightforward — the supreme accuracy of the design and etching sees to that.

I have built quite a number of engines with outside Walschaert's but the valve gear in this kit was, in every way, just light years ahead of the rest. I have probably built complete locos in the time it took to fit it all together but rarely have I made anything quite so satisfying. To show the kind of expectations that this kit raises in the builder, there was the unfortunate incident of the valve spindle. I had, as instructed, let a length of 1.5mm OD brass capillary tube into each piston valve head to take the valve spindles that, prototypically, are worked by the oscillation of the combination levers. Absent-mindedly, I used tube from my own stock that had a slightly thicker wall thickness than that supplied with the kit. As a result, I had to use 0.7mm wire for the spindles instead of the 1mm wire specified. I felt quite irritated by

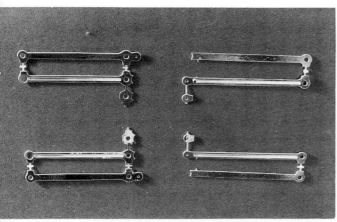
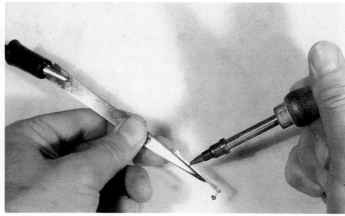

Left: *Fold-up coupling rods take much of the pain out of alignment. Note the additional thickness on the bosses – very prototypical.* Right: *One way of soldering up coupling and connecting rods – holding them in long pointed tweezers with the earth lead of the RSU clamped to one end.*

Left: *The rods have been fettled and generally cleaned up – not that they need much preparation. They are beautifully designed and etched and deserve to be seen at their best.* Right: *Using a carborundum disc to chamfer the front of the knuckle joint so it will clear the big end.*

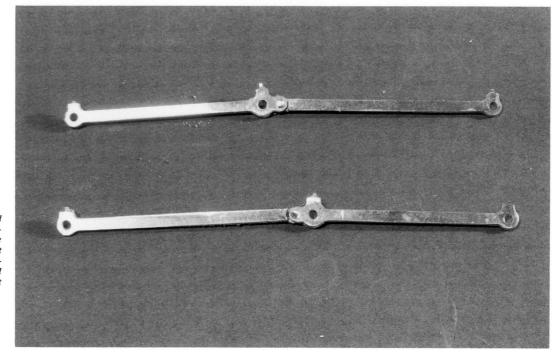

Proper knuckle-jointed coupling rods follow proto-type practice. The rods are drilled to take a 1/32 rivet and the rear face is counter-sunk. The rivet is passed through and the end cut off short.

Right: *The Bradwell kit uses adapted Exactoscale suspension units. The U-shaped nickel plates allow each assembly to be located in its frame cut-out using standard hornblock alignment jigs — this is not normally possible with conventional sprung hornblocks.* Far right: *Now that's what I call a hornblock — big, chunky bearings sliding in substantial brass flanges, each of them individually paired. The twists of wire are hangers for the springs.*

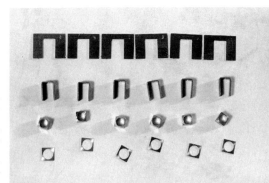

Left: *The centre set of hornguides has now been soldered in place, secured by an axle to get it aligned properly.* Right: *Setting up the centre hornguides. These checking procedures may appear over-cautious but I have been caught out often enough to prefer prevention to cure.*

Left: *Here we go again — no matter how many times I perform this operation, the adrenaline is always flowing as I set up the alignment jigs and fit the coupling rods. The success of the whole project depends on the accuracy achieved at this stage.* Right: *Even with alignment jigs, hornguides don't just shuffle into place automatically. The one on the right will need squaring up before being soldered into position.*

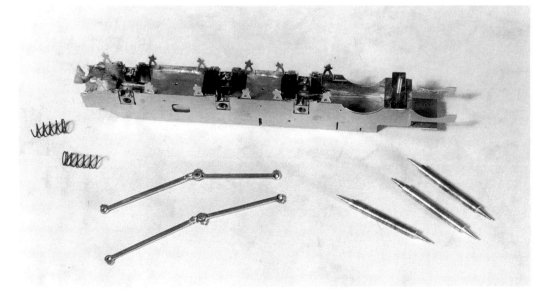

The worst part of the job done — time to relax with a nice cup of tea.

Each wheelset is quartered up in turn with the GW Models wheel press. Note that the hornblocks and washers are already in position on the axle. The back-to-back gauge provides a useful double-check for accuracy.

A trial fit of the rods — with the holes opened out to a running fit on the crankpins — shows everything working smoothly, first time.

Wheels in place, dummy spring assembly screwed down and the suspension springs installed. The instructions — unlike many — make perfect sense throughout. Because they are so comprehensive, they may at times make things seem more complex than they really are. I haven't fitted the gearbox yet as I wanted to ensure everything else was running smoothly.

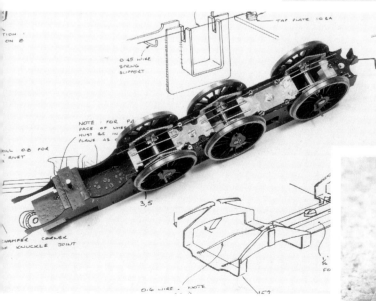

The bogie, before fitting the springs. An improvement on the usual cast blob, wouldn't you say? As with the frames, the concept is unequivocally P4 but the needs of OO and EM people are readily accommodated.

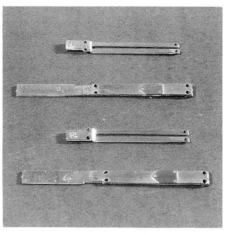

Above: Crosshead castings with 1.25mm nickel wire soldered in place for piston rods. Right: The slidebars are two-part laminations with a detail overlay, already fitted here.

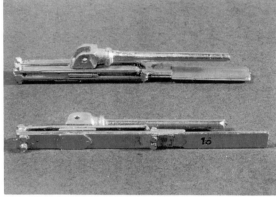

Left: The slidebars are pinned together for alignment. After soldering with the crosshead trapped in position, the pins are cut short and trimmed to represent bolts. Right: What a ravishing piece of engineering the completed slidebar/crosshead assembly is! This is design work of the very highest calibre.

this lapse, as if I'd badly compromised the work by using wire that was 0.3mm finer than it should have been; and yet we are looking at a component which is so nearly invisible to the eye, that it is normally omitted altogether.

The detail that, to me, best summed up this kit was the slidebar assembly. On a real steam locomotive the slidebars are massive steel forgings, maybe six inches by three, that look nothing remotely like the flimsy etched plates supplied in most kits. This skimping and simplifying doesn't mean they run any better — the reverse, in fact. I have made a lot of outside cylinder engines and I usually spend more time on fettling the slidebars and crossheads to get a close, smooth fit than on any other part of the assembly. Under normal circumstances you either get an overweight crosshead and severely malnourished slidebars, or parts that are so loose and floppy that the crosshead charges around all over the place. Major remedial work is needed on both and often I opt for complete replacement.

Not so here. The designer has produced the characteristic three-bar Gresley pattern to as near scale dimensions as makes no difference, and it runs beautifully. His approach, however, sounds like a formula to terrify the beleaguered modeller. To get the right dimensions, three layers of nickel

A quick check with the slidebars, cylinders and motion bracket temporarily fitted to the chassis to reassure myself that everything will go where it is meant to go. Things are looking good, but how often have I had to reach for the files at this stage?

The completed crosshead/slidebar assemblies, before cleaning up. The little end of the con rod pivots on a rivet passing through the crosshead, the rear of which is countersunk to allow the rivet to be soldered and then cut short.

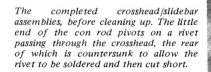

Looking at the real thing, I'm struck by the differing thicknesses of the rods and the knobbly appearance of the joints. Walschaert's valve gear is far more three-dimensional than many kit makers seem to assume, but Dave Bradwell's perceptive eye captures these qualities to perfection.

are sandwiched together, with a cast brass crosshead running between them. Each slidebar needs drilling, riveting, pinning and soldering in perfect alignment, and one layer has to be carefully joggled. And yet, amazingly, everything went together with stunning precision, first time, not because I'm any great whizz at metal-forming but because of the idiot-proof way the kit had been conceived. I took the customary care soldering up the layers but I didn't feel that any particular demands were being placed on my abilities to shape and assemble these components, other than to be nimble of finger and deft with the iron. After routine cleaning-up of the crosshead castings and a couple of wipes with a fine file to remove the cusped edges from the running surfaces of the slidebars, that was about it — and it didn't hurt a bit. The cast crosshead worked first time too, running the full length of the slot in perfect alignment and without a hint of a wobble or a snag.

The skeletal cylinder assembly trial-fitted to the frames. I don't think I have ever known a chassis kit where the alignments were so perfect.

TENDER MATTERS

The tender chassis is a simple one-piece fold-up etch suitable for all three gauges without modification. Because I had decided on a tender-mounted motor, I needed to drill and tap 10BA holes to take

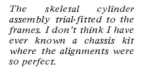

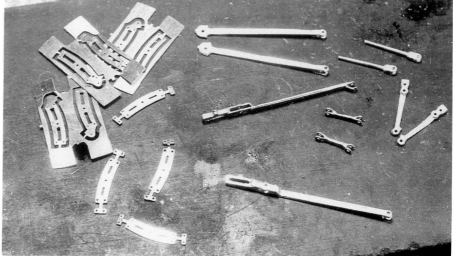

There are five of these parts sandwiched together to make each expansion link. Every one needs a 0.35mm hole drilling in each corner (a dimple is provided as a start) with four extra holes in each of the outer layers — a grand total of 56 tiny holes. I broke three bits before I'd finished the first . . .

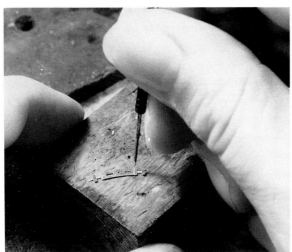

Left: *Small drills do not come cheap and, with another fifty holes to go, I decided to improvise. I found an old, worn-out set of reamers, picked out the finest, snapped off the end and, having ground the tip to a point, used this instead. Needing only periodic resharpening, it did the job very well.* Right: *Cylinder assembly tried in place on the chassis and clearances checked between connecting rods and front crankpin.*

I was another whole day fitting this lot together — and yet it was one of the most rewarding modelling experiences I can remember. The quality of the die-block says it all. For a moment we lesser mortals can breathe the same air as Tony Reynalds or John Hayes.

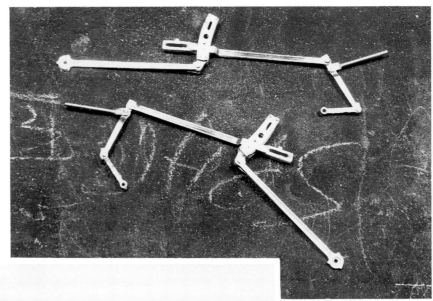

Trial-fit of the motion with the expansion link pinned to the motion bracket so I can check that everything moves as it should — which it does.

the securing screws for the motor plate. I usually have to have these things in bits a few times before I'm happy and it helps if the whole assembly can be taken apart if the need arises. As we shall see, it did . . .

The tender springing was very easy to set up, but I was especially taken by the arrangements for fitting the brake blocks. These are a two-part assembly — hanger and brake shoe — to circumvent the familiar difficulty of getting the shoes aligned with the wheels on anything other than a rigid chassis. Dave's suggestion is that we lightly rivet the shoes to the hanger, allowing them to pivot. We then solder the hangers into place and check that they are truly vertical, fit the stretchers and then adjust the lie of the brake blocks. Once this is satisfactory, the shoes can be soldered in place. A paste flux is obviously the one to use, as acid will attack the wheel

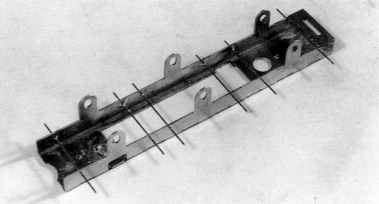

Left. After being folded up in the vice, the alignment of the tender chassis is checked by sighting along the axles. Finger tweaking will put right any discrepancies. Right: Lengths of 0.45mm wire are soldered across the chassis — they have the dual function of supporting springs and brakegear.

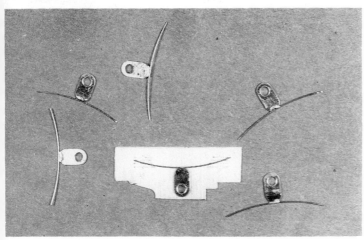
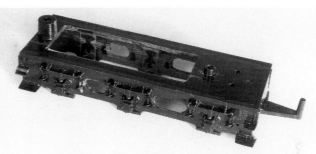

Left: Once assembled, the setting of the tender springs is checked with this simple gauge, nattily etched into the fret. Right: Tender frame moulding with centre section removed to clear motor and the dummy brake detail cut away. The edges of the frame openings have been bevelled to reduce their apparent thickness but otherwise I was happy to go with the proprietary product. Tow-hook retained — for the moment at least — to help with test running.

Left: Mounting plate for the motor, made from nickel silver. The forward lugs deter the 2:1 gearbox from wanting to revolve around its own axis. Note edges rounded off for safety. Right: Original arrangement of motor and 2:1:1 gearbox, test-mounted on the tender chassis.

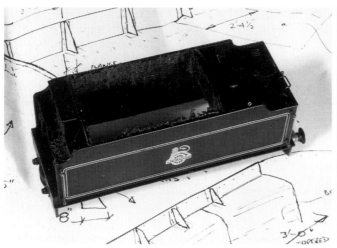
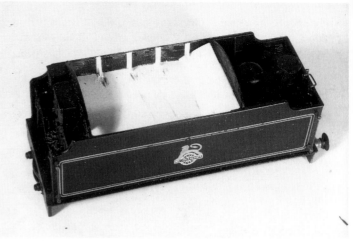

Left: *The moulded coal has been cut out of the Replica tender. Dave Bradwell's drawings show what needs to be done.* Right: *A new tank top is made from Plastikard and the bracing gussets are added in Microstrip.*

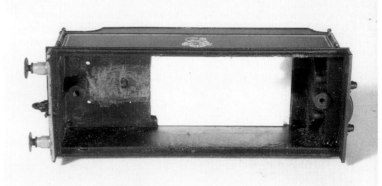

Left: *The fire iron tunnel is formed from 15-thou brass. See how the correct taper has been incorporated at the cab end. There should be a self-trimming hopper but, as it will be covered in coal, I was happy to omit it.* Right: *Tender body from underneath, showing how the new tank top rests on a ledge of Microstrip.*

tyres and cause corrosion. White spirit gets rid of any residues of Fluxite.

THE TRANSMISSION

Captivated by some video footage that showed a tender-first B1 with a trip freight, drifting smoothly and slowly towards an adverse signal, I decided to build an engine with similar running qualities. This meant choosing a suitable motor/gearbox arrangement. The kit is designed to take an RG4 on the centre axle, which is fine in P4, but in OO, and possibly EM as well, there is no way the gearbox is going to fit between the hornblocks without serious filing. I chose to put a Mashima 1628 motor in the tender, fitted with the largest flywheel that would go in and driving a 2:1:1 two-stage Exactoscale reduction gearbox, which, via a couple of ball-and-socket joints, would power a 30:1 gearbox hung on the rear axle of the loco. This, I reasoned, would give me a muscular, slow-running engine

that would be ideal for local freight and shunting work.

I built and bench-tested the drive train well ahead of time but didn't install it until the chassis and bodywork were well advanced. In keeping with the Swiss-

watch engineering of the chassis kit, all the components were from the Exactoscale range. This transmission system is a great favourite of mine, being compact (the worm gearboxes are smaller than a postage stamp), beautifully designed and very

Several changes of plan were necessary before I reached the optimum arrangement of the drive train. Cardan shafts do not like steep angles.

Left: *Exactoscale worm gearbox in pieces, with size comparison.* Right: *The two gearboxes complete and ready for installation.*

smooth running, especially when the gears are lubricated by packing the inside of the box with a grease such as Pronatur or Labelle 106. I run mine in by driving them in the chuck of a mini-drill for half an hour or so; you could use a lathe if you have one. After a couple of sessions of bedding-in they run silently and cold and, more importantly, they stay that way.

The way I conceived the drive train for this B1, the 2:1:1 reduction box would be fitted directly to the tender-mounted motor, driving the 30:1 box on the rear axle via a cardan shaft with Exactoscale ball and socket couplings at each end. Ideally, of course, the transmission should be as close to a straight line as possible, but this was not possible in an engine with such deep frames and large wheels as a B1. By making the driven shafts as long as practicable, the best I could do was to have the cardan rising upwards at an angle of approximately 15° from the horizontal, from a point midway between the two leading axles of the tender.

Component parts of the Exactoscale flexible coupling, with cardan shafts and ball-and-socket joints. The neoprene tube slips over the joined shafts.

This worked pretty well on the bench but benches tend, as a rule, to stay still and not to bob up and down vigorously, exerting all kinds of pushing and pulling forces in several dimensions at once while they try to haul dead weight around. A vast amount of torque was being expended simply on getting the sleeving to flex and it was obvious, once the system was installed in the loco and current applied, that all was not well. The 1628 got very hot and bothered, which is unusual for this design, and the power output was uneven. The top speed, too, was much less than my calculations had predicted, which suggested that the drive train was soaking up a lot of the motor's considerable power output.

It was clear, the way I had installed the transmission, that the levels of friction

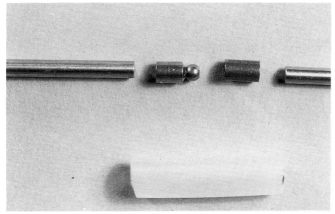

The inner workings of the Exactoscale 2:1:1 reduction gearbox.

Worm gearbox in place on rear axle, showing the ball end of the Exactoscale ball-and-socket joint that will link it to the motor in the tender. Without weight, the chassis is slightly 'up' on one side, remedied by a half-turn of the relevant spring adjusting screw – all part of the plan and covered in the instructions.

involved were too great, even though each component worked beautifully in isolation. In the end, I took out the 2:1:1 box and drove the worm gearbox direct, with the cardan at an angle of about 10°. Things were much better, but even this arrangement soaked up more than enough energy to cause concern. If an angled drive is unavoidable, then the use of a very powerful motor, with sufficient torque to overcome the loss of output, seems to be essential. Even the 1628 wasn't quite man

enough here, and in a later chapter we will see the massive Mashima 1833 (nominally an O gauge motor) successfully installed in a flywheel-driven Bulleid Pacific.

To get the cardan at a much more sociable angle, I discarded the screw-in motor mount that I had made and sawed away part of the tender chassis to get the Mashima — now epoxy-mounted to a simple plastic block — tucked down between the tender frames with its tail in the air. The drive is more or less straight

from the output shaft and it connects with the gearbox input shaft at an angle of about 5°. With a nice heavy loco and a lead-packed tender to cushion motor vibrations — the all-up weight in fighting trim is in the region of 500g (1lb 2oz) — the running was vastly improved. I felt much happier too, watching that marvellous silky movement that only a fully sprung locomotive can produce.

On the B1, the cardan runs directly under the tender fall plate. The cab floor

The final — and most successful — configuration of the tender unit, with the motor low down in the frames with its tail in the air, and the cardan in an almost straight line.

Interim version of the tender motor unit, with pick-ups on the leading axles and the electrical connection with the engine ending in tubular plugs that will mate with sockets under the cab floor. Despite losing the 2:1:1 box, the cardan was still too steeply inclined for comfort.

Left: *The clearance for the cardan shaft under the cab floor is very tight. Note the sockets for the motor leads.* Right: *The slot cut into the tender front to allow for lateral displacement of the drive shaft. There is a similar arrangement on the loco dragbeam.*

A temporary drive shaft attached to the gearbox allows me to turn the chassis over by hand to test valve gear clearances. This is not only the finest and most complete set of Walschaerts I have ever made, but also the only one where nothing whatever needed shortening, lengthening, tweaking, twisting, filing, cajoling, packing or pruning.

The pick-ups are duplicated — two per wheel — for improved current collection. They run from busbars soldered to copper-clad strips. The tubes on the extreme left are sockets into which the motor leads are plugged.

on the body moulding is too high (see below) and when a scale-height replacement is fitted, it only just clears the top of the gearbox input shaft. This effectively precludes the use of Exactoscale's 40:1 gearbox which is 25% deeper than the 30:1 version. It will certainly go in, and it would probably give slightly better low-speed running than 30:1 (although it was good enough for me and I'm pickier than most) but accommodating the cardan as well would, I imagine, call for a bit of backhead carving and some further mucking about with the cab floor. This kind of thing is fine, as we shall see, in the murky depths of a Bulleid Pacific, but the cab interior of a B1 is very visible and is best left alone.

SETTING UP THE CHASSIS

A sprung loco chassis needs a lot of care in the final adjustment to running condition and I was grateful that I could strip this one down to basics to attend to such matters as spring adjustment and weighting without other things getting in the way. Having evenly weighted the body up

to approximately 6oz (170g), I made a little Plastikard gauge for determining the ride height of the loco and then altered the height of the screws that secure the springs until the loco sat level but not quite flush with the gauge. I then added a couple more ounces of lead, distributed evenly, to increase the adhesion and bring the body down to scale height above rail level.

The tender needed particular attention to weighting, for a number of reasons: to establish the correct ride height, to ensure the proper function of the spring suspension, to deaden the noise of the motor and to damp vibrations from same. I added lead along the inner sides of the tank and packed more into the rear, behind the flywheel. I used the minimum amount that would do the job; there is space to add more, but this would add to the dead weight that needs to be hauled around. As it is, the tender weighs 6oz (180g) which is probably as much if not more than most whitemetal tenders. Without proper attention to weighting and especially to the way the motor is mounted, it is quite possible

for one of these big cans to generate enough torque to flip the tender over bodily when under load.

As well as the effectiveness of springing — in motion, this big, heavy loco has a lovely gliding feel to it — the other main thing I learned was how much easier life is if a chassis is assembled as a series of modular units. I like the modern tendency towards loco and chassis kits that not only go together, but also come apart. It can be very useful to be able to take off the valve gear, remove a wheelset and generally make adjustments without major surgery, especially if, like me, you are one of those people who doesn't always get everything right first time.

LOCO BODY MODIFICATIONS

I think, with hindsight, that it's best to get the chassis running and the body correctly weighted and positioned before making any cosmetic alterations to the plastic moulding. I didn't, and ended up knocking bits off the half-completed body. Because the detail is so good to begin with,

Left: The dummy front frames are marked for removal. I got rid of them with a craft knife. The steps can go too.

however, reworking the B1 is not an especially complex operation. Such improvements as need to be made are helped by the fact that the cab and most of the other fittings come free with a bit of firm persuasion. Then, once I had stripped the body of the unwanted details — handrails, chimney, dome, smokebox door and buffer heads — it was a simple matter to replace them with scale components. Most of these came with the chassis kit and the rest were improvised in the usual way from brass and Microstrip. Other than the detail parts that came with the chassis kit, I spent very little money on the cosmetics of this model, beyond the small net cost of the raw materials. I find this approach very satisfying and closer, in many ways, to the true spirit of finescale modelling.

Left: The underside of the running plate is then filed flush. The chassis is a very snug fit and we don't want anything fouling it. *Right:* Compensating perhaps for the care I put into upgrading RTR locomotives, I get an obscene amount of pleasure from the preliminary assault on their fabric. The weapons of destruction are simple — craft knives, cheap files, and a razor saw.

The ensuing wreckage.

I took out Replica's cab floor which is seated much too high and has the wrong shape of inner splashers — these should be square, not round. The new cab floor was from scribed 20-thou Plastikard, trimmed to a snug fit and welded into place with Liquid Poly. The splashers were simple boxes of 10-thou, though dimensions and clearances obviously need to be checked against the chassis and to be adjusted or compromised as necessary. I made a pair of bucket seats from Plastikard with the characteristic ribbing added in Microstrip. When everything had set, I fitted new cab handrails, using Alan Gibson's 'short' pattern of stanchion.

The AWS reservoir in front of the cab is from brass rod cut to length. I replaced the ejector pipe that runs along the left-hand side of the boiler with a new one out of 0.9mm brass wire, with fuse-wire fixings. The chimney, dome and smokebox door that came with the chassis kit were a commendably snug fit and I used merely the thinnest smear of epoxy to hold them in place. The dome isn't correctly seated in some of the photographs but I was able to put it right before painting.

In terms of the work involved, the main hassle I found was getting rid of the old handrails. The metal stanchions were glued in very solidly and, when persuaded with long-nosed pliers, kept snapping off. The remains had to be dug or drilled out before I could fill the resulting holes with Miliput, drill them out afresh and start all over again. This was a hassle, and I think there's a case for leaving the handrails as they come, plumpish knobs notwithstanding.

Photographs of my chosen prototype revealed it still had its electric lighting at

Left and right: Most of the alloy handrail knobs came out cleanly when persuaded with pliers, but some merely snapped off. I had to grind down the stumps with a dental burr, drill them out and fill the resulting holes.

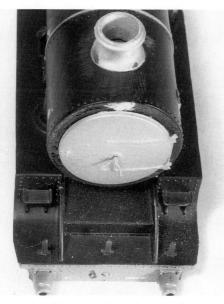

Left: Detailing components need to be aligned with care — wonky chimneys and off-centre domes look awful. A magnifying glass — or the camera lens — quickly reveals anything that isn't as it should be, like the dome . . . Right: The hollowed-out chimney is wonderful and Dave Bradwell also gives us two types of smokebox door. What a kind man he is! I was surprised we didn't get a steam generator, too, but what we have is more than generous.

No. 61201 has a B17-type smokebox door (Nos. 8301-10 only had these from new) and the Stone's electrical generator mounted on the front running plate.
                                                                                                           A. N. H. GLOVER

Left: *The basis of the Stone's steam generator is a length of 2mm brass rod with collars cut from capillary tube. It can be held in a pin chuck to make it easier to work.* Right: *The cable conduits are from 0.7mm brass wire let into holes drilled into the brass rod.*

Left: *The finished item. In the absence of a drawing I was working from photographs but I think the rudiments of the thing are here.* Right: *The pipework locates into holes in the smokebox, drilled slightly oversize to allow room for manoeuvre. The gaps are then filled with black Plasticine.*

the relevant period (early 1960s) and so I turned up a Stone's generator from 2mm brass rod with the flanges and other details made from thin collars of capillary tube, filed down as necessary. The various conduits came from wire, set into holes drilled in the smokebox. The lights themselves are simply made by drilling a length of 40-thou square Microstrip to accept brass pins stuck in place with solvent. When set, I cut off the tails of the pins and then cut the strip down into little cubes, the head of each pin representing the lens (Chris Pendlenton makes the body of the lamp out of brass bar, drilled for a little puddle of Krystal Kleer which represents the lens). The lamps were then stuck on to the exist-

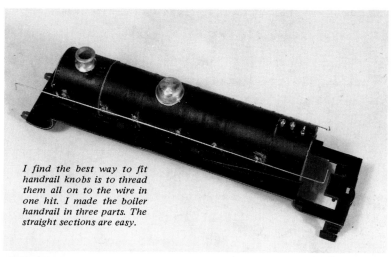

I find the best way to fit handrail knobs is to thread them all on to the wire in one hit. I made the boiler handrail in three parts. The straight sections are easy.

Left: *The curved part is more tricky, and I rarely get this right first time. The handrail wire is formed around a steel bar and — with the knob for the smokebox front now attached — the bends are put in and the straight sections trimmed to length.* Right: *When I'm satisfied with its shape, the completed front part of the handrail is offered up and fitted into the handrail knobs on the smokebox sides. I don't push it fully home, instead leaving a little recess at the rear so the straight sections can just about get a purchase in the same handrail knob. A wipe of solder helps the handrails stay put. The aluminium acts as a heat sink and protects the plastic.*

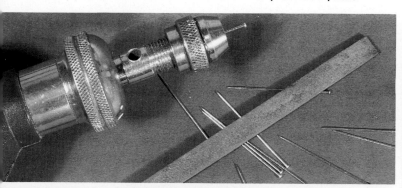

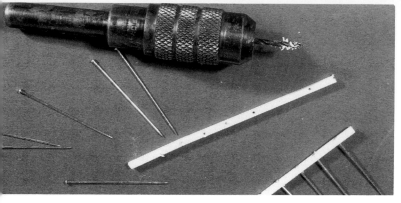

Top left: *To make the lenses for the Thompson-pattern electric lights — also found on L1s and some of the Pacifics — a brass pinhead is thinned down almost to nothing.* Left: *A line of holes is drilled in a length of 60-thou microstrip and lightly countersunk on the front. The pins are then inserted into the microstrip, secured with solvent and the ends snipped off.* Above: *Finally the strip is cut into lamp-sized sections. I usually make a lot and pick the best. Once in place on the model, the electrical conduits are added from 5-amp fuse wire. One of the double lamps in the centre — the right-hand one, I think — has a red lens, to act as a tail light.*

Cab of No. 61332 at Gorton Works on 2nd May 1953.

H. F. WHEELLER

ing lamp irons which are just about the right length. They are probably best left off until immediately before the model is painted. The wiring, copied from photographs, should be added from 5amp fuse wire. On the prototype, it usually looked a bit untidy.

I like to take my time about detailing work, spreading it over several sessions and alternating it with the more technically demanding stuff, such as fiddling with gearboxes and transmissions. If this kind of cosmetic modelling is 'about' anything then I would guess it is the slow and patient accumulation of detail in response to observation. The key to success, I am sure, lies in having the right reference material to hand and the technical skills to make use of it. So I checked things like whether or not my prototype had the smokebox step that was fitted to many B1s — it didn't — and did it have AWS at the relevant period — it did. You get an AWS protection plate with Dave Bradwell's kit, but I didn't bother with the magnet below it which, from previous experience, can impede the bogie swing. Left unresolved, pending further research, was the ashpan detail — some B1s had a rod-and-crank arrangement (with a little triangular cover plate on the footplate, ahead of the cab on the right-hand side) and others didn't. I chose to omit it, at least for the moment. It is usually easier to add detail than to remove it.

Steam heat pipes, curiously, seem to be modelled only rarely and I've never seen

Left: *I've drilled holes in the wrongly shaped cab splashers and then I will scalpel out the webs that remain.* Right: *Replica's cab floor is several inches too high and doesn't align with the tender – so out that comes too.*

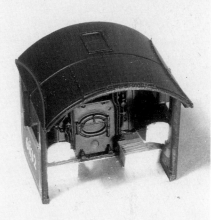

Left: *New, scale-thickness cab floor, scribed to represent 6in planking. Correct square-pattern splashers have also been fitted.* Right: *Bucket seats with the characteristic ribbing reproduced in Microstrip.*

Left: *The ejector pipe is a length of 9mm wire suitably shaped and with fixings added from fuse wire.* Right: *Pipe runs are prototypically crooked.*

No. 61409, at Sheffield Victoria in July 1962, paired with an all-welded Group Standard tender with integral coping plate. This was one of ten engines built at Darlington in 1950 which had tall lamp irons but no provision for electric lighting.

one with the hose removed, as they very often were in the summer months, leaving the valve mounted just below the buffer beam. This detail was from the neat ABS casting, ref U29. The large LNER date-of-build plates on the forward frame were brass blanks from 5522 Models; at first, the North British-built engines carried the distinctive diamond-shaped works plates on the centre line of the smokebox but many subsequently lost them as smoke-boxes were swapped around. There are two short grab rails above the front steps, mod-elled from 0.33mm wire. Hoist with my own petard, I had just about got this lot on when I realised the moulding didn't have any lifting holes at the front end, so I had to go in very carefully with a 0.7mm drill. Something else I almost missed was the conduit running along the left-hand foot-plate valance of AWS-equipped engines, immediately below the beading; 0.33mm wire is about right and if you want to do the tiny split pins that hold it in place, you're on your own.

REWORKING THE TENDER

Replica's tender is moulded in two parts, frames and body, which simply screw together with the usual self-tappers. With my tender-powered transmission, a large opening needed to be carved out of the

plastic-moulded chassis to allow it to slip easily over the inner chassis once the motor, gearbox and flywheel were in place. I also had to create space for the drive shaft running forward to the loco (all that is needed is a cut-out beneath the coal plate) and to carve away the moulded-on repre-sentation of the brake gear, not forgetting to bevel off the visible edges. All the other work was concentrated on the tender body and there was rather more of that.

The tender handrail stanchions came away rather more easily than the ones on the loco and I replaced them, having filled the holes with Miliput, with Alan Gibson's 'short' variety. Note that on the real thing, unlike the RTR model, the handrails extend some inches beyond the stan-chions, top and bottom. No doubt they snagged a fair few enginemen's sleeves in their day — BR diesel shunters were built with the same pattern of handrails but

Tender rear detail — lighting conduits from 0.33mm wire, vac pipe from MJT, steam-heat pipe by ABS.

later, in response to complaints, they were cut off flush.

Dave Bradwell very kindly sent me copies of his drawings showing the inside of the coal space on a Group Standard tender. I felt it would be a nice idea to model a half-empty tender that showed the fire-iron tunnel and the flanges inside the top raves, but I didn't bother with the self-trimming hopper at the front because of all the electrical bits underneath. This work entailed removing the rather generous filling of plastic coal and building a new tank top. The coal appears to be a separate moulding from that for the main body. It also incorporates the rear coal plate, no doubt to enable Replica to produce the two versions of the Group Standard tender that I mentioned earlier. My 'coal' seemed to be pretty solidly glued in place, however, and so I took it out with a piercing saw. You could also drill a series of holes around the edges and cut through them but this is dirty work and creates clouds of bits.

The jagged edges that result from this surgery can be smoothed off with progressively finer files. It would be a good idea, at

the same time, to lightly bevel the exposed edges to reduce their apparent thickness. We now have a decision to make. There should — except on the flush-sided GS tenders — be a line of rivets along the inside top edge of the tender side sheets and the front and rear coal plates. It would certainly be possible, if time-consuming and eye-straining, to add these rivets in the form of minute dots of Microstrip, à la Geoff Kent. Personally I would prefer to make up thin overlays using my riveting tool but on the B1 this would add to the thickness of an already over-scale moulding. Reluctantly I did neither, and instead thinned down the edges as best I could.

The removal of the coal leaves rather a weak tender structure and it would be as well, before any detailing work is carried out, to get a new tank top in place to strengthen the moulding. I made this from 20-thou plastic sheet 45mm × 28mm, supported lengthways on battens of 60-thou square Microstrip. In BR days a sloping panel was added at the rear of the coal space, rising until it was level with the top of the tender sides. This is represented by another piece of 20-thou measuring

11.5mm × 28mm, the edges being bevelled to lie flush. The inside of the tender is braced on each side by triangular gussets and these were cut to size from 10-thou Microstrip.

The tunnel for the fire irons was more of a challenge although the idea was simple enough. I cut a length of 15-thou brass 43mm × 10mm and bent it down the middle in a vice to give a curved edge. I used the invaluable carborundum disc in my mini-drill to cut a chamfer in one end to accommodate the sloping panel against the rear coal plate. The forward 3ft of the tunnel is tapered outwards and upwards and to do this I cut a 12mm slit with a piercing saw and then bent the edges out until the amount of taper looked about right. To fill the gap I soldered a stub of 2mm brass rod into the void and filled any chinks with 145° solder. After rounding off this fillet with an emery-board file, I glued the fire iron tunnel in place with contact adhesive.

FINISHING

Tempering a last-minute urge to finish the model as one of the handful of B1s that, in

The classic 'lid-off' shot beloved of MRJ. It never ceases to surprise me that I should ever get to this stage, with the chassis running nicely and most of the detail on.

the early months of Nationalisation, came out of Darlington and Cowlairs in LNER green, but bearing BR numbers and lettered 'BRITISH RAILWAYS', I stuck to the original plan and finished the loco in late-period BR livery, well weathered. Although many mixed-traffic classes — the Stanier and BR Standard class 5s, for instance — were latterly turned out in plain black, the B1s were always fully lined out.

I gave the loco and tender bodies a gentle scrub in washing-up liquid to get rid of finger grease, moulding release agents and other nasties, and then sprayed them with Halford's own-brand satin black acrylic car paint. This yielded a finish as smooth as any I've seen from a professional model-painter (mental notes duly made) but this wasn't the effect I was after. The next stage was the lining-out, for which I used a Bob Moore pen and neat Humbrols. The grey — on a dirty engine, something that's more of a muddy cream is preferable — was applied with the standard head. I find that with red-on-black it's difficult to get sufficient body of colour using red paint alone, especially with the fine head that I was using here. I prefer to apply a roughly equal mix of red, white and yellow. The resulting flower-pot shade goes on much better — the white makes it virtually self-undercoating — and of course it's nearer to 'scale' colour anyway. The boiler bands are transfers from the PC/HMRS series, applied with great care to minimise those tiny silvery patches,

Protec's polyacrylic primer is ideal for brushing on to brass details applied to a plastic body.

caused by minute air bubbles, that give the game away.

This wasn't my best-ever lining job but it didn't matter too much because most of it would be gently diffused and obscured by weathering. Sometimes, on a well-weathered loco, I will omit parts of the lining completely, especially any tricky bits such as reverse curves or crescent shapes. As long as some at least of the main bits are present — cab sides, tanks and tenders — it is surprising how the eye can be deceived into 'seeing' lining when it isn't there, especially if just the odd section or two of the difficult stuff is included, a

corner here, a straight length there. All that is needed is a gentle build-up of weathering in the area concerned to make us think the lining is just out of sight, under the coat of grime. Of course, I didn't reckon I could get away with such short-cut shenanigans here and I did the whole lot. The running plate lining, which continues on to the tender, was something of a pain to apply and I was peeved to find that I'd lost the greater part of it under the weathering.

The grubbing-up process was much the same as for the 4F. Note the various end-of-steam touches such as the electrification

Beneath a wintry sky, a well-weathered No. 61016 Inyala bringing a train of empty coal wagons into Huddersfield on 9th November 1963. This picture shows the riveted pattern of Group Standard tender, with raised coping plate. Note the water-filler characteristically left open.

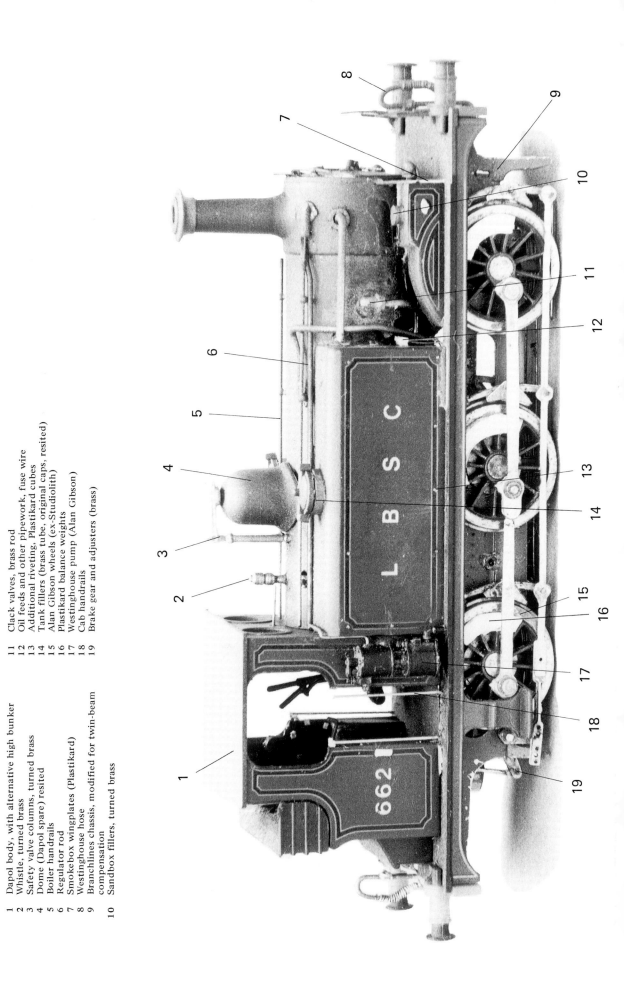

1 Dapol body, with alternative high bunker
2 Whistle, turned brass
3 Safety valve columns, turned brass
4 Dome (Dapol spare) resited
5 Boiler handrails
6 Regulator rod
7 Smokebox wingplates (Plastikard)
8 Westinghouse hose
9 Branchlines chassis, modified for twin-beam
   compensation
10 Sandbox fillers, turned brass

11 Clack valves, brass rod
12 Oil feeds and other pipework, fuse wire
13 Additional riveting, Plastikard cubes
14 Tank fillers (brass tube, original caps, resited)
15 Alan Gibson wheels (ex-Studiolith)
16 Plastikard balance weights
17 Westinghouse pump (Alan Gibson)
18 Cab handrails
19 Brake gear and adjusters (brass)

CHAPTER FOUR

THE GHOST ENGINE

A BRIGHTON TERRIER BASED ON A DAPOL BODY AND A BRANCHLINES CHASSIS KIT

With 1,165,194 miles already on the clock, Colonel Stephens got little return on the £1,750 he paid for the former Shadwell, *and even this was £50 more than the engine's 1872 building costs. Acquired for the Edge Hill Light in July 1920, the engine was laid aside in 1925. It is seen here, entirely abandoned, in 1935. The unknown photographer obliged posterity by pulling back the ragged tarpaulins that, for twenty years, partially covered the engine.*   AUTHOR'S COLLECTION

I never knew the Brighton 'Terriers' at first hand, which is ironic because I was at university in the town and indeed lived there for some years afterwards. But by the time I came to get some letters after my name, these picturesque little engines were long gone from the obscure shunts and pilot duties that they had performed for so long.

Outwardly demure and elegant, they seem, to modellers at least, to be the archetypal locomotive for a branch line or light railway, although they packed more of a punch than their diminutive appearance might suggest. My introduction to these quintessentially Victorian locomotives was strange to the point of surreal, and came in the early hours of a cold, damp morning in Ayrshire. It was one of those monumental weekend shed bashes that seemed to occupy much of my youth in the 1960s, when I wasn't busy playing colts rugby or chasing girls (mostly unsuccessfully) round the local discos. We'd already done

Stranraer shed at dawn — a two-hundred mile detour to pick up half a dozen engines — and in the grey light of early morning we pulled up outside Butlin's holiday camp near Ayr. No one was stirring in the chalets and the interior of the coach was pretty lifeless too, a mass of humped bodies stupefied by stale, unwarmed air.

I rubbed the condensation from the window. There, in the drizzle, was the familiar bulk of *Duchess of Sutherland,* utterly dwarfing the diminutive engine parked next to it, the erstwhile *Martello* of the LBSCR. It was the first Terrier I had seen and I guess there was some excitement about it — preserved locos were still pretty thin on the ground back then and anything pre-grouping Southern was a distinct rarity for me. I made a note of the numbers, as the slumped figures all around me began to come to life and drowsily grasp what the fuss was all about. When curiosity had been satisfied, our driver

revved his engine and we headed off for Aberdeen by way of Ayr, Hurlford, Greenock, the Glasgow sheds and points north, a thousand numbers or bust.

Compared with a Duchess, I guess the Terriers would seem pretty small in stature but I came to build this model after a spell of working on industrial locomotives. After a Doxford crane tank or a Black Hawthorn, Stroudley's little tank engine seemed massive. All that room inside the boiler and between the tanks! A coal bunker begging to be filled with lead to bring weight on to the rear axle! Four-foot driving wheels! The scope for improvisation seemed enormous.

Few modelling projects are simpler than a six-wheeled tank engine — at least in theory. Having made one or two, I like to ring the changes and experiment with new ideas because half the fun of any building project, for me, is figuring out how I am going to tackle it. This can, and frequently does, take a very long time. I tend not to sit down and consider the possibilities, rather do I prefer to wait for inspiration to float up from my subconscious. So I get on with other things while, like an underground river, the modelling options trundle gently through the left hemisphere.

What finally came through the ether was a Dapol body (pretty obvious), a Branchlines chassis kit (again, fairly predictable), Alan Gibson wheels and a Mashima 1224 motor with the highly adaptable Backwoods Miniatures 'Contorto' gearbox in its 108:1 configuration. There's no reason why the model shouldn't be built with a less spectacular reduction (50:1 or even 38:1) if dead-slow running is not a prime consideration, or that the chassis shouldn't be built as per instructions. However, I had been getting a bit bored with simple beam-compensated systems with a rigid driven axle so I decided to go for an equalised twin-beam set-up with a floating rear-axle drive and a pivoted front axle.

THE PROTOTYPE

I hope readers will have gathered by now that I never make a generic model, always preferring to replicate a particular locomotive at a particular time in its life. Researching these minutiae is, for me, another very pleasurable part of the modelling equation, especially if it's a class I've not been familiar with. The story of the Terriers is exceptionally well documented and needs only the baldest summary here (see my list of background reading for more information). Quite apart from minor detail differences, the Terriers came in two major versions — A1 and the reboilered A1X class — and there was a considerable number of livery variations, right through into BR ownership. To add to the mix, a fair number were sold out of service both in LBSCR and in Southern days. Some, bought by the Admiralty, gravitated to Scotland — one for the 'prototype for everything' department? — while nine of them eventually ended up with Colonel Stephens, who used them on

lines as geographically remote from traditional Terrier territory as the Weston, Clevedon & Portishead and the Shropshire & Montgomeryshire.

One of the LBSCR disposals was motor-fitted A1 No. 674 *Shadwell*, which entered service in October 1872 and ran more than a million miles before being sold to the Colonel in July 1920. Like A1X rebuild No. 673 *Deptford*, which the great man had bought earlier, *Shadwell* was destined for the Edge Hill Light Railway. Opened in 1920, this was a purely mineral line in which the Colonel had an interest. It conveyed ironstone brought down by rope-worked incline from quarries at Edge Hill, Oxfordshire to the Stratford-on-Avon & Midland Junction Railway interchange sidings at Burton Dassett, just over two miles away. I believe from the less than convincing evidence of a couple of photographs of these engines at work, that *Shadwell* at least was never repainted from its Marsh brown livery; other than to carry

At least one representative of most classes is camera-shy and one of the more elusive 'Terriers' is No. 42 Tulsehill, spelt by the LBSCR as one word. Withdrawn as early as 1926, it remained in totally original condition for all its (by 'Terrier' standards) comparatively short life. Note, among other details, the early-pattern brake shoes.
AUTHOR'S COLLECTION

a new number, 2, and the letters 'EHLR' on its tanks.

Unfortunately for the Colonel and the other investors, the ore deposits soon gave out and by 1925 the line was moribund; its temporary closure became permanent. The two Terriers, along with the EHLR's motley collection of rolling stock, were simply left to moulder in the sidings at the foot of the incline (there was also a Manning Wardle 0–4–0ST tucked under a bridge at the top) and here they remained for twenty years, undisturbed except by local youth and visiting railway enthusiasts. Not until 1946 were the locomotives cut up on site by James Friswell & Company of Banbury. Perhaps some obscure legal tangle explains their strange and ghostly survival; with working Terriers to maintain elsewhere, it is surprising the Colonel's men did not rob the Edge Hill pair for spares. The Southern, at one stage, got so desperate that they actually bought back one of his redundant Terriers — old No. 83 *Earlswood* and latterly *Daphne* of the Shropshire & Montogomeryshire — and towed it to Eastleigh for cannibalisation. Maybe they simply forgot about the two ghosts of Edge Hill.

I first became aware of these derelicts through some highly atmospheric photographs by H C Casserley, showing the line in its latter days. I'm afraid I'm one of those people — anathema, no doubt, to the heritage industry — who much prefers his historical artefacts to be weed-strewn, rusting and remote, rather than stuffed and mounted in some theme park. I immediately felt drawn to the tattered tarpaulins in which *Shadwell* was shrouded and the faded remains of its LB&SCR lettering

Among other accretions, the former Waddon *gradually gained a Wainwright boiler. Drummond chimney and Ramsbottom safety valves. In 1932, it entered service stock as 680S, but by 1937 the engine had been again rebuilt with an A1X boiler and coal rails. As it retained the short smokebox with wing plates, this created a real hybrid among the 'Terriers'.*
AUTHOR'S COLLECTION

Reboilered to A1X class in 1911 — note the extended smokebox and the sandboxes resited below below the running plate — the former Knowle *was one of four 'Terriers' that went to the Isle of Wight in 1929, acquiring the unique extended bunker of the island engines and a new identity as IOW No. 14* Bembridge. *The quartet returned to the mainland in 1936 and* Bembridge *became plain No. 2678 once more.*
AUTHOR'S COLLECTION

and number showing through the markings of later EHLR ownership.

Many years later, the desire to produce a 'light railway' engine for this book gave me the chance to make a model of this remarkable survivor — the last engine in the country, I should imagine, to retain pre-group livery.

PRODUCT REPORT

Real-life Terriers have a 'light-on-their-feet' look but Dapol's chassis is so clumsy that it distracts the eye from the excellence of the body moulding. This is a pity since, like their J94, it runs rather well at slow speed. With its outside brake pull rods (alas also rather over-robust) some attempt clearly has been made to give this loco a decent set of underpinnings, but the fixings for the proprietary couplings destroy the illusion. Tension-locks are bad enough on any loco (they scale out roughly to the size of a baby grand hung under the buffer beam) but on one the size of a Terrier the impact is catastrophic.

First impressions of the bodywork are very good, however. Sure, the handrails are too heavy and the Westinghouse pump is poor, but the plastic moulding is, on the whole, very successful at conveying the prototype's special delicacy. I was impressed by the roof (and indeed the whole of the cab moulding) while the shape and proportion of the tanks and boiler were dimensionally correct. These, to me, are the key features of a Terrier, though others may pick up on the engine's extreme narrowness (barely seven feet overall) in relation to its length.

Because the fundamentals of the moulding are right, the rest is largely cosmetic. Inevitably, with an RTR model, we have a 'bitzer', with various features from different periods run gaily together. The smokebox front — for this is an original A1 we are looking at here, not an A1X rebuild — should be flush with the leading sandboxes instead of protruding by a scale three inches and there are no wing plates either. The chimney, on the other hand, is marvellous, the distinctive Stroudley taper captured to perfection. I wasn't quite so sure about the dome; it looked slightly undersized in comparison with photographs and yet it measured up well enough against the drawings I was using. Unfortunately, for an A1 at any rate, it wasn't in the right place, though it's about OK for an A1X. The model has a vacuum ejector on the left-hand side, which was a Southern addition,

Dapol's body moulding is really very good, even in its unadorned state. The plated steel handrails do rather sing out but there are some lovely touches, such as the chimney and the cab roof. They capture the elusive character of the prototype in a manner to which the old Ks whitemetal kit could never aspire. Surprisingly, I don't think there's ever been a decent etched kit.

and a blank smokebox door numberplate, which is appropriate only to BR days. Some details jar — the clacks looked good in profile but turned out to be moulded in heavy relief, the tank fillers were a bit odd and in the wrong place for both the A1 and A1X versions, while the whistle and safety valve columns, so elegant on the prototype, simply showed the limitations of plastic moulding.

I was, however, very taken by the finishing and lining out, which hasn't always been Dapol's strong point. To reproduce the ratty state of *Shadwell* in its Edge Hill days, I had acquired a body in Marsh colours, depicting LBSC No. 662. I didn't fancy doing all that lining and then taking 90% of it off again — the weathering alone would be enough to think about. As supplied from the factory, the engine lacks the outer panels of dark brown and, of course, it only carried this livery after being rebuilt to A1X in 1914, in which form the real No. 662 (which also has the large Isle of Wight bunker) is now preserved at Bressingham. On the whole, though, I felt I'd got the best possible start to the project.

This turned out to be a pretty straightforward build, though it was far from being a quickie. Once I started pulling the moulding apart, I found few things to get alarmed about — there was nothing that couldn't readily be taken off and replaced, and, better still, there was little to buy in by way of extra components (not that many Terrier add-ons are available from the trade). In fact, a natty detailing pack of

optional extras came with the spare body I bought. This contained pipes for the feed-water heater with which many of the Terriers were fitted, a smokebox extension ring and replacement dome to convert the boiler to an approximation of the A1X style (though you would need to lose the front sandboxes and fabricate a new smokebox saddle), a set of extended coal rails as found on many prototype engines, and, for reasons best known to Dapol, a set of Ross pops. I thought this detail pack was A Good Thing. It shows the manufacturer realises that not all modellers run things straight out of the box and it also adds value to the product at little extra cost to the manufacturer.

CHASSIS

Various chassis kits are or have been available for Terriers and I chose the one designed and produced by Andy Mullins of Branchlines, which can be built either rigid or with simple beam compensation. This captures rather well the extraordinary delicacy of a Terrier's underpinnings and as it comes it's very good, though there is no mention of the diameter of compensation beam and pivot to use, despite the holes being ready-etched in the sideframes to fit something specific. Here, however, I opted for full compensation using a pivoted front axle and twin equalising beams on the centre and rear axles.

I stole all the details of this system from High Level Kits' superb Andrew Barclay 16in 0-6-0T, which I reviewed in *Model*

Railway Journal No. 82. I learned a lot from
this kit — as I have with all Chris Gibbon's
products — and I'm surprised more
etched-kit manufacturers don't make use
of the twin-beam system it embodies. It's a
lot easier to install than single-beam compensation — only one pair of hornblocks
to fit, for a start — and I'm convinced it
gives a smoother ride than any rigid-axle
method. My only caveat is that it might be
difficult to fit a gearbox into narrow-
chassis 16.5mm models, but this Terrier
was to be in P4 so I had no problems.

The only modification that equalisation
entailed on the etched chassis was the need
to open out the centre and rear axle holes

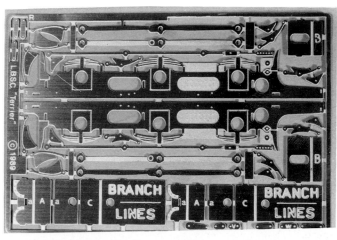

Crisp, clearly defined detail on the Branch-lines Terrier chassis, with alternative spacers for the different gauges. Note the choice of wooden or steel brake shoes.

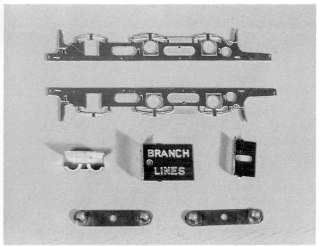 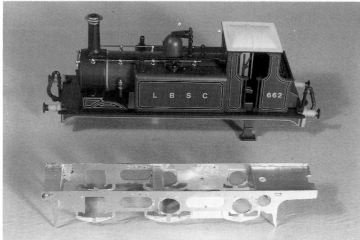

Chassis components with modifications to allow for twin-beam equalisation. This, hopefully, will give added refinement in slow-speed running by nullifying the 'clunk' of fixed axles over badly aligned rail joints.

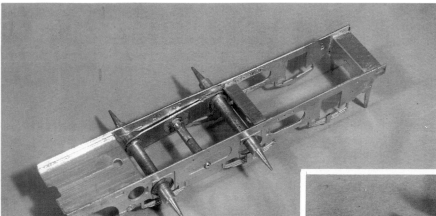

Above: *It's a ten-minute job to solder up the chassis. Terriers were very airy around their frames and underpinnings — Andrew Mullins has caught this quality well. Beams temporarily installed in the chassis so the alignments can be checked.* Right: *Twin-beam equalisation on the Terrier chassis is a straightforward operation. The pivot tube is made in two halves.*

to around ³⁄₁₆in to allow a little vertical movement of the beams that carry the actual bearings (they can be mounted thick-side inwards or outwards, according to preference). Obviously I had to make the equalising beams myself, using the coupling rods as templates. Since the beams also carry the axle bearings, it's important that the centres are correct. I didn't use any sophisticated measuring devices but I took a lot of care, centre-popping the marks and gradually opening up the holes by running up through the drill sizes until I could get a tightish push-fit on a pair of ⅛in top-hat bushes. A central hole to the diameter of the pivot (I used ¹⁄₁₆in brass rod) should also be drilled as the exact mid-way point and a corresponding hole drilled in the chassis using the beam as a template. The alignment of all the holes in the beams needs to be carefully checked, either by passing rods through and seeing that they line up or by using the coupling rods in standard jig axles.

Over the pivot rod there is a pivot tube of 2mm brass, to which diameter the central hole in each beam should be opened out. The pivot tube is in two halves — to allow the beams to pivot independently — each of which is exactly half the width of the chassis. Once cut to length,

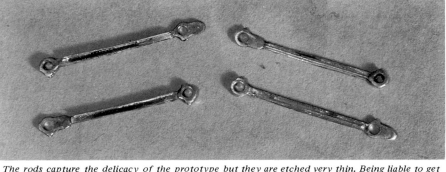

The rods capture the delicacy of the prototype but they are etched very thin. Being liable to get bent while being handled and especially when crankpin holes are being opened out — a catch or snag with the reamer can be disastrous — I soldered a length of 0.33mm brass wire on the back, low down so it cannot be seen. This greatly strengthens the assembly and allows brutes like me to proceed in safety.

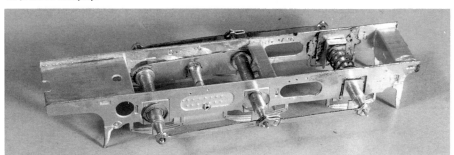

Left: The front axle runs in conventional MJT hornblocks which are lined up in the usual way using jig axles. Right: A length of 1mm brass rod, soldered to the front spacer, provides the pivot around which the front axle rocks. This blocks the front body fixing screw but the rear screw is perfectly adequate on its own. Most of my plastic loco bodies, in fact, are made to be a push-fit on the chassis, with maybe some Blu-tack for security.

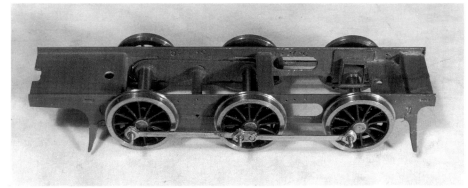

The chassis has been primed and the wheels fitted and quartered by eye. This last operation is so much easier with an even number of spokes, where two pairs of spokes will always be at right-angles to one another. The rods are then fitted and the chassis tested for smooth running. I lost a couple of tight spots by opening out the crankpin holes.

these are pushed into the enlarged pivot holes in the beams and, after checking that everything is square, soldered into place; this can be done with the whole shebang jigged up in the frames.

WHEELS

I used Alan Gibson's 3ft 11in wheels for this loco. These are from the original Protofour tools so, unlike the majority of the Gibson range, they do not have an integrally moulded hole for the crankpin, merely a locating dimple which has to be drilled out by the builder. To do this I used the power tool set in a vertical drill stand and, as with the beams, I went at it very carefully. There appears, at the time of writing, to be no alternative wheelset. As far back as 1989, Ultrascale were promising a Terrier pattern wheel which has still to materialise. Sharman has a couple of 4ft diameter, 12-spoke wheels but with a crank throw much greater than the scale 16in of a Terrier. This may cause problems with the externally-mounted brake pull rods and, in P4 at any rate, the rear crankpin nuts would very likely be clouting the cab steps. In any case, the short crank throw is a feature of the Terriers that, once you become familiar with them, is one of their most characteristic attributes

GEARS

Most loco drive trains — typically a medium-sized can motor with 38:1 gears — are designed to work best with locos that are usually seen running at a scale 20–30mph or more. Such set-ups, which I have used many times, are fine in general use but don't give a lot of control at very slow shunting speeds. Ease back a notch too far and the engine will likely stall, because the motor hasn't got enough revs to sustain the momentum.

A lot of real engines never went much faster than about 20mph, anyway, and some spent most of their working lives going about much more gingerly. The Terriers, according to Hamilton Ellis, could show a sprightly leg when the occasion demanded, but mine was to be very much in the light-railway calibre. So, when I model such an engine, I prefer to fit a gear train that enables it to run at very gentle speeds without the motor cogging and without the constant risk of a stall. Assuming no speed higher than about 20mph is required, my preferred solution these days is to fit a slow-revving motor and a very high-reduction gearbox.

The best way to shorten motor shafts is to use a carborundum cutting disc. This creates clouds of filings so, to keep them out of bearings, brushgear and other sensitive parts, I pierce a hole for the shaft in some kitchen foil and then wrap the motor up tightly, like a boiled sweet. Wear plastic safety goggles while cutting.

The extraordinary 'Contorto' gearbox, marketed by Backwoods Miniatures but designed by Chris Gibbon of High Level Kits, here assembled in its sawn-off 108:1 configuration to suit the Terrier. It's quite difficult to find a main-line prototype into which this unique articulated design will not fit.

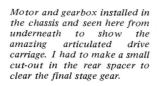

Motor and gearbox installed in the chassis and seen here from underneath to show the amazing articulated drive carriage. I had to make a small cut-out in the rear spacer to clear the final stage gear.

In pursuit of an optimum level of slow-speed running I have in recent years used various combinations of double, triple and even quadruple reduction gearboxes. Most have their drawbacks — noise, bulk, cost, component quality, all of which factors can be considered singly or in combination — but the range produced by Backwoods Miniatures fully satisfies my personal desiderata. Used with powerful high-quality motors such as the Mashima 1224 or, where space permits, the 1628, slow-speed running is close to the optimum — always assuming, of course, that the builder has paid attention to the other factors in

the equation, such as wheel quartering, pick-up design, weighting and compensation. I used Pete McParlin's 'Compacto' 54:1 design in the 4F to give an enhanced slow-speed performance and a respectable top speed in the region of a scale 40mph or so. For a purely shunting design such as this Terrier, with so much tempting space between the side tanks, I used Backwoods' 108:1 'Contorto' to slow things down much further — my engine will do no more than 20mph flat out.

The reduction is not the only remarkable feature of this gearbox. It is also artic-ulated to enable it to slither down under

Wheels and rods on, test leads attached to motor terminals and we're off, with the chassis running on a perspex block. No matter how many times I do this, it's always an anxious moment watching those first few revolutions. It is surprising how many factors can affect smooth running — even a crankpin nut a quarter-turn too tight can cause a bind (or perhaps it's just the way I build 'em).

The marks in silver pen show where a little plastic needs to be carved from the underside of the Terrier body to clear P4 wheels.

fireboxes and cabs to reach rear axles, or to double back on itself, or even drop straight down for high-boilered prototypes such as the BR Standard classes. It can be built, from the same etch, in several forms and ratios to suit individual requirements. On a Terrier, this means you can keep the back-head intact — with a more conventional rear-axle mounted gearbox, I would imagine some of the firehole door/floor area would need to be cut away to accommodate the worm, a compromise which always annoys me.

PICK-UPS AND BRAKE GEAR

Ordinary rim-acting wipers would be fine on a Terrier; with the pull-rods being on the outside of the brake blocks, there is no chance of them making contact. The leads or busbars would, however, need to be routed carefully to avoid them showing through the big hole in the frames.

With a twin-beam chassis, unfortunately, wipers can be difficult — where do you stick the PCB strips? Once again, the solution came directly from the High Level Kits Barclay 'sixteen inch'. The pick-ups are soldered to tiny slivers of PCB filed very thin, attached to the brake cross-members and linked electrically by

The chassis up and running, awaiting rear-end brake cylinder detail.

A Terrier has a very open-looking chassis and the current-collecting arrangements need to be discreet if their inner secrets are not to be exposed to prying eyes. I soldered tiny slivers of PCB to the brake cross-members and ran the 0.33mm pick-up wires from these along the outside of the springs. The lengthways connecting wires — being placed as close to the centre line as practicable — are quite well concealed when seen from normal viewing angles.

fine wire. Unorthodox, undoubtedly, but brilliantly successful in operation.

The rest of the chassis is straightforward. The kit allows for early (wooden) and later (steel) brake blocks but there were individual variations on the prototype. A nice touch is the system of reversing rods, just visible under the boiler. Unfortunately, this feature would have fouled the rear of the motor, and had to be omitted.

BODYWORK

Unlike some proprietary mouldings, the Dapol Terrier breaks down into its constituent parts very easily. The cab unclips, the smokebox front pulls out and in ten minutes time the unwanted details such as the misplaced dome and the overscale handrails were in the bin and I found myself wondering, as I contemplated the scarred remains, just why I'd started.

Before I got very far, I decided I would have to make a couple of compromises. The moulded front splasher goes right across from one side to t'other and should, for a scale model, be cut away to make two individual splashers, remembering to allow for the appropriate back-to-back distance of the wheels. Unfortunately, the tank fronts are also solid and this is less easy to deal with, at least the way I built the chassis. My reverse-mounted Mashima 1224 butts right up against the surplus centre section and, if it were removed, the brush tags and wires would probably be on show. Reluctantly, I left this part of the moulding alone although, in truth, it is normally in shadow. Blue sparks from the

Steps need thinning on most RTR mouldings, both for a better appearance and, as with this Terrier, to avoid being clouted by passing crankpin nuts. Clearances — especially in P4 — should be checked right at the start. See the difference by comparing the right-hand step with that on the left.

commutator, though, would rather let the side down.

The other problem is that the cab step backing plates are not quite wide enough. They need to be thinned down anyway at the back to clear the crankpins in P4 but, the way I read the situation, scale-width steps would still be a shade too close to the nuts for comfort. I had used Alan Gibson's crankpin nuts which are fine for most locos with round fixing bosses but a bit over-scale for a loco the size of a Terrier and I guess this may be where the problem lay.

The holes and scars that resulted from the session in the operating theatre were filled with Miliput and while I was waiting for it to set I turned up some simple fittings from brass wire, tube and washers — a pair of clacks, sandbox lids and various

The body comes apart pretty easily. The cab is screwed and clipped into place but the rest is mostly a push-fit.

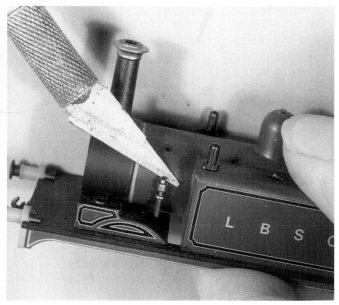

Left: *Slicing off the clacks with a scalpel blade.* Right: *I took off the incorrectly sited dome with a razor saw.*

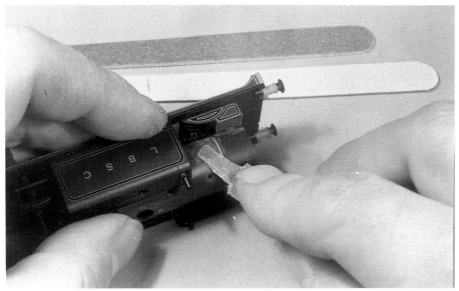

Emery boards – shaped as necessary – are fine for rubbing down plastic.

others outlined below. Very few detailing parts are available from the trade for a Terrier, so I felt it might make a pleasant change to try and go it alone for once and to see how far I could get. I do enjoy this side of things although I was getting a bit long in the modelling tooth before I realised how easy it is, even if, like me, you only have a mini-drill to use as a power tool. Very little of what I churn out bears much comparison with proper lathe-turned work but the spirit is there. I find it helps to run the drill much faster than usual when turning brass — it seems to cut cleaner when you do this.

Whatever you're making, the knack is to look at that obscure object of desire, be it a set of safety valves or a bell or whatever, and try and figure it out as a sequence of cuts. Other parts can be broken down into sub-assemblies. Something more complicated, like a brake stanchion, might seem intimidating until you reduce it into con-

Left: *After the over-scale rear spectacle guards have been scalpelled out, the scars are smoothed off with a rotary abrasive tool.* Right: *Those clumsy cab handrails can come off for a start.*

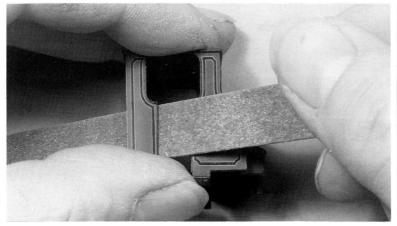

Left: *The edges of the side sheets are judiciously bevelled to suggest that they are made of 1/8in iron plate, not three inches of concrete.* Right: *With a bit of work, it's surprising how the inherent chunkiness of plastic can be disguised. Once we've got rid of the clumsy and inaccurate bits, we can begin to see the underlying refinement of Dapol's body mouldings. At the same time, we can check clearances on the chassis.*

Above: *Before any delicate detail goes on, I like to work out what kind of weighting is required. The Terrier body comes with moulded weights for the smokebox and bunker but these give nowhere near enough mass to persuade the equalised chassis to work efficiently. Here I have cut extra slugs of lead to go inside the tanks. Sheet lead — for roof flashing — comes in rolls of different thicknesses from a builder's merchant. The one down the road lets me have off-cuts and odd lengths very cheaply.* Top right: *The moulded coal has been removed so I can pack the bunker with lead. More will be added once the bunker extension is in place but this will have to wait until the rear window has been glazed and the spectacle guards added.* Right: *On the moulding, the coal door intrudes into the cab but it should really be flush with the rear spectacle plate. I preferred to leave it as it was in order to cram in as much lead as possible, but later had a twinge of conscience and took out the centre section (the rest being hidden by the sandboxes). The Isle of Wight Terriers had a much larger bunker which would allow even more rear-end weight to be added.*

Left: *In place of the neat but rather puny weight provided by Dapol, I stuffed even more lead into the smokebox to bring the weight of the body up to 80g (3¼oz), nicely balanced around the centre driving wheel, which was the centre of gravity of a real Terrier. Trials had shown that with this loco I should be aiming for an all-up weight of around 150g (5oz) and the first test runs with the weighted body in place were most encouraging.* Right and below: *The over-dumpy smokebox front is reduced by rubbing it face-up on a big fine-cut file until it's wafer-thin. Plastikard wing plates (necessary for an A1) are added at this stage.*

stituent shapes — in 4mm scale all it basically warrants is a tube with a collar at either end, a handrail knob or split-pin sticking out at the top and a length of wire with a right-angle in it for the handle. Beadings, flanges and other embellishments can readily be added in 5amp fuse wire.

Making a set of fittings for the Terrier kept me out of mischief for a few hours. I don't, incidentally, always expect to get these things right first time — there are quite a few holes-in-one but some items need to be remade several times. The Salter safety valve columns are a case in point; the first one was useless, the second brilliant,

The brake cylinder detail (improvised from brass rod and fret waste) fills out the rear end nicely.

Left: The hole where the original dome was located can be plugged with plastic sprue filed to shape, likewise the locators for the tank filler caps. Miliput will hide any gaps. Right: Dapol's cab floor moulding has a curious hump to clear coarse OO wheels. I cut it out . . .

Left: . . . I filled the gap with a new 'planked' floor and added proper splashers. This is best done with the body mounted on the chassis. Right: A Terrier's cab was incredibly cramped. Here I have added sandboxes and other intrusions from Plastikard. According to the GA drawing, the handbrake leans forward into the cab at an angle of approximately 8° from the vertical. Assorted dials and gauges augment the cab interior. The Westinghouse pressure gauge is another of my little turnings.

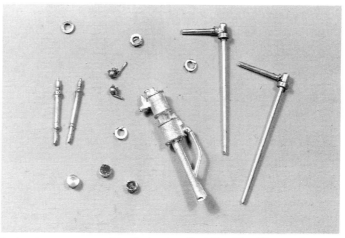

Left: *There's no great mystery to the materials used for pipework. Soft brass wire — as opposed to the hard stuff sold by Alan Gibson — is very pliable but soon snaps if worked too vigorously.* Right: *These are some of the details for the Terrier that I made from brass rod and tube, and seen here before cleaning-up and refinement. The Westinghouse pump is the Alan Gibson lost-wax casting, mastered by the inimitable Roy Link. The whistle must be hiding.*

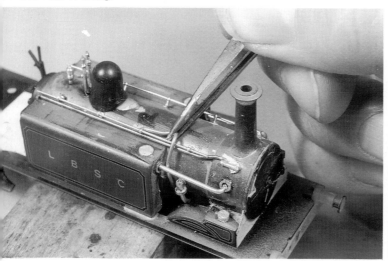

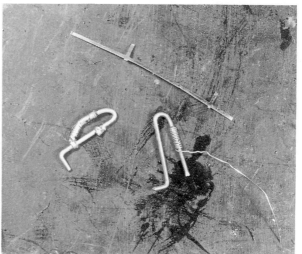

Left: *Once the brass details start to go on, the mutilated hulk of the bodywork looks a lot more appealing. But there's a long way to go yet. Doing the plumbing involves lots of bending, offering up, tweaking and refitting. Fortunately, the pipes on the EHLR Terriers were more than a little bent.* Right: *Westinghouse pipes are finer than vacuum brake hoses. They are easily made by winding 5 amp fuse wire around 0.7mm brass wire bent to shape and soldered up on a block of paxolin.*

The tank and boiler-top arrangements seem to vary considerably between engines, and decent high-angle photographs, unfortunately, are hard to come by. This was my best guess. The tank fillers were adapted from the Dapol items. This seems to be about it, as far as the pipework goes, at least until the cab goes on and I can plumb in the whistle and the Westinghouse pump. First, I think a good wash is in order.

Left: The coal rails that protect the rear windows are made by soldering four parallel lengths of 0.33mm wire to a length of fine shim. Another piece of shim braces the bottom of the assembly. The extension bunker has now been added – this comes as an 'extra' with the Dapol loco. Right: The cab handrails have been fitted and the Westinghouse brake pump has been plumbed in. Apart from the couplings (Exactoscale, of course), the pump was the only 'bought-in' item on the whole loco.

the third snapped off with the prize in sight and the fourth just about squared up to make one of a pair. Some prototype engines, incidentally, seem to have a longer 'spike' at the top than others but always the two are identical. I wondered about making a Westinghouse pump but Alan Gibson's casting is exquisite and I agonised no further. The globe lubricators on the smokebox front of my Terrier (they are absent on the A1X) were fudged from some old 'fatso' handrail knobs discarded from a kit, whilst the moulded tank filter caps were cut short and fixed on to short lengths of thin-walled 5mm OD brass tube. Another prototype detail worth checking is the whistle; most seem to have retained the original style but Isle of Wight Terriers had a unique 'organ-pipe' pattern whilst the whistle of EHLR No. 2 was mounted much higher than any of the others.

Pretty well everything else was made out of wire of various gauges — the boiler-top plumbing, the brake pipes, the coal rails to protect the rear cab windows (various patterns were evident on the prototype). The cab fittings, however, were mostly in Plastikard apart from a couple of gauges turned from brass rod. The sand-boxes and splashers were simple boxes assembled in situ, the cab floor was scribed 10-thou, and I was happy to retain the rather neat moulding for the reverser quadrant.

FINISHING TOUCHES

I took a lot of care over building up the heavy weathering that was such a feature of the Edge Hill Terriers. It is very difficult, however, to describe this kind of work in

I hope this view suggests something of the transformation that has been effected, and the level of work involved. The brass bits have been lightly undercoated — red acrylic car primer — and a line of rivets applied around the tank, using tiny cubes of 5-thou in best Geoff Kent fashion.

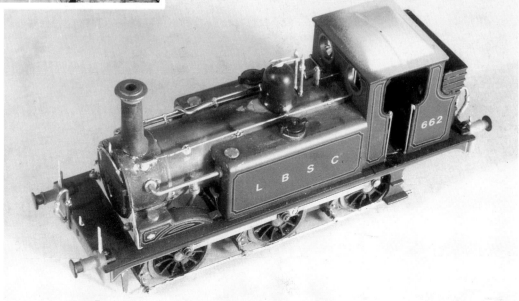

Lamp irons are set in holes drilled into the buffer shanks. It seems incredible that the erstwhile Shadwell should have retained its prominent route-indicator brackets on the mineral-only Edge Hill Light Railway.

step-by-step terms, since so much of it is improvisation and observation, rather than an empirical process such as building a chassis. I tend to airbrush a good overall coat of grot on to the engine fairly indiscriminately and then get to work, building up colour and texture in particular areas, rubbing it away, generally dabbing and blobbing for some considerable time until I feel satisfied that I have reached an approximation of the image in my mind.

It has to be said, too, that many fine models have been ruined by poor weath-

ering. My best counsel is firstly to refer the reader to Martyn Welch's marvellous book, *The Art of Weathering* (Wild Swan, 1993), and also to the many fine colour albums which have been published showing steam in its heyday. Secondly, I would suggest that you always have reality in mind — you don't find many working steam locomotives these days but, just walking and driving around, I come across all manner of inspiration for weathering effects, from heavy machinery and plant to buildings and road vehicles. All is grist to the mill

because, unless you are very careful, it can be very easy to adapt the kind of general-purpose weathering approach seen on so many models — a general pass from left to right and back again with a kind of track-colour brown, and then another waft of sooty-grey over the top. Like lime-streaking from clacks and safety valves, it's become a kind of modeller's shorthand and, unfortunately, it rarely looks anything like the way real engines weather. Observation is the keynote. Technique is only 10%, if that, of the equation.

The easiest form of weathering to execute is the extremely dirty locomotive. The model is rarely finished this way by intention. Usually the builder sets out to distress it lightly but overdoes things and ends up with a very grubby engine. I know this because I've done it myself, on several occasions.

One of the hardest qualities to suggest at all accurately, however, is the really degenerate look. To capture the feeling of near-total neglect, you need to go way beyond the familiar look of over-emphatic rust and grime. You need to do it very deliberately and very carefully, to study or recall or work out what a locomotive that has not been cleaned for years actually looks like. This is an awful lot harder to achieve. It is not at all the same thing as being over-enthusiastic with the airbrush.

The first step was to study the Edge Hill Terriers as they appear in Casserley's evocative photographs taken in the summer of 1939, their paintwork bleached to a dull brownish-grey, rust almost completely covering the boiler and breaking through along the tank sides, a few tired fragments of tarpaulin clinging to the

dome. Then I tried to imagine what they had been like in earlier years. I wanted to portray an engine that suffered neglect but was also in working condition, as the former *Shadwell* might have looked on its last working day on the doomed Oxfordshire mineral line, its crew resigned to impending redundancy, the whole undertaking suffused by a feeling of hopelessness. Of course, there are no colour photographs of the EHLR that I know of

but I have seen plenty of latter-day industrial railways in a similar parlous state.

The first step was to prime the body with red oxide car aerosol, gently drifted over the visible brass components but leaving the lined-out tank and cab sides untouched. I carefully rubbed away the number and LBSC lettering and added the number 674 and the legend 'LB&SCR'. These were hand-painted in white; they would be only very faintly visible under

the top coat of faded paint, and the odd error or rough edge can be fudged quite easily. I then mixed up Humbrol gunmetal and leather to create a sooty grey-brown and airbrushed this over most of the engine, followed by lighter and darker mixes of the same shade. Then I got to work with Carr's powders. I have the lot, but the ones I use most frequently are a couple of rust shades, a sooty black and the very useful creamy white. This last, brushed liberally over the tank and cab sides, rear and roof, gave the desired faded paintwork effect. The other colours were worked in as seemed appropriate; the boiler and coal rails are quite heavily rusted, the cab is sooty, the firebox area below the footplate looks like the paint has been burned off, and so does the smokebox. Some parts were treated to several applications of colour until I got the effect I was after. This all happens in a slow-motion blur and is next to impossible to describe sequentially; the best I can offer is this retrospective analysis of what I think I must have done.

I got the airbrush going again — this was on a hot day in the garden, deliberately selected to try and recreate the conditions under which Casserley took his photographs — and re-sprayed the chimney and smokebox a sooty brown-black. I hand-lettered 'EHLR' on the tanks using a Bob Moore lining pen and toned this down with more white powder, letting just a hint of the lining show through. We have the customary oily patches (gloss acrylic varnish from Protec) around the lubricators, coupling rods and wheel centres, but the Westinghouse pump is very flat, the oil caked on to suggest its years of

disuse. On a working engine, of course, it would be absolutely dripping with oil.

As well as powders I used Caran d'Ache crayons to create little pockets of local colour; the front boiler band is also drawn on in this way, in brown and olive green overlaid. Streaks and dribbles were improvised either with heavily thinned Poly-S weathering acrylics (it is extraordinary how little pigment one really needs) or with lighter fuel, which leaves a nice 'tide mark' as it evaporates. The Exactoscale screw couplings are blackened with gun blue. There is no conventional brush painting on this loco at all, other than the odd drop of pigment introduced on the tip of a oo sable and flooded on with thinners. I knew exactly the effect I was after and once it had been achieved in any one area of the locomotive, I left it alone. Of course there will always be an unpredictable

element caused by finger marks and overlaps and accidental abrasions but these can be made good by thin paint or powder or both. The randomness of the marks is highly effective on top of the basic logic of the overall scheme.

The key to achieving this pinnacle of decrepitude is restraint. If you really let rip, blasting the engine with the airbrush and sloshing powder all over the place, it will simply look overblown, and totally unrealistic. Every mark should be made for a reason, because you understand why it is there — seepage from a pipe union, the shiny patches on the cab sides where the crew's overalls have rubbed. This loco was weathered much as one might paint a watercolour — with discretion, subtlety and an eye for nuance. There may be an element of serendipity in the way colours and textures merge, but, for the most part, one is exercising considerable control. I can do a basic weathering job on a loco in ten minutes flat but this one was the main focus of a weekend.

I wasn't keeping a tab but I would guess at least six or seven hours work went into painting EHLR No. 2. I enjoy this kind of thing anyway but my pleasure knew no bounds when, chatting to John Hayes when we were picking up our competition prizes at Scaleforum, he said how much he liked the way I'd finished it, how strongly it reminded him of the photographs. My No. 2 had won best of breed for converted proprietary locos and the great man's A3 swept the field in the kit- and scratchbuilt category. I offered him a straight swap but he said the Pacific was already spoken for . . .

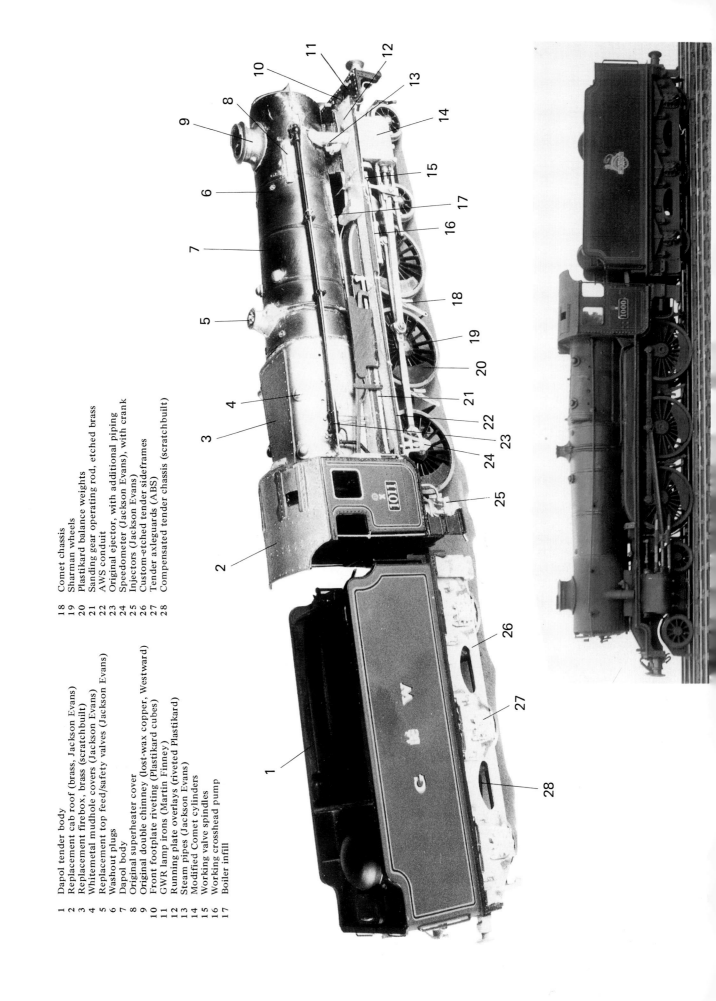

1 Dapol tender body
2 Replacement cab roof (brass, Jackson Evans)
3 Replacement firebox, brass (scratchbuilt)
4 Whitemetal mudhole covers (Jackson Evans)
5 Replacement top feed/safety valves (Jackson Evans)
6 Dapol body
7 Original superheater cover
8 Original double chimney (lost-wax copper, Westward)
9 Front footplate riveting (Plastikard cubes)
10 GWR lamp irons (Martin Finney)
11 Running plate overlays (riveted Plastikard)
12 Steam pipes (Jackson Evans)
13 Modified Comet cylinders
14 Working valve spindles
15 Working crosshead pump
16 Boiler infill

18 Comet chassis
19 Sharman wheels
20 Plastikard balance weights
21 Sanding gear operating rod, etched brass
22 AWS conduit
23 Original ejector, with additional piping
24 Speedometer (Jackson Evans), with crank
25 Injectors (Jackson Evans)
26 Custom-etched tender sideframes
27 Tender axleguards (ABS)
28 Compensated tender chassis (scratchbuilt)

CHAPTER FIVE

KEEPING UP WITH THE COUNTY SET

A HAWKSWORTH COUNTY USING A DAPOL BODY
AND A COMET CHASSIS KIT

I'VE always felt drawn towards the County class 4–6–0s, without ever really knowing why. Perhaps it's because, like the only other Great Western classes that I have an urge to model — the spectacularly pugnacious 1500 class pannier tanks and the equally brutal Aberdares — they don't fit in with the accepted Swindon canon. For over fifty years there was a remarkable homogeneity to GW locomotive design, from the Saints and Stars right through to the BR-built double-chimney Castles. Having been professionally involved for many years with corporate identities, house styles and such-like, I feel I ought to admire this continuity more than I actually do. The Counties seemed to represent a challenge to that epic hegemony, a paradox, a diversion, a contradiction. In this nonconformism, I believe, lies the seed of their appeal to me.

It's obvious, isn't it, that they're not quite the ticket. Those elongated splashers, the bulbous cylinders, the sadly graceless chimney, the slab-sided tender — it's like a freelance model of the kind that used to feature in the *Model Railway News* of the late 1950s, a Priory class or some such knocked-up from a Hornby-Dublo Castle in an attempt to produce something 'in the Swindon style' by someone who doesn't really speak the language. This kind of renegade offering offends the purists but it pleases me no end. I get the same feeling looking at such 'almost but not quite' engines as the CIE 800 class 4–6–0s (more of a Henry Greenly design than a Celtic Royal Scot) and many of the North British Locomotive Company's designs for the export market.

My acquaintance with Western Region steam was never intimate, though I can recall every second of an idyllic afternoon at Wolverhampton Low Level, with three Kings, an auto-train and a 47xx to provide me with a microcosm of the Swindon empire. In consequence, I only ever saw one County. This was *County of Middlesex* itself, simmering away on Mold Junction shed in an autumn Sunday dusk in 1963. I took a picture but, in such low light, it was predictably indistinct. I was disappointed that the last survivor, *County of Chester,* wasn't preserved on withdrawal in 1964, despite ambitions to the contrary, because with its demise went my chance to get a better snap. Maybe that was why I've

The classic shot along the sea wall at Teignmouth. The viewpoint emphases the angularity of the County class — they look more an engine made up of bits of other GW classes than something designed from scratch. I like them . . .

B. M. BARBER

Another timeless moment. Because of their mixed parentage (there was a definite LMS look about the boiler and the tender frames) I think the County class wore the BR lined black a good deal more happily than GW engines of impeccable pedigree. The acute angle is kind to the original chimney of No. 1000 County of Middlesex.   COLLECTION R. S. CARPENTER

always rather fancied a model of a County. I will never, I am sure, have a layout on which I could justify running it.

MODELLING PHILOSOPHY

My innocence of the prototype had a significant effect on the way I tackled this project. I tend to build models not as models but as images of the real thing. I know that this is what we are all supposed to be doing but some people clearly have different attitudes, where engineering skills have dominance over the more interpretative approach that I adopt. Often these guys make exquisite models of prototypes that they could never have known at first hand, and their locomotives are conceived and executed purely as models, beautifully painted, their brasswork gleaming. The fact that they are based on real-life originals that were hot to the touch, smelled of all kinds of things and made a lot of noise, seems to be irrelevant — they are models pure and simple. My kind of modelling, however, is all about capturing character and I am afraid that I find these masterpieces of miniature engineering to be cold and sterile, however admirable the execution of detail and however hard I wish that I could aspire to such finesse.

Occasionally, though, the skills of engineer and artist come together and we find ourselves in the company of genius. In this respect it's impossible — or at least I find it so — to ignore the wonderful Great Western 4–6–0s that have appeared in *Model Railway Journal* over the years. These are the work of scratchbuilders like Guy Williams, John Hayes and Tony Reynalds and kit designers of the calibre of Malcolm Mitchell and Martin Finney — and they don't come any better than that. I took on board a lot of what they have achieved although Guy Williams' account of his scratchbuilt County in *More 4mm Engines* came too late for me — mine was already finished. All the same, I think that, for once, I've been infinitely more influenced by models than by the real thing.

It seemed futile to try and show that I could do something just as good in plastic, because I knew I couldn't. To me, building a Great Western 4–6–0 seems like the modelling equivalent of playing Hamlet, only my performance would be more village hall than Stratford-upon-Avon. I had a mind to see what could be done using a proprietary body, an off-the-shelf detailing kit, a few bought-in bits, scale wheels and a chassis pack plus, of course, a liberal measure of improvisation and a

knowledge of what had gone before. This wasn't going to be a matter of sticking a few bits on to a proprietary loco — like the books and *MRJ* articles that were my guiding light, it was about making a finescale model, but not via the customary route.

My starting point for the project was a rather ropy Dapol body moulding, acquired as a spare. The makers must have been taking an enormous risk when they introduced their RTR model in the mid-1980s, although model railways were on a bit of a roll at the time. Jamieson had done a kit ages long ago and more recently there has been an etched kit from Falcon Brass, not forgetting the rather nice M&L whitemetal design, which has subsequently been upgraded by Alan Gibson. On the whole, though, the County class has never been popular with modellers, and you rarely see a decent model of one. The GW people are very particular, I find, and don't seem to have much affection for the class,

or indeed for anything else that isn't 100% classical Swindon.

Most of the mouldings that I've used as the basis for finescale models have been, in themselves, not too bad at all. Not so with Dapol's County unfortunately. It has a lot of good points — some nicely moulded rivet detail, a fine copper-capped single chimney and a pretty reasonable stab at a Hawksworth tender body. Since I had a number of County class drawings at my disposal, thanks to the good offices of David Geen who flies the Swindon flag up in Hartlepool, I could see that in most respects the model seems to have followed Colonel Templar's drawings in J H Russell's book pretty faithfully. There are things that aren't right, though, and they are quite tricky to correct. All the Great Western 4000 gallon tenders had a common wheelbase — 7ft 6in × 7ft 6in — but for some freakish reason Dapol have done theirs at 7ft 3ins × 7ft 3ins, which makes a fine mess of the tender sideframe

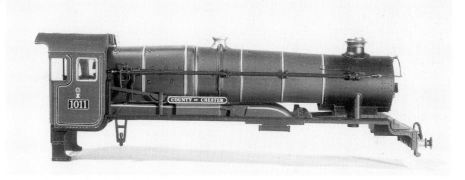

The body moulding isn't the finest the world has ever seen but it has its good points, such as the smokebox, the cab sides and a well-detailed buffer beam.

Not much needs doing to the tender body, beyond replacing the moulded handrails and lamp irons. It is the correct overall width for a 'County'. I understand the 'Modified Halls' had tenders 6in narrower, which is perhaps why they were never exchanged between the classes.

From sideways on, the full horror of No. 1000's chimney is revealed. A fortuitous leak allows us to see the little valves on the steam pipes.

H. J. STRETTON-WARD

moulding and is obviously going to call for a new chassis. I suspect they may have measured off the old Skinley blueprint, which quotes the correct dimensions but is reproduced to a scale very slightly smaller than 4mm/ft.

Turning to the loco body, things get worse. The shape of the cab roof looks totally wrong even to a non-GW type like me, we have a bottomless boiler and, worst of all, the various sloping surfaces on the firebox have been heavily fudged, presumably in order to accommodate the RTR mechanism. The firebox of a real County is quite wasp-waisted but the moulded one looks like a human torso after a protracted binge on carbohydrates. Having bitten the bullet and bought the bits, I contemplated

the remedial work that would be entailed and began to wish I'd gone for the 'Modified Hall' that was the first option suggested by my publisher.

PROTOTYPE CONSIDERATIONS

It was inevitable that I should choose to model *County of Middlesex,* but running not as I had seen the loco in 1963 but as it looked in 1956, the main reason being that I had some decent photographs taken at this date. In fact the County class were comparatively free of detail variations between individual locos, which meant the research wouldn't be quite so demanding (we can save that for the Bulleid Pacific). The predominant difference relates to superheater covers. The engines were delivered from Swindon with three-row superheaters, whose cover on the offside of the smokebox was distinctly flat-faced (but not quite as flat as Dapol's pattern-maker has it). Many (but not all) engines were fitted in the late 1950s/early 1960s with enlarged four-row superheaters that had two covers, one above the other on either side of the handrail, and much more rounded in profile. On some engines there is also a small square inspection panel below and immediately to the rear of the safety valve/top feed housing on the right-hand side only. Its presence or absence (it could be the light, of course) seems to have nothing to do with date and it is found on

The shape of the firebox isn't just dubious, it's totally wrong. Complete replacement is called for. The cab front is too high also.

engines with either type of superheater cover.

There is also the matter of chimneys. No. 1000 entered traffic with an enormous double chimney, even more bulbous a conk than that fitted to the Kings, but the others at first had an orthodox and rather elegant single chimney of traditional Swindon pattern. Severe steaming problems were experienced with both designs. No. 1009 was the subject of many experiments with draughting arrangements, and acquired a nasty double-stovepipe chimney. As a result of these tests, between 1956 and 1959 the whole of the class acquired a new pattern of double chimney. This was lower and narrower than that originally fitted to *County of Middlesex* and it just didn't look right, generating much

discussion in high places as to its aesthetic merits. Still, it worked a lot better than the old, single blastpipe version and that was what really mattered.

Other class modifications were slight. The test-bed loco, No. 1009, was often seen with an indicator shelter, as was No. 1000 at various times, while No. 1002 ran with a self-weighing tender for a while in the mid-1950s. The whole class, in fact, swapped tenders quite regularly, but only with other Counties (County tenders were 6in wider than those fitted to Modified Halls and Castles). Otherwise, apart from the disposition of pipe runs, the thirty engines of the class appear to have been virtually identical. They were outshopped in lined GW green with the G-crest-W tender emblem. In early BR days they

were reliveried in 'mixed traffic' lined black — and very handsome they looked too — but from mid-1955 a start was made on repainting them in passenger green as they were outshopped.

CHASSIS CHOICE

Neither of the proprietary chassis kits that are available for the County is really quite what it seems, despite each of them being specifically described and packaged as a County chassis. The Perseverance/Puffers design has an interesting multiple-beam compensation system and some nice-looking cylinders, but the frames are identical to their kits for the Manor, Grange and Hall classes. This must mean that at least one of them isn't right and I suspect it's the County — the frames are nowhere

The single chimney was more flattering but led to poor steaming.

D. B. HART

near deep enough for a loco with 6ft 3in driving wheels, as opposed to the 5ft 8ins wheels of the smaller 4–6–0s. If this is not attended to — and the kit instructions are predictably mute about any modifications that need to be made — the discrepancy will cause problems with cylinder alignment, wheel pitch and the ride height of the body. The brake hangers and balance weights, too, appear to be designed for the small-wheeled 4–6–0, while the bogie isn't at all right for a County — it's the bar-framed kind used on the older Swindon 4–6–0s but which was replaced by a new plate-frame design on the Modified Halls and Counties. In fact, looking at the main chassis etch, I couldn't see anything that was even remotely relevant to a Hawksworth 4–6–0.

I decided to buy the Comet version instead. At least their kit is different to the one they do for the Grange/Manor, even if it is billed as being equally suitable for a Hall. The Halls, of course, had 6ft diameter, wheels but I felt, all the same, that this version was a lot closer to my prototype than the Perseverance kit; once assembled, it fits the unmodified Dapol body perfectly. The brake blocks align quite well but there are no balance weights — an irritating omission on all Comet kits. The cylinders are Comet's GW two-cylinder pattern and the thin whitemetal wrappers will need a little tweaking to make them suitable for a County. Many makers subscribe to this one-size-fits-all philosophy but one understands the production economics. Though lacking compensation, the bogie etchings look very attractive and include optional overlays for both the GW standard bar frames and the later plate-frame variety which is correct for the County.

CHASSIS

This was so bog-standard that, after the description of the chassis for the 4F, it scarcely needs any more than a perfunctory mention here. Although I was using

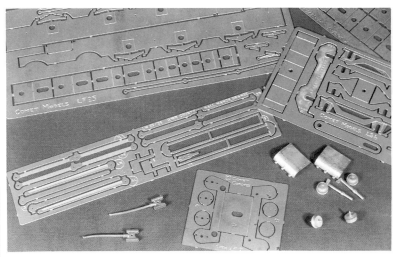

All the chassis components came from Comet with the exception of the spacers, which were Perseverance, left over from another kit.

The rear spacer carries the body fixing screw. To make sure it was in the right place and at the right level, I set it up so it could be tack-soldered on site. I even allowed clearance for the wires that support the rear brake hangers, which was unusually prescient of me.

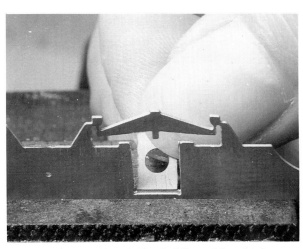

Having cut through the half-etched lines with a piercing saw, ready to accept the hornguides, the waste brass is gently tweaked backwards and forwards until it snaps loose.

Once more unto the jig . . . As the scorch marks suggest, this has seen a lot of use, largely because it works reliably, every time. I have tried sprung jigs but I didn't get on with them — which is not to say that others don't.

Comet components, I was greatly influenced by the way Guy Williams describes building a couple of Hall class chassis in *The 4mm Engine.* I opted to use beam compensation, Perseverance hornblocks and the RG4 motor that seems almost mandatory for a Swindon 4–6–0.

The chassis was soldered up, the rods were made and the hornblocks installed in exactly the same way as I outlined earlier. Although I am firmly convinced of the merits of building chassis that can readily be taken apart again, this one was actually much more solid than usual. Comet's

cylinder assembly is, quite rightly, meant to be screwed into place, but I wanted to make the valve gear work instead of using the dummy whitemetal casting for the valve spindle that is supplied. To have working valve gear and a moving vacuum pump that was also detachable would have

Left: *Just like the ads — I was most impressed by the snug fit of the Comet chassis when offered up to the proprietary body. This has always been a hallmark of their work.* Right: *A little judicious sawing and filing is needed to get rid of Dapol's dummy front frames. With the cylinder front and rear profiles in place on the chassis, I can check that everything is square and level and that we don't have daylight in the wrong places.*

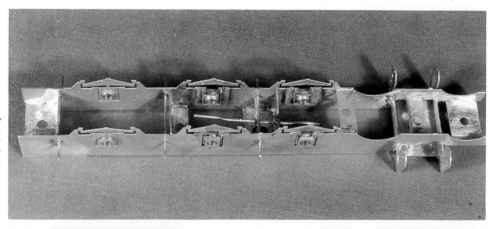

Now we have the basic chassis soldered up and the hornblocks in place. I usually leave fitting the brake hanger wires as late as possible — I tend to catch my fingers on them.

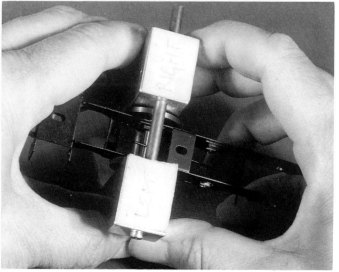

Left: *Having sprayed the chassis black, I've prepared the wheels by removing moulding pips and other detritus. One pair is mounted in the GW Models wheelpress, ready to be fitted to the front axle.* Right: *Having added a couple of shim washers to soak up sideplay, the wheels are force-fitted on to the axle, exerting equal pressure from both sides. You can do this by hand, as here, or in a vice. The quartering is perfect every time.*

called for some elaborate bracketing arrangements and I chose to do as Guy had done and soldered the cylinders up integrally with the frames, with fixed support brackets for the valve gear and vacuum pump. This is jumping ahead a little, of course, but I mention it here because one does need to anticipate these things and plan accordingly.

Building to P4, I used some discarded Perseverance spacers, taken from my spares box. The oo ones supplied on the frame etch are extraordinarily narrow, as they are with all Comet kits. Unless workers in this gauge really are intent on using Romford wheels and coaxing the loco around 12in radius curves, Comet's EM spacers would be a wiser choice. This would give a

13.5mm overall chassis width, which gives adequate sideplay and a monumental improvement in appearance.

Driving wheels are from Sharman. The bogie and tender wheels, though, are Alan Gibson's — I think they are just that bit finer than the Sharman product. Ultrascale, of course, are finer still.

This was the first loco I had built for some time with an RG4 and I was reminded of how easy it is to install. The assembly of the chassis was routine and the only problem I encountered was a persistent short from the brake gear. Like the Castle class, the leading and middle pair of wheels of a County are very close together and quite a bit of discreet tweaking of the brake hangers was necessary to avoid electrical contact. With Guy Williams' book open in front of me, I soldered up a simplified version of the compensated

Above: *Before fitting the motor, I temporarily added the rear wheelset and the rods to check that all was in order and that the wheels would turn over smoothly. Using good axle jigs and a wheel-quartering press means that I can be pretty well 100% sure all will be fine, but I like to make certain. Nasty things can happen if a chassis binds under power because of faulty quartering or poor hornblock alignment.* Right: *Whether it's through conscious intention or not I don't know, but most plastic RTR bodies have adequate clearance for P4 driving wheels. A very different position obtains with cast kits, where gouging out great hunks of white metal from inside the splashers is a horrible but necessary job.*

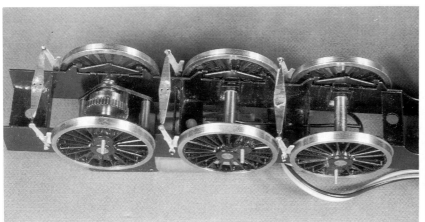

Left: *I thought I'd get the brakes on now, while I had the chance. This saves fiddling about behind coupling rods. The cross-shafts aren't quite the right shape but they were conveniently to hand, being left over from a BR Standard Class 4. The pull rods go on later.* Right: *Hidden behind the brake hangers but visible in this lengthwise shot, the pick-ups are simple 'backscratchers' of 0.33mm hard brass wire, soldered to transversely-mounted strips of copperclad which, in turn, are linked by busbars of 0.7mm wire. The right-angle bends reduce the whippiness of fine wire and facilitate the inevitable tweaking that goes on before everything works satisfactorily.*

brake gear but I left this as late as possible in case I needed access to anything mechanical or electrical that was playing up.

BOGIE

One of the distinctive features of the County class — and of the Modified Halls, for that matter — is the prominent and rather ungainly-looking transverse plate at the front of the bogie. This makes no difference if the bogie is to be built rigid but it knocks on the head any idea of having an equalised bogie with pivoted side-frames, which is the way I usually prefer to build 'em.

Being a modeller of industrial locomotives as well as the main-line stuff, I have built a fair number of small four-coupled engines and the last half-dozen or so have all had the same basic chassis design — fixed rear (driven) axle with front axle riding in hornblocks and pivoting around a central bar. It's very easy to install and it works — so this is how I decided to model the County bogie.

As supplied by Comet, the bogie has integral OO spacers which had to be ditched and replaced by P4 ones. Once I had the basic frame soldered up using 2mm rods to aid alignment, I slightly elongated the front axle holes to allow a little vertical displacement — little more than a millimetre is required, if that. I then bent up a short pivot arm out of 0.9mm brass wire and soldered it to the central spacer so that it bears on the front axle; it can be tweaked, if necessary, to give the correct ride height. Wire retainers hold the wheels in place.

Reams of technobabble have been written about the behaviour of bogies on model locomotives but, in my painful mechanical ignorance, I seem to get by reasonably well by lead-weighting the truck as heavily as is practicable and securing the bogie to the chassis by a centrally mounted pillar or screw which makes contact *below* the axle centre line (this seems to be the important bit). A slot is opened out in the main stretcher to offer a degree of side control and allow the bogie to lead the loco into curves, so you don't get that great yawing motion that characterised my three-rail *Duchess of Montrose* hitting a small-radius curve at speed. There's no great finesse to this method but it works. It's also the way they do these things at Pendon and I wouldn't argue with that.

The bogie uses simple compensation to stay on the track — note the central pivot beam. The lead weights help with stability while the hole will be elongated into a slot to help with side control on curves.

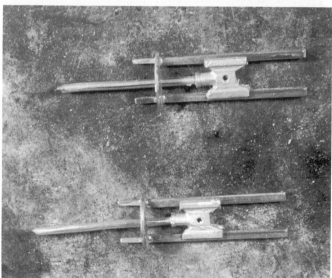

The movement of the crossheads on the slidebars wants to be perfectly smooth and this is achieved by careful filing and polishing. These Comet slidebars are a fold-up etch and need to be dressed to get rid of the inevitable cusp. Real slidebars are chunky steel forgings and scale out a little thicker than these. Rather than thin the slidebars still further, I prefer to file off any metal that needs to be removed from the sliding channels of the crossheads.

OF SLIDEBARS AND CROSSHEADS

First track trials with the basic chassis were, for once, as smooth as silk, and it was at this point, inevitably, that Nemesis struck. I had offered up the completed slidebar/piston rod assembly to check clearance of the front crankpins when I noticed that, at back dead centre, the crosshead was well out of the slidebars. Folk memory, confirmed by photographs, reminded me that on Great Western 4–6–0s, the crosshead at the rearmost point of its travels is right at the end of the slidebars, and closer inspection revealed that, assembled as instructed, the latter were approximately 2mm too short. Quite how this should be escaped me for the moment. The two-layer etched

slidebars are folded up in a basic flat box shape and the front and rear vertical portions are then snipped off at a clearly defined line. Had they ended up short through carelessness on my part, perhaps, or was it a design fault? I don't know and maybe it doesn't matter, but the solution was comparatively painless.

The front part of the slidebar is a fold-back half-moon shape which represents the rear cylinder cover. The slidebars pass through this and into holes etched into the rear face of the cylinders. The cylinder etch contains separate, circular rear covers which, when Comet slidebars are used, are superfluous. I found that by soldering these circular covers on to the innermost ends of the slidebars, and then carefully removing the half-moons, I could create the longer slidebars that I needed. This was very much a solution born of necessity, seeing as I'd already soldered up the slidebar/piston rod assembly, but if I were building another chassis from the same kit, I'd be inclined simply to cut away just that part of the rear spacer section that lies between the slide-bars. This isn't how you're meant to cut them but it would leave just about enough extra length on the slidebars, which is what we're interested in.

With the crossheads running nicely in the slidebars I could solder the assembly to the chassis. Alignment is easy because the cylinders and slidebars are parallel to the tops of the frames, not inclined as they are on many classes that I am familiar with. The pistons and connecting rods at back dead centre should also he horizontal in relation to the frames and this can be checked by running a suitable length of rod out of the pistons; it wants to follow a straight line from the gland through each of the wheel centres. Maybe, with the

cylinders made up as a separate sub-assembly as Comet recommend, these alignments are arrived at automatically, but I thought this was very much the kind of point that might have warranted a mention in the instructions. For a real steam engine to work, the fully extended piston rod and con rod need to be in a

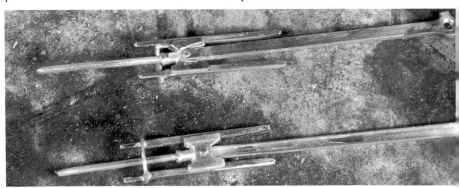

straight line across the back dead centre of the driven axle and this incontrovertible mechanical fact obviously governs the angle of inclination of the cylinders and slidebars. Many model locomotives (including some of my own, I have to say) ignore this point and look weird in consequence. I've seen a Pendon loco where this

Experience taught me to take a sliver or two of metal off the outer ends of the slidebars to give extra clearance for the connecting rod – this is done on prototype locos for the same reason. I also opened up the recess in the rear face of the crosshead to give the con-rod a little more room to move. Often these modifications, in the event, prove unnecessary but prevention is always better than cure. Very few kit instructions mention this kind of thing and the inexperienced builder is left to flounder as he contemplates an immobilised chassis.

The rod helps to align the slidebars with the wheel centres. I have tack-soldered them in place on the cylinder rear face and to the motion bracket, and when I'm satisfied that the crosshead runs smoothly, I will run in a good fillet of solder and generally clean up the rather scrappy situation that is evident here. The M2 bolt, by the way, is somewhere for the crocodile clip on the negative lead of my RSU to grip while I'm soldering up brake gear and suchlike.

I had reached this stage when I discovered the slidebars were too short. The text reveals the remedial surgery that was involved — the scars are pretty obvious in this shot of the end result. However, a few passes with file and scraper will work wonders.

fault was readily apparent, so even Jove nods sometimes.

To get clearance behind the slidebars I had filed the boss of the front coupling rod down to half-thickness and, instead of using a crankpin nut, simply reversed a suitably shortened crankpin bush (with a thin washer at the 'wheel' end) and secured it to the crankpin with Loctite. The surplus crankpin was cut off and the bush filed down until it was flush with the front face of the rod. I got this wheeze from Chris Gibbon of High Level Kits and it works very well on my P4 models.

So, the rods were in place and everything ran nicely. I was surprised, however, by how splayed the connecting rod looked in comparison with the coupling rods — it was more like OO, in fact, whereas real con rods are parallel to the coupling rods. I hadn't actually measured anything up beforehand but I got the feeling, studying the slidebar assembly in situ and marvelling at the unusual amount of daylight that was shining through between front crankpin and con rod, that Comet had quietly pushed out their slidebar centres to give more clearance and stop the rod clouting the front crankpin. This is a practical solution to a perennial problem and I'm sure many modellers will have reaped the benefits without realising what's going on — but I think it's a bit naughty all the same. In my book, every whisper that is taken over and above the statutory 27mm or so between slidebar centres is a crime against civilisation. In consequence, I found myself in the extraordinary position (in P4 at any rate) of performing a little alchemy with files and soldering iron to reduce the amount of clearance available to me and to get the rods more closely parallel.

WORKING VALVE GEAR

Having built some cam-driven automaton figures in wood, I thought it would make an interesting challenge to have working valve spindles; they are hardly prominent but seem to contribute to the character of a GW engine. In *The 4mm Engine*, Guy Williams outlines a suitable method using a pivoted arm driven by the piston rod, but I chose another system derived from his earlier book, *Model Locomotive Construction*. The motion is transmitted by means of a thin wire striker attached to the piston rod which engages with suitably spaced stops (in my case, short lengths of wire attached to brass collars) on the spindle itself. The displacement is not great, no more than a

The skeletal right-hand cylinder/slidebar assembly with a token attempt at the glands and other fittings. Note the arrangement of the front crankpin — a very effective way of creating adequate clearance.

The working heart of the model, ready for track testing. In this case, everything went beautifully first time (for once) but there is no point moving any further until the usual blips, glitches, tight spots and shudders have been identified and eliminated.

Simple wire strikers are used to create moving valve spindles. The various linkages on the spindle itself are represented by chain shackles from the PC Models screw coupling etch — a useful source of improvised detail. The slidebars, practical but obviously fictitious, are hidden by the valances.

The crosshead-driven air pump is mounted on a little bracket soldered to the frame. The pump itself is easily made from brass tube, with turned collars at either end. As with the valve spindles, the syncopated movement of the piston is utterly captivating and yet incorporating these working features added little more than an hour or so to the construction time.

scale six inches or so, but once you realise it's there, it does catch the eye. I found myself looking at other models of GW engines and realising how few seemed to have this feature — even on the Malcolm Mitchell Grange that represents my only previous excursion into Swindon territory, the valve spindle isn't designed to work.

The position of the stops and hence the amount of travel is determined by trial and error, while much depends on the nature of the wire that is used for the striker arm. After experiments with various gauges, I found Alan Gibson's 0.33mm brass wire gave the best results, being whippy enough to soak up any excess travel but strong enough to do its job. I put a little loop in the wire and soldered it to the extreme end of the piston rod. Moving parts in the immediate vicinity should, of course, be well oiled while the soldering iron is about; we don't want anything going solid on us.

Making a working vacuum pump was simplicity itself! The pump is brass tube with a collar at one end and a square section at the other, whilst the rod that runs from the right-hand crosshead is 0.7mm brass wire. The support for the pump is bracketed out from the chassis and soldered in place quickly, using the RSU well cranked up.

Assembled as its designers intended, with dummy valve spindles, the Comet chassis fits the Dapol body without any

Chassis more or less complete, with the Comet castings added to the cylinders and the front and rear sandboxes (from the Jackson Evans detailing kit) superglued in place. The sandpipes can wait till later — they'll only catch on something.

adjustment except to remove most of the moulded screw locator under the cab and the dummy front frames. However, the various working fittings that I'd added fouled the thickly moulded footplate — on the real thing, of course, they're tucked in behind the valances — and I had to carve away quite a bit of plastic to get everything tucked snugly away out of sight.

It's as well, by the way, to get the body sitting nice and level as early as possible and certainly long before any of the detail goes on. We don't want any of it to get knocked off while we perform major surgery to correct anything that's obviously skew-whiff, like footplates that are higher at one end than the other. It is amazing how one little bobble can upset the alignment and I spend a lot of time looking and checking and filing as necessary. Far and away the best tool to use in carving away plastic is a burr in a mini-drill — run it fast enough to cut cleanly but not so fast that it melts the plastic. The result may not always look very pretty but who checks under footplates for scars and blemishes?

BODY REWORKING

I built this model after a long spell of making almost everything myself, and I reckoned it was time I found out what the trade could offer by way of detailing components. Whilst there are some makes that I have learned to avoid, I have always been impressed by the Jackson Evans range of after-market bits and pieces. The list isn't enormous but the castings are good and the etchings are equally plausible. These products formed the basis of this work, coming in a bespoke 'County detailing kit' which, at very reasonable price, offered a surprising number of well-crafted bits and pieces. Crownline also do an add-on improvement kit for a County which, on closer inspection, turns out to be the self-same Jackson Evans components with some extra bits such as vacuum pipes and brass buffers.

The older generation of plastic loco bodies were one-piece mouldings but I was surprised, when I came to take it apart, just how many separate bits were in this County. Most of the details like the whistles, whistle shield, reversing rod and ejector pipe were simple push-fits that didn't put up any fight when I pulled them loose. Not so the cab unit, unfortunately. This slides in over a slot in the firebox, but

Above: *A fair amount of plastic needs to be removed from the underside of the footplate to clear the various moving parts. The remedial work isn't too taxing with a mini-drill and a selection of burrs.* Right: *Here we see body components for the 'County' from, among others, Jackson Evans, Martin Finney, ABS, Westward and Blacksmith. The nameplates are by CGW, the finest by a country mile.*

The 'County' body is stripped for action and shows signs of the protracted struggle to get the cab off.

Left: *The 'cage' for the firebox is two hefty slabs of brass, shaped to the appropriate profile and joined by 1mm rod. The wrapper is 5-thou brass sheet, a fairly hard grade. The top curves are already started, using a 3/16in drill bit as a form tool.* Right: *The wrapper is tack-soldered to the formers.*

Left: *The rear firebox former is tacked in place one step at a time, followed by the front former. The block of wood helps with coaxing the wrapper to shape. I try to avoid excessive finger pressure on the wrapper, as this will cause buckling.* Right: *The formers in place — the soldering's a bit messy but everything holds. Now I will run some big fat seams in along the back edges.*

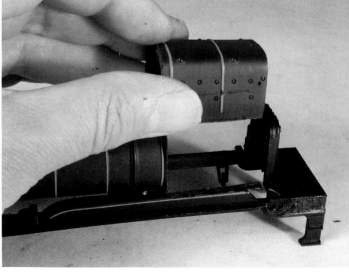

Left: *I wouldn't know if every last nuance of every last chord is perfect but this is already starting to look a lot more like the shapely Swindon firebox than Dapol's effort. Here I've been dressing the top front corners — inside there is a big thick fillet of solder at this point, to allow me to file down into it with impunity.* Right: *Satisfied that the firebox isn't going to be the greatest disaster since the Ford Edsel, I can remove the moulded version.*

the bottom of the side sheets had been solidly glued in place on the rear running plate. Quite a bit of persuasion with an extremely blunt scalpel was called for before the two parts separated and even though I used the minimum leverage, some of the valance came away with the cab. We tend as modellers to be a great deal more adept at assembling things rather than dismantling them, and the procedures on some proprietary models are not at all easy. Separating the body and chassis of the Lima class 59, for instance, makes stripping down a watch mechanism while wearing boxing gloves seem like five minutes' harmless diversion.

The Jackson Evans kit is comprehensive, including such tiny and commonly missed features as the valves on the steam pipes. But with the weight of those exquisite Mitchell/Finney kits on my shoulders, I felt that some considerable refinement would still be necessary over and above shaking a tube of cyano at the detail components. The major item needing attention is the firebox which, as we have seen, is totally the wrong shape — the detail kit doesn't even begin to address this problem. I took the precaution of making a replacement before removing the existing moulding, in case things went horrifically wrong. There are various ways one could go about it, but I followed the method outlined by Guy Williams in *The 4mm Engine,* using a metal 'cage' to support an overlay of 5-thou brass.

The ends of the cage were cut from solid brass and the spacer rods are 1mm hard brass wire, which I found perfectly adequate although ⅛in is usually recommended by the Men Who Know. I soldered the cage up, checked it for squareness, tweaked it as necessary and then part-formed the wrapper at the top shoulders, using a drill bit as a form tool. A thickness of only 5-thou is not great and perhaps one should use something a little sturdier, but it is very easy to work even in a non-annealed state and, provided you do not attack it with a hammer, seems surprisingly resistant to dents. Thicker metal will, of course, need annealing before it can be worked and it is painfully easy to mark it while it is soft. It is worth noting that, if you can wait a day or two after annealing to allow whatever chemical process is going on to arrive at its conclusion, the brass will be much more scuff-resistant but still be just as amenable to bending.

The first trial fit, with the firebox loose, isn't too alarming. The splashers will obviously need to be widened with thin Plastikard overlays, but we'll come to that in due course.

After riveting them, I have added the various cover plates on the firebox and drilled out for the washout plugs. The burring caused by drilling can represent the rim around the holes.

The washout plugs are stubs of 0.7mm wire, set into holes drilled into a backing plate and then filed square.

I cut the wrapper a millimetre or two oversize and tack-soldered it from the outside — a centre line on the wrapper would have helped with positioning if I'd remembered in time to draw one. When I was satisfied that it wasn't too far out of true, I ran big thick fillets of solder around the inside, trimmed it to size and then rounded off the edges, taking especial note of the highly characteristic curves at the top front corners. Once things were looking reasonable, I began to add the details such as riveted overlays at the top and sides (which help to strengthen considerably the thin brass wrapper) and the washout plugs, for which holes had to be carefully marked out and drilled. These could be done before the wrapper is formed but I had a false start with an earlier attempt in which I pre-drilled the holes in the flat. Inevitably I got something not quite true when I came to solder it to the formers, and all the holes ended up in the wrong place.

I'm aware that the brass firebox may appear to be a paradox in a book which is primarily concerned with moulded bodywork. As I said earlier on, I'm not unwaveringly loyal to any particular material and I will use, by and large, whatever is most suitable. But I did, out of interest, make an alternative firebox in plastic. Surprisingly, this was a great deal harder to produce than the brass version; the cage, though made of stout stuff, was nothing like as

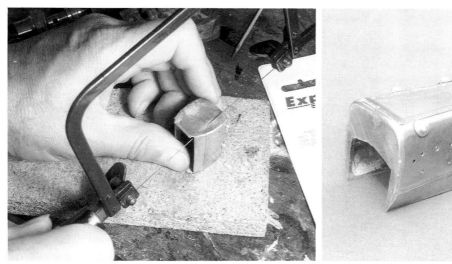

Left: *The firebox front and rear need to be cut away with a piercing saw to clear the RG4 motor/gearbox. For reasons of stability, this is best done last.* Right: *Now that it's complete and ready for installation, I would like to think that my brass firebox is at least a modest improvement on Dapol's clumsy effort.*

I thought I would check to see how the new firebox mated with the (virtually new) cab (see page 103). As you can see, even the loose fit is pretty good, though this was the first time the parts had come together. I don't think you could have a clearer illustration of the advantages of working from scale drawings – you know everything will fit. I rarely use fillers – if the parts are cut and shaped accurately, you shouldn't need to.

A razor saw takes off the unwanted boiler details, such as the top feed.

stable, whilst coaxing 5-thou Plastikard around its curves (and getting it to stay in place) was next to impossible. I gave up when it became obvious that, despite putting considerable effort into trying to make it work, I was getting nowhere at a rate of knots. Modellers who are in mortal fear of basic metal forming might want to try this approach, but I wouldn't recommend it. The brass cage method is far easier. The third option — and I put it forward quite seriously — is to graft the firebox and boiler from the Hornby 8F on to the Dapol cab/footplate/smokebox assembly. Swindon built a batch of 8Fs immediately prior to the County class and the dimensional similarities are marked.

Once I was pleased with the firebox, I cut out the old one and got to work on the body. The stripping-down operation had left me with a bare hulk with just a few more details, such as the steam pipes, smokebox door dart, chimney and safety valve cover to get rid of. This is not difficult but it calls for a knowledge of what tools to use in which circumstances. The object of the exercise is to a leave as little mess as possible to clean up afterwards. Of course, we can always use a little filler if the knife slips but it's best to avoid making too many nicks, dents and abrasion marks in the first place. As the photographs suggest, I am quite a messy worker but hopefully it all comes right in the end.

Like many proprietary locomotives, the County bodywork is designed to fit a solid metal chassis with integral weights at the front end. In consequence it has a hollow-bottomed boiler that needs bulking out to

Left: *Small dental burrs are useful for winkling out recalcitrant bits of plastic without removing detail you wish to keep. Here, the moulded superheater header cover comes off without making a mess of the smokebox rivets.* Right: *This little circular-saw attachment in my mini-drill lets me get into some awkward corners. It needs to be run quite slowly or things start to melt.*

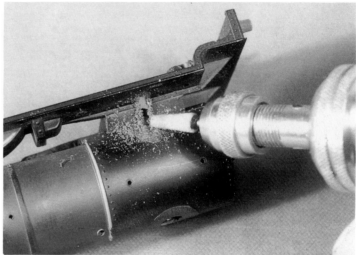

Left: *We finish off with a scalpel. As you can see, I prefer to use a bluntish blade for this kind of refined hacking. A sharp blade can dig in and take off too much.* Right: *Shaped abrasives are very good for working in tight corners.*

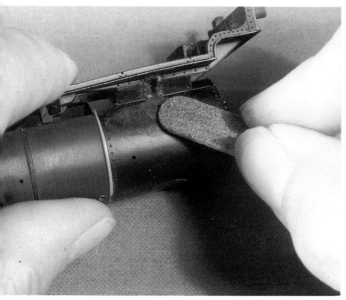

Left: *I use ordinary emery boards for the final clean-up. They can be shaped to penetrate nooks and crannies.* Right: *We finish off with a rub from some 400-grit emery. Most of this area will be concealed by the steam pipes and the new footplate overlays, but we still want to leave a tidy job.*

Left: *As more and more of the bodywork is removed, the structure starts to become unstable. Here I am using a block of wood to support the footplate while I file away at the area where the motion covers used to be.* Right: *After an early-morning hour of sawing, filing, scraping and cajoling, this is what we have ended up with. It looks, as I am readily aware, an absolute fright. So I'll go and have some breakfast and then we'll see what we can do about it.*

Left: *Body rebuilding begins with a new filler piece for the bottom of the boiler. This is made up from layers of 20-thou Plastikard, bent to shape and sprung into place. The exact shape is best determined by trial and error; I made four before I got it right. The 'plug' is secured inside the boiler by strips of 60-thou Microstrip. Once it's fitting snugly, I use a lot of Liquid Poly to make sure it all stays put.* Right: *Adding successive layers increases the strength of the filler piece and enables it to be filed to match the taper boiler profile.*

This is not an exact science and a little filler will be necessary when I come to tidy up.

Left: Riveted overlays for the running plate are made from 5-thou Plastikard. This is a long job calling for great concentration. I find some soothing music helps – Duruflé's wonderful Requiem *is my usual choice, a different version each time so it doesn't become monotonous.*
Right: More overlays conceal the gaps in the splashers where the over-wide moulded firebox was cut away.

its full circumference. As we found with the 4F, fitting a replacement segment of parallel boiler is straightforward enough — you just take a suitably-sized rectangle of Plastikard and curve it to shape — but doing the same thing for the taper variety is not easy. It helps to be able to fit some kind of circular formers inside the existing boiler, if possible, but the interior shape of the County moulding militates against this.

My method of filling in the boiler was first of all to make a best-guess filler piece of 20-thou and then bend it roughly to shape between my fingers. Actually I made a few before I got one that fitted about as snugly as I could reasonably make it. I used this as a template for two more filler pieces and then solvent-welded the first one in place, using strips of 60-thou strip as anchor points inside the boiler. I then added the two outer wrappers and, when the solvent had set, sanded them down to the correct tapered profile. This area is normally in shadow but the low-angle profile view is very convincing.

There is a lot of riveting along the running plate edges and front platform of a County but this has been omitted entirely by Dapol's pattern-maker. I felt it ought to be there and so I made overlays out of 5-thou plastic sheet which I embossed in my Graskop rivet tool. These are welded in place using Liquid Poly. Making a single piece to fit around the frame extensions at the front end is perfectly feasible but I wasn't entirely sure of the pattern of rivets in this area, so I opted to lay them individually, from tiny cubes of Microstrip. Of

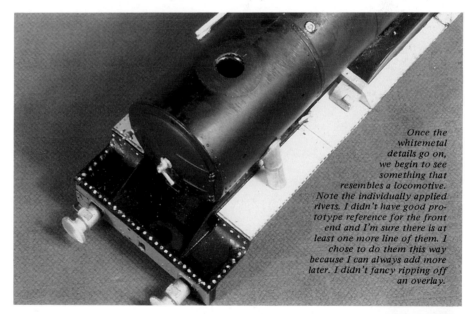

Once the whitemetal details go on, we begin to see something that resembles a locomotive. Note the individually applied rivets. I didn't have good prototype reference for the front end and I'm sure there is at least one more line of them. I chose to do them this way because I can always add more later. I didn't fancy ripping off an overlay.

course this is mind-numbingly fiddly and a great strain on the eyes, but the job is done in the end. Once more accurate information is to hand, I can add or remove rivets at will; this would be much more difficult with overlays.

That was about the sum of the hard work on the body and the rest was a comparatively easy coast. The various replacement castings and etchings go on painlessly although constant reference to pictures is necessary to make sure everything is where it should be. The castings needed the usual cleaning up for part lines but were pretty good on the whole, although I felt the mudhole covers were perhaps a shade over-prominent and could take a little filing-down. I used quite a mix of adhe-

The cast copper chimney – from Westward – was a mass of moulding part lines, calling for careful work with an oval file.

Left: *The cab's back on, and more of the boiler fittings. But still no firebox . . .* Right: *There is a surprising amount of detail on the running plate of a 'County'. Jackson Evans do the bits very well — I think their stuff is excellent.*

Left: *This is the moment where the success or failure of the entire project hangs in the balance — the new firebox is moved into its final position. I have used epoxy to secure it to the rear of the boiler. Note that the top of the firebox has been tack-soldered to the cab front to get the backward slope of the firebox right.* Right: *Plastic-bodied 4−6−0s are notoriously nose-heavy. To balance things out, I packed lead into the firebox and every other aperture — note the big lump between the frames at the rear end. I've also given* County of Middlesex *a lead cab floor — this makes it higher than scale but the moulded floor is slightly too low, and anyway the fall plate can be juggled to lessen its visual impact. A few grammes in the right place can make all the difference and I felt the compromise was justified.*

Right: *The curved smokebox handrail is tricky but worth the effort. I find several attempts are usually necessary.*

Right: *A brief flashback to see surgery to the cab begin by opening out the holes for the roof vents and building up the moulded roof to match the profile of the new etched cab front. The thickly moulded rear portion of the roof has also been removed. Actually the cab front is a little too high and needs filing down by 1.5mm, down to the line of rivets. I didn't spot this until later, too late for these photographs.* Far right: *The new cab roof is bent to shape and soldered in place.*

sives — cyano for very small parts such as the neat little casting for the lancecock, epoxy for that monstrous chimney (imagine trying to solder a big copper casting like that), contact adhesive for the things in between — not for any special reason, merely that I happened to have the tube open at the time. It was surprising how quickly the parts went on and to see a County begin to emerge from the grievously hacked-about hulk of the Dapol moulding.

I had pre-assembled the cab with a new front and roof of correct profile (etches from the Jackson Evans kit) and before refitting it I got rid of the moulded handrails and thinned the sides to give the required 'sheet metal' look. This was now ready to slot back in place over the backhead moulding. Though stripped of all detail ready to have a new backhead fitted on top of it, this part of the moulding (originally forming the firebox rear) has an important structural function in securing the cab to the footplate and has to be retained.

With the cab seated correctly, I slotted the new brass firebox into position. This baldly factual statement belies the considerable amount of work in measuring, cutting, forming and filing that had gone into making sure it fitted snugly. Because everything had been checked and double-checked against drawings and photographs — you cannot simply 'make up' something like a firebox — all went well. Once this was done I put the remaining detail components in place, including reinstating the nicely moulded ejector pipe that had been removed from the Dapol body. The final act was to detail the cab, centring on a new backhead made from thin lead sheet and

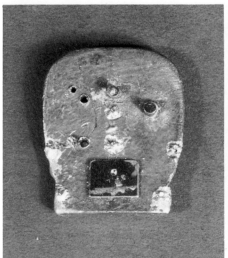 

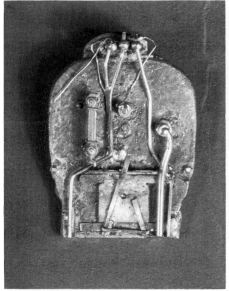 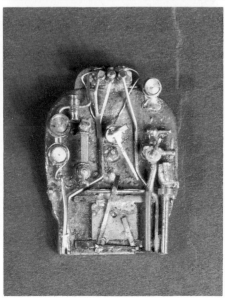

Stages in the production of the backhead, from the beginnings with a lead base to the finished item. The gauge glass — slightly oversize — is a casting but the rest is improvised from fret waste, wire and a few handrail knobs. It took several hours to assemble and still fails miserably by comparison with what the Pendon boys can produce.

I can see a dozen small details that still need to go on, but if it doesn't look like a 'County' by this stage, it never will. Before I can think about painting it, I also need to take a long hard look at the model and clean up all the blebs and blemishes as well as sorting out all the things that have become bent, fallen off or simply ended up in the wrong place. And I still haven't put the cab roof right . . .

glued in place over the old one. I had the Swindon drawing of the cab controls to go on but no photographs. However the cab layout of the County is well nigh identical to the Halls so I stole with impunity from the published wisdom of Messrs Williams and Hayes.

TENDER

As usual we have dummy outside frames and axlebox detail while the real work is carried out by an inner chassis. The GW 4000 gallon tenders all had a 7ft 6in × 7ft 6in wheelbase and whilst it would be perfectly feasible to use the same Comet etch that I employed on the 4F, I preferred to make the tender chassis myself. I don't think it's a good idea always to rely on trade products and, for the inexperienced, a scratchbuilt tender chassis is quite simple and makes excellent practice for the more serious stuff that may come later.

Once again I had a good long look at how Guy Williams had done things with his Hall. I cut the basic frames out of two strips of 1mm brass, sweated together and then sawn so I got an identical pair. Normally I would mark out the outline but here I simply made a photocopy of Guy's drawing and stuck it down on the workpiece with PVA glue. The best tool to use for working this double thickness of brass is a piercing saw with a fairly meaty blade. Once the basic shape has been sawn out, it can be refined with successively finer files.

Before the frames are separated, we need to drill for brake hangers and the compensation beam. I wasn't taking any prisoners

The speedo bracket is a super little casting, as are the injectors – the latter are soldered directly to the chassis. The crank from the rear wheel isn't physically connected to the speedo but it looks like it is.

and opted to use 0.9mm brass wire for these. We also have to drill the axle holes very carefully. I start with a small hole, maybe 1/32in or so, and then open up with larger drill bits, finishing off with a tapered reamer to make a smooth sliding fit for a 2mm axle. I opened up the two leading axle holes to make slots for the compensation — a decent Swiss file is fine for this. As with the bogie, only a millimetre or so of displacement is needed, but care should be taken to make the slot truly vertical and to avoid any fore-and-aft slop.

Spacers came from my seemingly bottomless box of fret waste and were someone's EM chassis spacers which, with the good solid brass I was using for the frames, gave around 15mm overall, which is fine for P4 with its 17.67mm back-to-

back. I soldered the front spacer to one frame and the rear one to the other, then put the two sides together on my wooden jig. We saw this in use with the 4F and it really is a remarkably useful contraption even though it took all of ten minutes to make. My oak blocks, which are planed truly square, help to hold everything in place while the flux sizzles and the solder flows. A quick check to see that everything is as it should be and then an extra spacer can be carefully soldered in the middle — carefully, because we need to solder one side and then let it cool before doing the other. If both are soldered at once, one side will surely expand faster than the other and leave the hapless builder with a banana-shaped chassis.

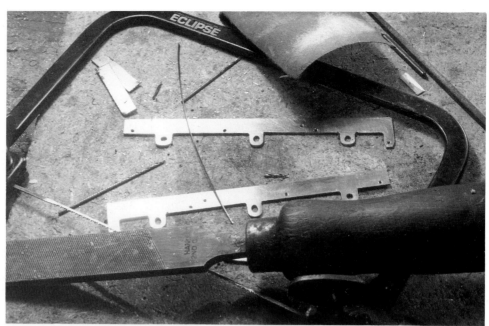

Amid the usual litter of broken piercing saw blades and drill bits, the dummy inside chassis for the tender begins to emerge. It was copied from drawings in Guy Williams' The 4mm Engine – I assume that's what they were there for. The chassis is built out of 1mm brass and 0.9mm wire and could probably withstand being trodden on. Note the shape of the compensation beam, necessary in order to clear the cross-shaft for the brake hangers. The water scoop is one of Crownline's better castings. To form anchorage points for the chassis, M2 nuts are let into the moulding and secured with a hefty gob of epoxy. The cosmetic tender sideframes were custom-etched but the spring/axlebox castings are standard ABS products.

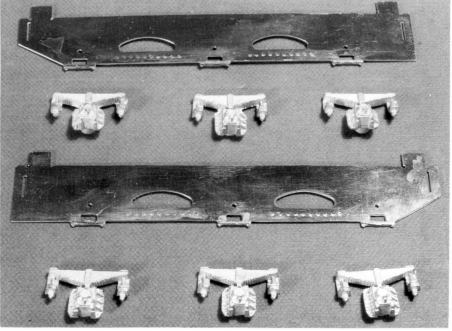

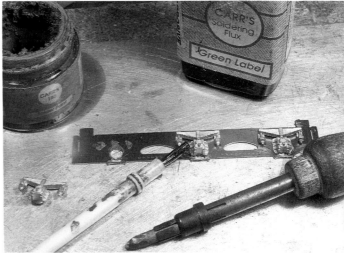

Left: *It's not always easy to solder whitemetal to brass or, as here, nickel silver. This is how I've learned to do it. The first stage is to tin the casting with low-melt solder, using Red Label flux.* Right: *A few spots of 188° solder paint are now added to the nickel sideframes, where the axleboxes will go (note the locating holes have been opened out). With the casting in place, flood the issue with Green Label flux. Then, with the RSU well cranked up, solder the casting in place. The heat is localised so you won't melt anything, but be careful not to touch the casting with the probe. Whitemetal-to-nickel (or brass) joints made this way are incredibly strong.*

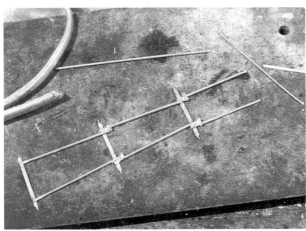

Left: *Simplified brake pull rods for the tender, made from 0.9mm brass wire filed flat and odd scraps of fret waste. Impetus and High Level Kits, in particular, provide a useful source of nice straight strip — the kits are pretty good too.* Right: *Underside view of the nearly-completed tender. The bracing angles on the sideframes are made from Microstrip, riveted in my Graskop press. I think this shot shows well the sheer diversity of the materials I use.*

Dapol's tender body checks out pretty well against the Swindon GA. I particularly liked the moulded front plate — not always an area where the RTR manufacturers make much of an effort — and the fact that the coal bunker was modelled virtually empty. Unfortunately, the exposed edges of the side sheets scale out to 6in across the beading and there doesn't seem to be much that one can do about it, save to really pile on the coal and have a good bit of spillage over the back plate, around the filler dome.

Cosmetic work is routine — just the replacement of moulded handrails, buffers and lamp irons. I note that the horizontal arm of the L in the sideways-on GW lamp irons is always pointing to the right when viewed from the smokebox end, but to the left on the tender rear. This is the kind of

detail that repays careful observation. You will also see that the tender steps are cranked, not straight as in the moulding. The Jackson Evans detailing kit includes replacement whitemetal steps of the correct profile which can be substituted, suitably thinned and with rivet detail to choice. Comet's lovely etched GWR steps are of a different pattern, more suited to the flared-sided tenders.

I mentioned earlier the curious business of the tender wheelbase. Obviously this cannot be tolerated and so the first remedy I tried was to cut off the moulded axlebox/ spring assemblies, clean up the frames and substitute whitemetal castings, correctly spaced. It was obvious from the first incision that the plastic wasn't going to cut at all well. It was greasy to the touch and it shattered when I put any kind of pressure

on to it. Stanley knife, craft knife, file, razor saw and circular saw all produced equally negative results and I was left with no option but to make my own outside frames.

I could have made these out of plastic, as we will see with the Bulleid Pacific, or I could have sawn and filed them out of brass sheet. However, this being the period of the Great Piercing Saw Blade Famine, I did neither and had them etched for me instead. Many kit-makers will do this either as part of their professional services or, if you buy enough of their kits and ask nicely, as a favour; there will often be space on a test etch for a one-off such as this, and etching services are occasionally advertised in the pages of *MRJ*. The replacement Collett-pattern axleboxes are from ABS and are very good. These were superglued

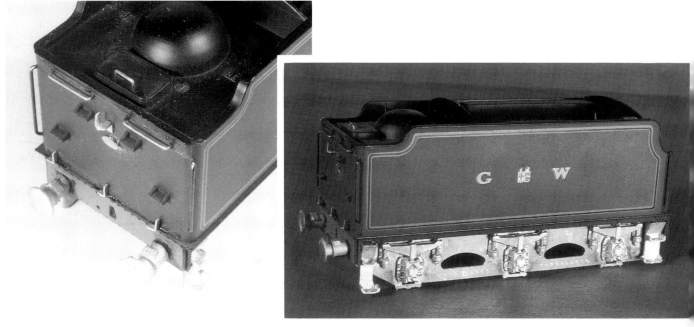

in place and then I fitted the cosmetic sideframes to the tender body.

PAINTING AND WEATHERING

Right up until the early 1960s, the quality of finish evident on Western Region locomotives, and especially the express passenger classes, was in a class of its own. I don't know how Swindon made them look so sleek and shiny but the products of most other paint shops looked distinctly second-rate by comparison. This concern for outward appearance seemed to encourage respect among the operating department and my own superficial impression was that everyday cleanliness was a good deal more prevalent on Western Region than elsewhere. Only in the last couple of years, it seemed, did depot staff lose heart and the remaining Halls, Granges and Manors began to look as filthy as anything Gateshead could turn out. The character of many locomotive classes, especially freight and shunting engines, is enhanced by their disreputable appearance but there was something 'not quite right' about the shabbiness of Western Region express engines once their glory days were past. It made me feel uncomfortable, like watching a once-great footballer or pop star who has gone on too long and run to seed.

Something else that disturbs me is high-gloss finishes, not least because I seem unable to spray them without blemishes. Like the camera, such a finish cruelly reveals the slightest imperfection on the surface, whether it is a tool mark or the motes of atmospheric dust that I can never

entirely banish. Since matt surfaces are much kinder in this respect, the filthed-up state of most of my models could be interpreted as a subconscious defence against inadequacies in my finishing technique — were it not for the fact that I'd been weathering for about twenty years before I consciously attempted to create the ex-works look on a locomotive.

For the County I wanted to capture the appearance of an engine that hasn't been shopped for a long time but has been regularly cleaned, if not always with great thoroughness. My ideas were supported by a half-dozen well-printed colour images from various angles. The first stage, after a thin coating of white primer, was to airbrush the body colour. Although I wanted to show *County of Middlesex* in mid-1950s condition, I used the later style of GWR Loco Green from Railmatch (ref 601) rather than the BR version. I am probably going to get hate mail for this but it does seem, from personal observation supported by photographs, that many Western Region engines were painted in a darker, more yellowish shade of green than the brighter, blue-tinged Brunswick green that was notionally the BR standard. I could be quite wrong, of course, but bearing in mind the Factory's propensity for going its own way regardless, I would be surprised if half a lifetime's supply of Loco Green was chucked out on Nationalisation.

I gave the green parts a light coat of semi-gloss varnish and then lined the loco with a Bob Moore pen, the orange first and then a black line down the middle. I

don't know if the professionals get it right first time but I usually need to do a lot of retouching under heavy magnification. If you work on an area too much, it can stand out and any bits that still won't come right for me at the third or fourth attempt tend to be hidden under discreet weathering. Boiler bands were ruled on to pre-sprayed parcel tape stuck to a sheet of glass, before cutting out with a new blade. I drew out several lengths and chose the best.

To get the 'oily rag' finish, I gave the loco a light weathering, concentrating on the frames, motion and smokebox but trying to avoid the green areas as much as possible. Spray drift will reach them nevertheless and it is important that it does so, because the next thing we do is to take a brush that is just slightly dampened with thinners and take most of the grubbiness off the green bits, being deliberately not too thorough and allowing the dirt to collect in nooks and crannies. Once the thinners has evaporated, some diluted Protec satin coating can be brushed over the green with a No. 2 sable, adding a little water here and there so some areas will be proportionally duller or shinier than others. The residual dirt shows through the sheen, especially in the firebox area, and this looks very prototypical, suggesting patches of blackened and discoloured paintwork in all the right places. I notice that the WR rarely seemed to clean smokeboxes — even on Kings and Castles — so this area can be as mucky as the cab roof, running plate and tender top.

CONCLUSIONS

The adaptation of moulded components for finescale models is often assumed to be a time-saving method and this can sometimes be true. But there were times during the construction of the County when I seemed to be making work for myself, and wondered whether I might not have been better off building from a kit. I think the point is that I enjoy making models this way, even if it is hard work at times. Midway through the build I happened on a conversation between two well-known modellers who were obviously talking about me. "He likes taking something that's a bit rough and having a go at it," one of them was saying, and I guess that sums my attitude up.

The remarkable Swindon finish, evinced by No. 1025 County of Radnor. *But as the close-up of* County of Oxford *shows, cleaning could be selective.*
COLLECTION
R. S. CARPENTER

No. 1011 County of Chester, the last of the class to survive in BR service, immaculate in final BR condition outside the factory, complete with the later versions of the double chimney and superheater cover.

The disciplines involved in railway modelling are many and varied but they do belong to a common pool of ideas. What we see in the County is the way techniques associated with scratchbuilding in metal and assembling state-of-the-art kits can be successfully applied to plastic mouldings. The brass firebox, the riveted overlays, the working valve gear — all these go to lift a humdrum plastic model to a new level. I don't for a moment think that my County bears much comparison with any of those brilliant Great Western 4–6–0s that we've seen in *MRJ*, but ideas do rub off. I stole plenty of things from Guy Williams and John Hayes and it's possible that readers might adapt some of my techniques to their own purposes. I like this notion of ideas and concepts passing from one to the other, mutating and evolving as they do. Without change, there is no progress and in all kinds of ways the County represents both.

No. 1028 County of Warwick at Canton in the early 1950s with a single chimney and three-row superheater. It is shown in 'Mixed traffic' black livery and I am told that Swindon favoured vermilion (buffer beam red) for the lining, instead of the deeper shade used by other works. Colour photographs seem to confirm this, although the early Kodachrome was especially sensitive to red.

K. R. PITT

1 Kitmaster tender sides, trimmed to correct length
2 New bunker, tender cab and front plate (Plastikard)
3 Original-pattern cab (Plastikard)
4 Original-pattern two-pane cab window frames (Albert Goodall)
5 Cab roof shutter, brass
6 Oval washout plugs (Albert Goodall)
7 Dome cover (Crownline)
8 Whistle (Albert Goodall)
9 Safety valves (Albert Goodall)
10 Boiler top casing in Plastikard
11 Original-pattern chimney, from sheet brass
12 Smokebox cowl (Albert Goodall)
13 Smokebox front (Albert Goodall)
14 New front end (Plastikard)
15 Electric lights (cubes of Plastikard)
16 One-piece buffer beam/pipe/step assembly (brass)
17 Etched smoke deflectors (Albert Goodall)
18 Bodyside overlays (Plastikard) on Hornby bodyshell
19 Beam-compensated chassis (Puffers, adapted for Dyna-Drive)
20 Alan Gibson wheels
21 Ashpan detail (Albert Goodall)
22 Injectors and related pipework, from wire
23 Cab steps, brass shim
24 Tender sideframes, riveted Plastikard
25 Tender axleboxes (ABS)
26 Compensated tender chassis (scratchbuilt)

CHAPTER SIX

THE BEAST

A WEST COUNTRY PACIFIC BASED ON A HORNBY BODY, PERSEVERANCE CHASSIS KIT AND SCRAPS OF KITMASTER TENDER

No. 34020 Seaton *with extended smoke deflectors, in early Nationalisation days, still in malachite but without ownership marks.*

COLLECTION R. S. CARPENTER

FOR three summers in a row — not entirely without my tacit approval — my parents decided on Bournemouth for our holidays. They'd found a hotel they liked and I'd discovered Southern steam.

After about half a day of pretended interest in the beach or the Winter Gardens or whatever they seemed to want to do, I'd drop into the familiar routine for the rest of the week: breakfast at hotel, pick up packed lunch from reception, walk to station, bunk the shed, catch the first steam-hauled train that turned up and hare off to Southampton, Eastleigh, Weymouth, Basingstoke or wherever I fancied a day's photography. Sometimes I would extract maximum advantage from my 'Holiday Runabout' ticket and simply charge up and down the line all day, behind Bulleid Pacifics and standard class 5s, returning black with soot, and just in time (after the quickest of quick scrubs) for dinner.

Anything south of Leicester seemed very different to my teenage eyes and the Southern was about as foreign as it got in railway terms. Concrete station name-boards and green enamel signs I could handle but the Bulleids were just weird. I was impressed by the sheer presence of the Merchant Navies but the unrebuilt Pacifics had something unique and magical. They were spooky.

For a start, they didn't seem to make any visual sense. Their hulking metal shrouds, heavily dented and rippled, gave little hint of what lay within, apart from the odd panel tantalisingly slid open to reveal a steam manifold or sandbox filler. There was a strange, neb-like cowl around the smoke-box front and a tri-part cab window that was an architectural detail from the 1930s. They all seemed to be different from one another — different livery details, different fittings, different tenders, different styles of nameplate. Many of them had replacement body panelling in various shades of green, with or without lining. I wondered if any of them, in their last few years at least, were actually identical. Later I came to doubt if any two of them were alike even when built.

Casual curiosity apart, an interest in locomotive minutiae was yet to develop in me. I preferred to hang, streaming-eyed, out of a carriage window on one of those hysterical sprints that were so characteristic of the Bulleids' last runs, but best of all I liked to stand on a platform end and watch a Pacific start a heavy train. Actually, it was more of an aural experience. Doors slammed, whistle blew, a hiss of steam and then there would be an explosion of sound and fury as the Boxpok wheels spun helplessly for a few seconds before the engine found its feet. It would crawl forward a few

inches and the volcano would erupt again, maybe several times. Unburned coal dust, cinders, black oily water — all would be flung heavenwards before descending on the marvelling crowd of onlookers. I have seen a Merchant Navy on the northbound 'Pines', sanders full on, take three or four minutes to get away from Bournemouth Central. The crews never seemed particularly concerned by it, although I don't suppose these uncontrolled skids did the fire much good, or the bearings.

The reason the Bulleid Pacifics looked so odd was that they'd been got at over the years by the operating department. In outward form, Bulleid's original concept had been a masterpiece of integrated design, considered from a purely aesthetic standpoint. But one by one, most of the features that gave them their distinctive character were bastardised — the front-end fairings, the cab, the high-sided tender, the livery. They were still handsome engines — and the fully rebuilt examples especially so — but the visual unity of Bulleid's air-smoothed concept had been irredeemably compromised. Apart, perhaps, from the Southern T9s, it is difficult to think of any classic British locomotive design whose appearance hasn't been loused up by insensitive meddling — from the clumsy tenders given to some of the Stirling and Johnson singles to the de-

A rare shot of the unnamed No. 21C164 — later to become Fighter Command *and, in time, to carry a Giesl ejector — on 9th June 1947, done up specially for a ceremony marking its entry into traffic as the 1000th engine built at Brighton. In fact No. 21C164 never left the works in this form. It was taken back into shops and given the new style of V-fronted cab (but still with the two-pane side window) and a fresh coat of 'photographic grey', minus the lining on the smoke deflectors. The second picture shows the loco in modified form outside the works on 1st July, after another visit from the official photographer.*   AUTHOR'S COLLECTION

valancing of Gresley's A4s and, most heinous of all, the ruination of his magnificent Mikados.

Though I was drawn towards a last-days-of-Southern-steam interpretation for this model (nameplates missing, tatty replacement panelling, general all-over filth) I decided this project should represent one of the West Country Pacifics in near-original form, but in BR Brunswick green with the early lion-and-wheel symbol. My choice fell on No. 34043 *Combe Martin,* which was still very much as built when, in the summer of 1951, it was transferred to Bath for work over the Somerset & Dorset, in company with Nos 34040/1/2. I never knew the S&D in its heyday but in recent years I have spent many idyllic holidays at a cottage close to Masbury summit and I feel a great empathy with the landscape through which the railway passed. Even now, when most of the trackbed has reverted to farmland, that marvellous sweep down to Wellow past the Iron Age long barrow at Stoney Littleton brings home to me the unique aura of this line. Though I'll probably never build the S&D parade-of-trains layout that has long been a favourite pipe dream, modelling one of the line's most charismatic engines seems like an agreeable compromise.

PROTOTYPE

I knew next to nothing about Bulleid Pacifics when I started this project, but then Paul Karau rang me one day and in that suspiciously casual manner of his suggested, apropos of many things, that it

might be nice, if only for his own benefit, to append a word or two about the different cabs and smoke deflectors and suchlike that characterised these engines. OK, I said in all innocence, and got to work. It quickly became obvious that the published wisdom was riddled with errors, half-truths and contradictions. In trying to put the record straight, what began life as a two-paragraph resumé almost became an article or even a book in its own right. The gist of this is printed here because it seems that — unless I've missed something very obvious — there is no one readily accessible, accurate and above all authoritative printed source of data on the visible differences among these extraordinary locomotives. The next best thing is the archive created by Albert Goodall, whose research into Bulleid matters, like his patience with enquirers, verges on the heroic. I am greatly indebted to Albert for much of what follows.

The detail variations among the Light Pacifics are truly enormous, especially in their unrebuilt form, and changes began to appear long before Bulleid's departure from Southern territory in 1949. I can only begin to scratch the surface here, so we might as well start at the beginning. One popular canard can go for a start: there was no intrinsic difference between the West Country and Battle of Britain classes. The distinction was a purely nominal one, created for publicity purposes. Holiday traffic being mightily important to the Southern, the first 48 engines, all originally allocated to sheds west of Salisbury, were given names with 'West

Country' associations. Nine Elms, Stewarts Lane and Ramsgate got the subsequent batches and, the war being not long over, play was made of the South East's RAF associations in the choice of names — hence the class designation. Every effort was made to keep the West Country class allocated exclusively to Western Section, a system of apartheid that lasted for over a decade and only really began to break down in the late 1950s. However, to demonstrate the kind of paradox that becomes all too familiar to students of Bulleid lore, Nos 34091–109 (built 1949–50) were allotted 'West Country' names but went new to both Eastern and Western Section sheds, whilst the last two to be built, Nos 34109–10, were nominally Battle of Britain class engines but went at first to Bournemouth.

Let's move on to more tangible details. Those light Pacifics built by the Southern Railway up to March 1947 (21C101–57) originally had short smoke deflectors and an extremely stylish, cowled cab with two-pane sliding windows. The cab, like the tender, was 8ft 6ins wide and enabled the Pacifics to work, in theory at least, over the Hastings line, which they never did in regular service. The square side sheets of the original cabs were swept upwards to blend with the top line of the casing.

Complaints from enginemen about drifting smoke led, within a very short space of time (1946–7) to the smoke deflectors being lengthened; the modifications were carried out quickly and almost all engines had been dealt with by Nationalisation in 1948. Engines from

21C158 on were built new with the longer style; on No. 21C162, the forward edge was curved inwards as an experiment. The front profile of these early-pattern smoke deflectors was flat but the later engines had plates with varying outlines — some were flat-sided whilst others were prominently curved, and a number of locos built with flat smoke deflectors later acquired curved ones. The variations appear almost random and the curved contours of the deflectors fitted to the BR-built examples, numbered from 34071–110, were different again.

Forward vision was another problem with these engines and in an attempt to remedy this, the cab sides were redesigned. The last engine to be delivered with the original square style of cab (but now carrying the new-pattern smoke deflectors) was No. 21C163, outshopped in May 1947. In an effort to give enginemen a better view forward, Nos 21C164–70 entered service with a V-fronted cab with the top of the sidesheets cut back. Nos 21C164–5 had, in fact, been built with the original cab but were modified before being released into traffic. These two engines only retained the two-panel sliding windows, as on the earlier engines, but they were replaced in early BR days by the three-panel pattern with which the rest of the V-fronted batch was fitted from new. This three-panel window was the style also adopted for all the BR-built Pacifics, on which the overall width was increased to 9ft, which precluded them from working on the Hastings line.

In late 1947 a start was made on converting the earlier engines to the V-fronted cab, beginning with Nos 21C151–7; all were given three-pane windows. Less than half-a-dozen engines (Nos 34015/19/24/34/8) were still running with their original cabs in 1955. By January 1956 No. 34015 was the last sur-

Many Bulleid Pacifics ran without nameplates at first. These pictures show No. 21C155 with the original short smoke deflectors, and No. 21C152 with lengthened ones. The class as a whole was in a continuous state of flux, with little or no consistency as far as outward appearance was concerned.

vivor of this group; not until March 1957 did it receive a V-fronted cab. From the early 1950s onwards the Bulleids also lost the distinctive wrap-around valance between the cylinders and the front platform and the character of the engines was beginning to change. It wasn't so much death by a thousand cuts as death by a thousand detail changes.

A slight digression, to maintain historical continuity — immediately prior to their involvement in the Locomotive Exchanges of 1948, Nos 34004/5/6 were fitted with V-fronted cabs and enormous, 12ft-long smoke deflectors. These features were retained until Nos 34004/5 lost their air-smoothed casing when they were rebuilt in 1958 and 1957 respectively. No. 34006, however, remained in original form and still had its unique extra-long smoke deflectors at withdrawal in 1967. The Southern had no water troughs and hence no scoops on its tenders and so, for the duration of the trials, these three engines ran with unlined black Stanier 4000 gallon tenders lettered 'BRITISH RAILWAYS' The engines themselves were in Bulleid malachite, lined yellow but with BR numbers in Southern style.

Back to the main story. All Light Pacifics built up to and including No. 34090 (entered service February 1949) originally carried Southern malachite green livery, with a triple line of yellow — sometimes called 'old gold'- along both locomotive and tender. There was also a broad black band along the front valance, the lower cab and the lower tender side sheets. Nos 21C101–70 were numbered in Bulleid's style, with 'SOUTHERN' on the tender in 'sunshine' lettering. The next twenty engines were delivered after nationalisation. They carried BR numbers and 'BRITISH RAILWAYS' on the tender, again in 'sunshine' style. No. 34090, though outshopped in malachite — and, uniquely, with green wheels to boot — had numbers in cream Gill Sans and the new BR 'cycling lion' emblem on the tender, which style of insignia was subsequently carried on other malachite engines. However, engines from 34091 on, built between 1949 and 1951, carried the new standard Brunswick green livery from new, again with the BR emblem and Gill Sans lettering. The black band — a stylistic nuance that served to increase the apparent length of the engine, making it appear fast and powerful — was retained throughout

each of these livery phases. All the earlier engines were eventually repainted in Brunswick green, the last engine in malachite being No. 34070 (outshopped March 1953). There were, inevitably, a number of anomalies and short-lived intermediate phases — engines running without marks of ownership, 21C numbers prefixed by the letter 'S' in early BR days, and so on. I might mention for completeness that, until the final details of livery were settled upon, Nos 34011/56/64/5/86/7/8 ran for some months in 1948 in an experimental shade of apple green, lighter than the LNER's interpretation. This was lined in red and grey, edged yellow in what would become the BR 'mixed traffic' style. The apple-green engines did not carry the broad black bands.

Light Pacifics in Brunswick green carried a unique form of the BR 'passenger' lining, with two parallel bands running the full length of the locomotive and tender, one high up on the air-smoothed casing and the other directly above the black panels. Even more unusually, instead of the standard style of two ⅛in orange lines on either side of a ⅞in black line, with ⁹⁄₁₆in green lines showing between, the Bulleids had ¼in orange lines butting right up to the 1¼in black line. When the tenders of many engines were cut down from 1952 onwards (see below), the narrow orange-black-orange lining along the air-smoothed casing was retained but the V-fronted cabs and tender sides were box-lined in the wider orange-green-black-green-orange fashion, which made for a dreadful clash of styles. The broad black band was dropped from the cut-down tenders although it was retained on the surviving high-sided designs. Engines which kept their high-sided tenders retained the original fashion of lining on cab and tender but I don't doubt for a moment that there were hybrid combinations.

The topic of liveries brings us on to insignia and the handsome cast smokebox ring carried by all Bulleid Pacifics built in pre-Nationalisation days. Red-painted, this device carried the name 'SOUTHERN' along with the date of construction. After 1948, the rings were removed and a cast

No. 34004 Yeovil *with the extra-large smoke deflectors – note the sliding panel for the sandbox fillers.*
AUTHOR'S COLLECTION

No. 21C101 Exeter *with 'Devon Belle' battens on the smoke deflectors and the original two-part side windows.*

J. G. HUBBACK, CTY. JOHN HODGE

BR numberplate was fitted instead, although some locos ran for a while with neither. In Southern livery the locomotive number was painted in 'sunshine' style on the front of the casing immediately above the buffer beam; a few engines carried painted BR numbers in the same letter-form (with the odd one still carrying its smokebox ring) before receiving cast number plates. The first 21 West Country class engines originally had black-backed nameplates, but from 1946 the background colour was altered to red. Battle of Britain nameplates were at first sky blue. Not all engines were fitted with nameplates from new and some ran nameless for several years. Around 1952/3 the background colour was, in theory, changed to black for both classes, but anomalies persisted; when the hitherto nameless No. 34026 received its *Yes Tor* nameplates in October 1955, they were red-backed, suggesting they may have been held in store for some time. However the nameplates of many Light Pacifics, of both the West Country and Battle of Britain classes, were repainted in red by depots after the engines had returned from works with black-backed plates until, from 1958, officialdom sanctioned a gradual reversion to the original colour schemes. Although the enamelled town or county crests carried beneath the

nameplate seem such a characteristic feature of the West Country class, less than half of the engines (29 out of 66) actually carried them. All the Battle of Britain class, except, for some reason, No. 34110, carried an armorial shield or some other appropriate device.

For all its complexity, this is, I have to say, only a general picture and I shall all but ignore the rebuilding of many of these engines from 1957 on — life is too short. There is much more to come in terms of specific detail — nothing is straightforward with the Bulleids — but to keep things in perspective and balance six things in our heads at once, we now need to understand about the tenders. The SR-built engines, 21C101–70, which were built to the Hastings line loading gauge, had high-sided, 8ft 6in wide tenders carrying 4,500 gallons of water. The top of the tank, rear-wards of the bunker, appears quite flat (actually it was gently curved). On it was mounted, flush up against the rear bunker wall, four large vacuum tanks. The tender rear, as built, was 4ins above the tank top. The BR-built Light Pacifics had, as well as a new smoke deflector profile and a 9ft wide cab, tenders with the water capacity increased to 5,500 gallons and a modified coal space, which was one foot shorter and six inches wider. These tenders were 9ft

wide overall. The central portion of the tanks between the fire-iron tunnels (visible behind the bunker) was raised up by one foot compared with the earlier batch and in consequence the cluster of vacuum tanks directly behind the rear coal plate was mounted that much higher but this time standing clear of the rear bunker plate by approximately 15ins.

Practical necessity, more than any other factor, was behind most of the changes to the outward appearance of these locos. Coal dust and water accumulated on the back platform, forming an unpleasant and potentially hazardous slurry. To make life easier for crews, BR lowered the tender rears of the 4,500 gallon tenders until they were level with the tank tops. There was also an acknowledgement that the high-sided tenders made tender-first running difficult, and so a start was made on cutting down the side raves of the tenders, level with the tank tops. Fire irons had previously been slotted into the open-topped gap between the side raves and the bunker, but now proper fire-iron tunnels had to be provided. The cutting-down of tender sides took some time and, extraordinarily enough, a handful of engines survived until withdrawal in 1963/4 with their tenders still in unmodified form, not just with the high sides but with the original

Surrounded on all sides by light Pacifics, No. 34011 Tavistock is shown here with the unique 'Devon Belle' wingplates, for which fixing battens were provided on the smoke deflectors. Many engines carried them until withdrawal, long after the 'Devon Belle' had ceased to run.
AUTHORS COLLECTION

No. 34086 with high-sided tender and V-fronted cab. Delivered after Nationalisation in malachite with 'sunshine' lettering, it acquired standard BR green livery and insignia after its first shopping.

No. 34043 Combe Martin ex-works at Eastleigh in 1952. There are a number of significant modifications compared with the condition in which I modelled this engine, including the cut-down tender, TIA doser tank, V-fronted cab and box lining.

high tender rear as well. The engines concerned were Nos 34069/72/4/5/8, all bar one of which were Exmouth Junction engines. The odd man out, Eastleigh's No. 34072, went to Barry scrapyard and was subsequently bought for preservation, although its tender had long been scrapped. The tender fitted to No. 34078 was, of course, a 5,500 gallon design. The high-sided tenders fitted to some Bulleid Pacifics in preservation, Nos 34023 and 34081, for example, are fakes, recreated with varying degrees of authenticity.

Cutting down the side raves revealed the very visible differences between the tender rears — the 4,500 gallon type appears flat-topped whilst the larger tenders are inset. At the same time as the sides were lowered, tenders of both sizes acquired a curved rear bunker plate which was absent on the original design. When rebuilding of the locomotives began in 1957, the official edict was that these engines (all with 9ft wide cabs, modified as necessary) should have the larger tenders. As the earlier engines were rebuilt, they too acquired 5,500 gallon tenders. Since there were eventually 60 rebuilds but only the 40 wide tenders originally fitted to 34071–110, not all the rebuilds could have them. Some had to have the 4,500 gallon version and in consequence ran with a tender that was six inches narrower than the cab.

To get at least part-way round this problem, a third variety of tender was introduced by BR. There were nine of these tenders altogether, built from 1958–60, five of which were allocated to Merchant Navy class engines and which used MN-pattern chassis. The four tenders of this type that were built for the Light Pacifics and originally fitted to 34031/9/46/59 had the same flush-sided 5,250 gallon, 9ft wide replacement body. They used existing frames, all Light Pacific tenders having a common chassis. On this pattern of tender, there was a high rear platform without the pronounced step-down behind the fire-iron tunnels that is found on the modified 4,500 and 5,500 gallon designs. The tender-top vacuum tanks were boxed in instead of merely being plated over (on the original high-sided design they were completely uncovered). No. 34031's tender passed to 34087 on withdrawal in April 1965 and in the August of that year 34104 acquired the tender from the now-withdrawn 34039. There was also a single 6,000 gallon self-weighing tender for test purposes which I believe may only have run with Merchant Navy class engines, but you quickly learn to take nothing for granted with the Bulleid Pacifics.

As well as the vacuum tanks, many of these tenders showed variations in detail fittings. Engines allocated to Bath for running over the Somerset and Dorset route carried a tender-mounted tablet exchanger for single-line working; this was on the driver's side above the front steps. Nos 21C166–70 entered traffic with the patented TIA (*Traitement Intégrale Armande*) water treatment system, identified by the large doser box on the back of the tender. Most of the Light Pacifics subsequently acquired this system but in 1955 BR began fitting a simpler type of water-softening equipment which had a much smaller cover; the exact position varies according to tender type. Engines so equipped carried a small yellow triangle on the cab-sides, but many of the class that were allocated to sheds west of Salisbury never received either system because the available supply was naturally soft. Once again, reference needs to be made to dated photographs and other reliable records because, inevitably, there were variations among all types. Albert Goodall produces an invaluable set of drawings of the major varieties of Bulleid tender but even these, admirably though they may paint the broad picture, can only scratch the surface regarding finer nuances.

Back, as threatened, to the locos. Having established the complicated general pattern of things, we can now look at some of the myriad further variations that are to be found among individual engines — they would be impossible to list in their entirety here, even if I were aware of them all. The buffers on the Southern-built Pacifics were of a stepped design very similar to the LNER Group Standard (Bulleid, of course, had been a senior colleague of Gresley's at Doncaster). Nos 21C131–45, however, had LMS-pattern buffers from new and this was subsequently standardised on the BR-built batch, although there are exceptions. Most of the Southern-built engines (in fact all except 21C106/13/19/22/3/8/9/32–40/4/5/55/8/60/62–70) carried a batten at the top of the smoke deflectors to which train nameboards for the 'Devon Belle' were once attached in the unique Southern 'wingplate' style; some engines had these battens until withdrawal. The first hundred Light Pacifics lacked dampers and this caused combustion problems when the engines were stationary for any length of time. To combat this, the final ten were built with a different ashpan arrangement incorporating dampers. In 1952, a new design appeared on some of the earlier engines, Nos 34011/43/65. Around 1957, Nos 34101–10 (all still in original condition) were fitted with these ashpans, which were also fitted to the rebuilt engines. The visible differences are marked but the modified ashpans fitted to the three engines involved in the 1948 Locomotive Exchanges did not cause any alteration in the external appearance.

One could go on almost indefinitely. As built, the Light Pacifics had rectangular hatches giving access to the sandbox fillers on either side of the nameplate position, with a third hatch immediately to the rear of the smoke deflectors. This last was plated over from the mid-1950s on. The final twenty built had round sandbox filler lids instead of the rectangular pattern. The new design proved troublesome — they rattled loose and let the rain in — and they were quickly altered to conform with the rest of the class; clear photographs of engines with round filler caps are rare. These never had front wheel sanding although they all carried slidebar covers to protect against spillage.

And still it comes pouring out . . . The first thirty engines to be built had a plain chimney with a streamlined fairing behind. The latter feature was absent on 21C131–45, which had lipped chimneys. The fairings were removed from the other engines around 1948 and the BR-built engines entered traffic without them but then, confusingly, the fairings seem to have reappeared on most or all of the engines by 1952. From 1954, the boiler pressure was reduced to 250psi and the safety valves, hitherto in a triangular cluster of three forward of the whistle, were resited in a shallow trough behind the dome cover. Most engines have the knuckle joint in the coupling rods behind the centre crankpin but on one or two it appears to be ahead of it. Between 1946 and 1948 No. 21C119 ran as an oil burner. The six engines built at Eastleigh (34095/7/9/101/2/4) very likely differed in minor detail from those erected at Brighton and probably with each other as well. Five engines changed their names at various times. After a while, you just want to stick your head in a bucket of water.

Later on in their careers, the remaining unrebuilt Pacifics acquired further modifications, the most noticeable of which were speedometers running from cranks on the nearside rear drivers, AWS battery boxes above the front buffer beams, with a step above it and a protective shield for the magnet below the buffer beam, and the permanent removal of access hatches on the lower cab side sheets and firebox casings. Early in 1960, No. 34049 lost its smoke deflectors entirely in an effort to improve the crew's forward vision; they were quickly reinstated, but with a modified top cowl. In April 1960 No. 34035 was outshopped from Eastleigh with an entirely new pattern of smoke deflector, similar to those fitted to Nos 34004/5/6 but swept round at the front to merge with the smokebox cowl in a style reminiscent of the original Merchant Navy front end. It quickly reverted to a more familiar configuration. Even as the rebuilding programme drew to a close, No. 34064 emerged from Eastleigh works in 1962 with a Giesl ejector. This kind of chopping and changing went on throughout the lives of these engines, even into the preservation era, during which time No. 34092 also acquired a Giesl ejector whilst No. 34023 was given a crest below the nameplate — something it never carried in its main-line days — but otherwise reverted to an approximation of its later Southern condition, with short smoke deflectors, a simulated high-sided tender and the original rendition of its name. A fair bit of component-swapping also went on at Barry and afterwards, and I feel one must be more than usually circumspect when looking at a preserved Bulleid in an effort to clear up the finer points of detail.

I guess I should only really talk about the unrebuilt Pacifics in any depth, because if I brought in the rebuilds we would be here all day and half the night. In every conceivable way and from every conceivable angle, the Bulleid Pacifics epitomise the case for building models only after the protracted study of dated photographs. This was certainly true of *Combe Martin*. This engine arrived at Bath shed in May 1951 still pretty much as built, but in Brunswick green with the large version of the original cycling lion emblem. This is how I think the Bulleids looked best and this is how I chose to model her, using for guidance a number of Ivo Peters' photographs taken in the summer of 1951. A year later, however, after a visit to works and a transfer to Bournemouth, she returned to S&D territory significantly transformed. From photographs one can see she has acquired a V-fronted cab, new ashpans of the pattern described earlier, and a cut-down tender with TIA doser. I dare say that, after the next shopping, things were different again.

The starting point — an untouched Hornby body. Note the fine rivet detail — all of it completely inaccurate — and the fairing behind the chimney, which is in the wrong place anyway. This will quickly be reduced to a bare hulk on which I will hang my interpretation of what a Bulleid Pacific looks like.

MODELLING OPTIONS

At the popular end of the scale, Hornby (née Triang) have been producing a ready-to-run Bulleid Pacific since 1961. Although I would discard the chassis and tender for finescale purposes, the loco body has possibilities. From the same era and going equally strong is the old Kitmaster plastic kit, subsequently reissued with minor modifications by Airfix and Dapol. This has its faults but it's a good cheap starting point and many presentable models have been built from it.

The conventional options open to the more committed builder are the Westward model, introduced in 1988 and still available from Puffers, and the more recent Crownline offering. The Westward design is a mixture of whitemetal and etched parts, whilst Crownline's is predominantly brass. Both give you, within the one kit, optional components to build some of the major variations we have just been looking at. This is convenient for the manufacturers, who don't have to package separate kits, but it does, of course, mean that you

are paying for a lot of parts you won't actually use.

Having seen the manufacturer's built-up samples, I wouldn't say either was exactly state-of-the-art. But the real crunch comes with the cost — you are looking at around £100 for each kit, exc w/g/m as the small ads would have it. Stick in an RG4 and decent set of wheels and you're easily looking at the cost of a bargain break weekend for two in a plush hotel. Your author, being more of the b&b/hol cott school of thought, decided to see what could be done for the price of an overnight stay at Mrs McGinty's flophouse. So we have here a Hornby loco body, a few scraps of a Kitmaster tender, a lot of Plastikard, diverse bought-in bits, Alan Gibson P4 wheels and a Perseverance chassis. I also decided to experiment with the transmission.

DRIVE SYSTEM

All that space underneath the air-smoothed casing cries out to be filled with interesting machinery. Ever since reading Chris Pendlenton's articles on his magnificent A1 Pacific in *MRJ* Nos 28 and 29, I have been drawn to the application of Dyna-Drive technology to model locomotives. The Dyna-Drive system uses a centrifugal clutch to smooth the take-up of power when current is applied to the motor. Hefty flywheels — of dimensions infinitely greater than those usually fitted to model locomotives — serve to further even out the torque, and give considerable momentum to the engine when it is on the move. The clutch cushions the start and the flywheels bring the engine to a smooth halt with the motor still idling, the clutch having automatically disengaged when power is cut. The impression of mass and momentum — the sheer aesthetic feeling of a hundred-ton locomotive on the move — is quite overwhelming.

In issue 84 of *MRJ*, I described the installation of Dyna-Drive in a Lima class 37 diesel. I used a standard conversion kit from Formil Model Engineering, who are UK agents for Brimalm, the system's Swedish manufacturer. But no one ever builds just one Dyna-Drive engine — the system has a seductive power all of its own and I particularly wanted to see if I could apply what I'd learned to steam locomotive construction. Formil don't, as yet, do bespoke steam-outline Dyna-Drive packs but that wasn't the point. Instead of thinking of Dyna-Drive as a self-contained off-the-peg system, I wanted to take its broad principles and integrate them with the kind of hardware most modellers will be familiar with.

Chris Pendlenton's *Hal o' the Wynd* has a loco-mounted motor and clutch driving a set of flywheels in the tender which, in turn, powers a bevel gearbox on the centre axle of the loco. I intended to do it in a linear way, with motor and clutch in the tender and the rest in the loco. The key components are the Brimalm clutch (imported by Formil) and the flywheels, which were made for me by a friend. The motor is a Mashima 1833, chosen because it is big, powerful and robust (it needs to be, because those four 24mm diameter flywheels alone weigh as much as many locos). I made the flywheel mounting brackets from 1/32in brass, soldered on to L-shaped spacers that, in turn, screw into the chassis spacers. The bearings are plain 2mm top hats; proper Brimalm Dyna-Drive brackets have integral ballraces which significantly reduce friction in the drive train. Brimalm also produce an exceptionally free-running, high-precision gearbox specifically designed for Dyna-Drive. The well-known Sharman gearbox would have been a less expensive possibility but a trawl through the depths of my 'solutions awaiting a problem' box revealed an ancient KTM 30:1:1 two-stage gearbox that exactly fitted the geometry of my proposed system. It had gears the size of pound coins and an alloy casing designed to withstand earthquakes. If anything was going to survive the pummelling of a big can motor and those massive flywheels, this was your man.

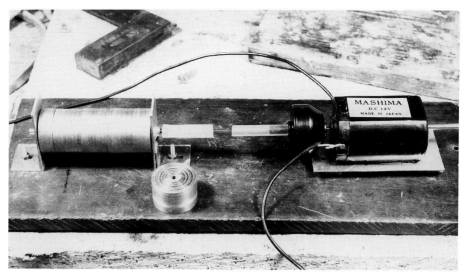

Before building the chassis, I made a few experiments with the Dyna-Drive system. My bench-testing rig quickly revealed that 16mm diameter flywheels simply didn't have the mass to generate the centrifugal force necessary for it to work effectively.

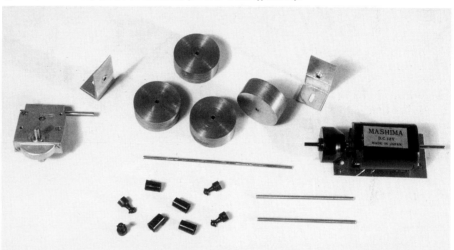

Components of the Dyna-Drive system ready to be installed in the Bulleid Pacific — from right, Mashima 1833 motor fitted with Brimalm clutch, 24mm diameter flywheels and mounting brackets, KTM 30:1:1 gearbox. In the foreground are the couplings for the cardan shafts. Things have come on a bit since the days when an X04 and Romford gears were mandatory for a 4mm loco.

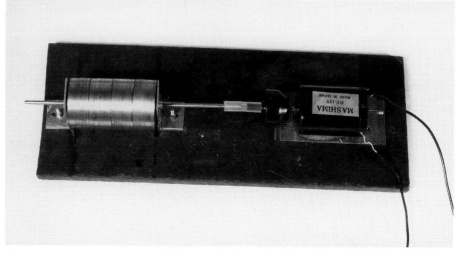

Results were infinitely better with 24mm flywheels, each of them 10mm thick. I found that four was the optimum number, although results with just three were more than adequate.

CHASSIS

All those universal joints and flywheels whirring around in their cradles would give me enough to think about and I didn't want to be messing about with anything fancy for the underpinnings. Going for the straightforward approach, I chose a Perseverance chassis kit for this loco. This is identical to the chassis in the Westward whitemetal loco kit and, on a purely cosmetic level, it looks pretty good, with some nice castings for the bogie and cylinders. Being based on dependable Flexichas technology, I guessed it would be more adaptable to the kind of application I had in mind than the eccentricities of the old Kemilway Bulleid chassis, while the Comet chassis is really intended for the rebuilt version with full outside valve gear. A fourth option would have been the Crownline Bulleid chassis (available separately from their kit) but I didn't know much about this and I didn't want to add too many unknown elements to the equation.

Having produced a working drawing of the flywheel/gearbox system, comparatively few modifications to the etched chassis proved to be necessary. It is designed for rear axle drive with the com-

The components of the Perseverance/Puffers chassis kit. Theoretically straightforward, it was to cause me a lot of headaches.

pensation beam on the two front axles, but I needed to reverse this arrangement in order to accommodate the gearbox at the front of the loco. This meant resiting the beam and opening out the front axle hole into a slot to allow me to get the gearbox in and out during the experimentation phase. Because of these changes, I had to rethink where the spacers would go and also how best to secure the supports for the flywheel mounting brackets, which entailed fitting a couple of extra spacers at the top of the chassis.

I built the tender chassis myself. This was a straightforward assembly, using 1/32in brass

for the sideframes with a continuous spacer between them, drilled for the mounting screws for the motor plate. The tender buffer beam assembly, including the rear-mounted vacuum cylinders, is a part of the same structure, although it was not added until later in the assembly sequence. The tender hornblocks were MJT (for 2mm axles) and the compensation was simple three-point suspension with a fixed rear axle. Of course we can't use coupling rods to set the axles up so I aligned everything with some good long lengths of 2mm steel rod. The plastic moulded brake blocks are from Alan Gibson. Static test

Using the Brook-Smith gauge to verify the back-to-back distance between the driving wheels.

The basic chassis is assembled, the gearbox is in place on the front axle and the flywheels are ready to be mounted. The gearbox shaft carries one half of an Exactoscale ball and socket joint (the other is on the flywheel output shaft). I used Bernard Weller's compact design because space is at a premium here.

The flywheels are in place and I've rigged up a temporary drive shaft so I can turn the chassis over by hand to check the quartering and for general smooth operation. Note the massive construction of everything. Much still needs to be decided — the distribution of weight, for instance. Tempted as I was to fit sub-beams and make the bogie and pony trucks work for their living, I felt the balance of the loco would be easier to ascertain with a chassis that was basically an 0−6−0 with simple three-point suspension.

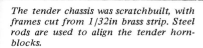

The tender chassis was scratchbuilt, with frames cut from 1/32in brass strip. Steel rods are used to align the tender horn-blocks.

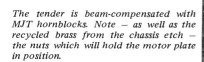

The tender is beam-compensated with MJT hornblocks. Note — as well as the recycled brass from the chassis etch — the nuts which will hold the motor plate in position.

showed that, even with everything screwed down tight, the motor generated no small measure of vibration and so it was obvious that a fair bit of weight would be called for in the tender — hence the robust construction.

A number of modifications proved necessary to the slidebar/cylinder assembly on the loco chassis. Having hit similar problems with previous Perseverance kits, perhaps I should have anticipated trouble.

The cylinders attach to a central spacer but this made them vastly over-width and the spacer had to be trimmed to get the outside face of the cylinders to line up with the body. The slidebars have some mysterious bend lines etched into their rear faces and I found the instructions were equally incomprehensible regarding the folds one was expected to make — there are no diagrams to help. Instead I put the slidebars together with spacers from fret

waste and also cut them down to scale length; they appear to have been designed to accommodate wheels with a massively over-scale crank throw. Assembled as supplied, the slidebar support bracket gives cylinder centres only a fraction narrower than the 8ft 6in overall width of the loco, so this too needed remedial action.

I thought this whole business was very poor — imagine the feelings of a newcomer to finescale, for whom this might be

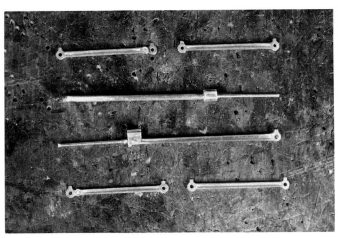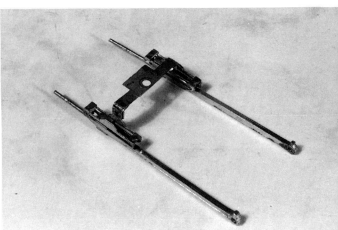

Left: Coupling and connecting rods for the 'Spamcan'. I made the con rods triple-thickness to match the massive construction of the prototype. The crossheads are my own fabrications, those that came with the kit being quite hopeless. Right: Connecting rods and slidebars fixed to the motion bracket.

Quite a lot has happened to the chassis here. The rods are in place, as are the cylinder/slidebar assemblies and the trucks. Pick-ups have been installed, running from busbars along the tops of the frames. Some preliminary cosmetic work has also been carried out around the rear end – cab floor, dragbeam and ashpans.

Right: Unfortunately, the pony truck was no better than the rest of the chassis kit, and ended up with near-total rebuilding. It might have been preferable to go for Comet's interpretation.

a first attempt at a 'proper' chassis. The compensated bogie was OK but I had trouble with the pony truck which, until I got serious with a file, fouled the bottom of the frames and the spacer from which it was designed to pivot. The least satisfactory part of the deal, however, was the crossheads. The instructions mentioned a cast set but none was provided. Instead, and without a word of introduction, a couple of fold-up crossheads appear on the slidebar etch, These were the craziest I have ever encountered, being far too wide and bearing no dimensional relation whatever to the slidebars that are supposed to support them. I put them on display in my Black Museum (open every Leap Year Day, admission free, allow several hours to see everything) and made my own. Fortunately the rest of the chassis was straightforward. A personal choice was to fit the firebox sides (whitemetal castings from Albert Goodall) to the chassis rather than to the body, while for practical reasons the frames also incorporate the cab door and interior detail, allowing me to lift off the body to attend to the intermediate cardan shaft.

TEST RUNNING

Results with the drive system were fascinating, as one might expect. The clutch, of course, cushions the take-up of power and makes for exceptionally smooth and impressive starting (though, remembering those platform-end pyrotechnics, I did wonder if this was altogether appropriate for a Bulleid Pacific). Mounting the flywheels on Brimalm's excellent ball-race brackets would unquestionably have cut friction and improved the over-run, but the momentum effect when slowing down and bringing the loco to a halt was clearly evident. Even running without the clutch — and the Mashima 1833 is certainly robust enough to get those massive flywheels rolling without turning itself inside-out in the process — the movement of the loco had that all-important feeling of mass and momentum. Big motors and big flywheels for me in the future, then — at least on this kind of engine.

Slow running on my P4 test track was virtually silent. Initial trials were conducted with an ECM feedback controller but I got much better results with the pure DC current of a Pentroller. At any kind of speed, though, I found the general noise levels were higher than on locos fitted with conventional drive systems and modern can motors. Isolation of components showed that the rattles were primarily caused by the build-up of vibrations in the drive train, exacerbated by one flywheel section which turned out to be not quite true on its shaft. These small shudders ended up in the worm gearbox and were, ultimately, transmitted to the track. Fitting a new flywheel brought a huge improvement. I am quite sure that, if I had used pukka Brimalm and Formil products throughout, the residual noise levels would have been reduced still further. A rigid chassis, of course, would probably have dampened the vibrations more effectively than my beam-compensated design, but in P4 standards you cannot build rigid engines of this size. With hindsight, I wonder if springs might not have been a wiser choice.

Continued experimentation certainly brought its round of surprises. The cardan shaft, in particular, appeared to have a disproportionate influence on things. If it's very long (say, 6–7cm or above) then it seemed to generate quite a measure of slap. Using a short shaft at a proportionally steeper angle, however, created a perceptible rise in the level of back-chat. As ever, the solution lay in the middle ground. Throughout these tests I had been using high-quality male/female cardan shaft couplings in friction-free Delrin but at one stage I rigged up a temporary transmission using nothing grander than neoprene tubing across the joints, and was amazed to find this in itself brought a significant softening of noise levels. Acoustic isolation, I am told, was what I had inadvertently brought about, although this was probably at the expense of some mechanical efficiency. This experience certainly demonstrates that the loco-tender coupling, though it might seem a simple affair, does need careful attention. There are a lot of forces at play here, in several dimensions at once. In many ways a tender loco is perhaps the most challenging application of the system.

Nevertheless, by the time I'd convinced myself that everything not only worked but worked very well, I was more confident than ever of the merits of Dyna-Drive. I feel that ultimate success with steam-outline models incorporating self-installed Dyna-Drive technology involves several circumstantially determined matters, which it is up to the individual to address and attend to. For me, one of the most critical factors was the effectiveness or otherwise of damping down vibrations from the motor, flywheels and cardan shafts, which means keeping everything tight, heavy and adequately lubricated (see below). Dyna-Drive works beautifully in simple twin-bogie diesels but the more complicated the engineering (compensation systems, outside valve gear, bogies and pony trucks) the more deviously things will find a way to rattle and hum unless every component is absolutely true. Model engineers should have no problems with turning flywheels and assembling gearboxes but the less gifted might be advised to stick with the pre-assembled Formil/Brimalm products. They are, at the very least, custom-designed for the job they have to do, rather than being improvised and adapted as many of my fittings were.

LUBRICATION

Bulleid's chain-driven valve gear, running in an oil bath, played merry hell with the operating department's peace of mind but in 4mm scale we don't need to worry about such things. Lubrication is, however, extremely important in any model loco and especially for one as unusual as this, for which the general-purpose 'dry' lubricants sold in model shops are woefully inadequate. I packed the gearbox with Pronatur grease (the same thing as Tri-Flow) whilst the flywheel bearings are lubricated with engine-grade Molyslip applied with a hypodermic — this stuff, in its own right, is almost as good as roller bearings. A washer is tightly fitted over the shaft at the outward end of these bearings to act as an oil thrower and keep the Molyslip away from the cardans. Molyslip, incidentally, should only be used when parts are well run-in; it is so effective at reducing friction that, used from new, nothing will bed itself in properly. Everything else that sees movement — from motor bearings to hornblocks and coupling rods — has a minimal amount of Zeuthe Ultra-Adhesive oil. This, as its name suggests, is a very 'sticky' oil that doesn't fly off at the turn of an armature or wheel and coat the rest of the loco in a black film.

THE LOCO BODY

A Bulleid Pacific, as interpreted by Hornby, is a curiously inconsistent thing. It has great thick smoke deflectors that protrude much too far from the body, cab sides that don't stick out far enough, front spectacles that resemble a gap that needs filling and a very odd front buffer beam.

The rivets on the bodyside panelling, however, are marvellous — if this were an etched kit, the old heart would be pumping away at a rate of knots. Unfortunately, almost all of them are in the wrong place — the result, I suspect, of the model being copied from one of F J Roche's notoriously inaccurate drawings. The detail on the top of the casing is equally fictional, while the chimney is miles away from where it should be, pushed back a couple of scale feet in order to line up with the smoke unit on the Triang 'Princess' chassis that, rewheeled, was used to power the original model.

The model has been in production since 1961 with little modification, although the sandbox filler openings are now more accurately positioned than they were and recent versions have lost the raised beadings for the nameplate surrounds and waist-level stripes. What I like about it is its shape. Hornby have never been very good at detailing but, on their day, they can do basic form and outline as well as anyone, if not better. Take their 'Duchess' off its chassis, remove the smoke deflectors and anything else that jars, such as the under-boiler 'web' where daylight should be, and in that raw hulk you have the essence of what these massive engines are about.

The same goes for the Bulleid. Forget those silly errors of detail and look at the moulding from a few feet away. It really is, well, like a Bulleid Pacific. All those curves and planes are pretty well as they should be. The Kitmaster/Airfix/Dapol 'Battle of Britain', by comparison, seems curiously angular and has strange dimensional discrepancies. To me, it fails to evoke the character of the real thing.

Others might regard Hornby's effort as being beyond redemption in finescale terms — certainly by comparison with an engine such as the Mainline Jubilee or the Airfix 4F. What I see, though, is a proprietary model with excellent possibilities. Add to that the existence of a great many detailing parts from the after-market trade — some good, some hideous — which we can either utilise or ignore according to preference, and we have the basis of an intriguing project.

REWORKING THE DETAIL

First things first. Even if Hornby had got the panelling right, I would probably have wanted to replace it. The reason for this apparent madness is simple. Whatever material they are made of, small-scale models of Bulleid Pacifics, A4s and stream-lined Coronations tend to have flawlessly smooth bodywork. If you look at the real thing, even in new condition, you will see ripples and distortions, all kinds of subtle hints that suggest the body is made not of solid plastic, but of thin sheet metal riveted or welded to an underlying framework. As time goes by, and the knocks and dents begin to accumulate, this feature becomes more and more pronounced until the engine ends up looking like the casing is made from crumpled tin foil. I felt I should have a try at replicating this feature on *Combe Martin*.

As far as I can see, the only way to produce accurate bodywork panels for a Bulleid Pacific is to make overlays, adding the lines of rivets with a suitable punch. For this work I use Dick Ganderton's 'Graskop' design. This is a marvellous tool and it works very well with plastic sheet — I don't have all that much specialist model-making equipment but this is one piece of kit I wouldn't want to be without. I made the side overlays from 10-thou Plastikard — it took a couple of hours, sitting in the garden on the first warm afternoon of spring, but I think the result was worthwhile. Albert Goodall's drawing of the Southern-built locos showed me where everything went.

The top of the casing is made in a similar way, but this time out of 5-thou which bends more easily. I anticipated

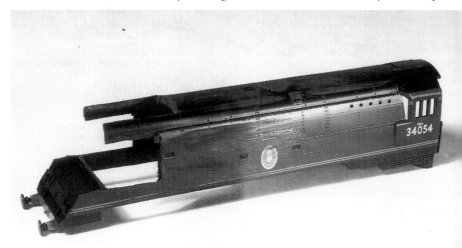

Most of the front end has been cut away and I have smoothed off all the detail on the sides and top. I have left the cab intact for the moment, so it can act as a reference point.

Work begins immediately on patching up, ready to receive the new overlays.

trouble in getting the overlay to keep its shape around the tight curves where the top joins the sides and I found it advisable to use a splint of square-section brass, held down with tape, to keep it in place while the solvent did its work. The curved sections of panelling alongside the chimney are quite narrow and it is difficult to persuade plastic sheet to hold its shape on so tight a radius. Instead, I made these separately, from 5-thou brass. This can easily be pre-formed and held in place with contact adhesive; if I built another Bulleid, I would make the whole of the top casing from brass.

Before any of this panelling is fixed in place, the join lines between panels are simply scribed in 'on the flat' with the tip of a scalpel. Originally I thought I would cut out and apply the panels individually, but the combined effect of handling and the various marks that had been made on the surface (most intentionally, some otherwise) seemed to suggest rippling well enough. Some of the lines of rivets on either side of these joints are staggered and it is gratifying for the modeller to find, when studying photographs, that where replacement panels have been fitted, a measure of unevenness seems to have crept into the riveting. When the engines were new, the rivets around the firebox and smokebox areas were much more prominent than those in the centre, which were so close to being flush that I decided to omit them from my model, leaving the scribed lines only to suggest the panelling.

Preparation of the body entailed removing most of the front end and filing flat all the raised detail. I used Albert Goodall castings for the smokebox front and cowl and made a new chimney from thin brass sheet, coaxed into a ring shape the way jewellers do it, on a tapered former. The smoke trough was made by cutting and filing a piece of 20-thou to an approximate fit and then offering it up, trimming as necessary. At this stage of its life *Combe Martin* was running without the streamlined fairing behind the chimney. The rest of the front end bodywork was improvised out of sheet and strip. Hornby's dimensions go haywire with the buffer beam and the panelling above it, so this too needed to be cut back and reworked. There is no doubt that, compared with the certainties of a good brass kit, this kind of modelling gets very messy but the medium is, in the literal sense, so very *plastic*, being readily amenable to tweaking, prodding, filling,

Some of the trickier details of the Bulleid Pacifics are perhaps best bought in where fittings are available from the trade. Clockwise from top we have here the smoke deflectors, ashpan sides, smokebox front, whistle housing, tender filler, TIA doser, cab windows, smokebox cowl, backhead (all per Albert Goodall), cab rear, roof shutter, dome cover and axleboxes (all Crownline).

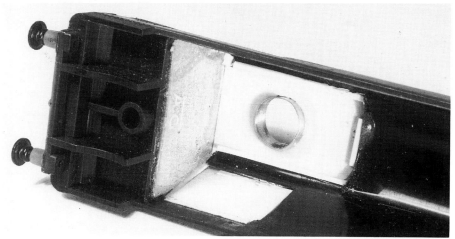

The cast smokebox door unit is integrated with the plastic bodywork. Good fillets of adhesive on the inside of the body look foul but add strength.

I made the original-pattern chimney of Combe Martin by rolling a 10mm diameter tube in 5-thou brass with the lip added in soft brass wire, filed flat. This underside view shows how it is glued into the smokebox. Evo-Stick contact adhesive gives a good bond between the various materials used in this model.

The tapered fairing behind the chimney was a feature that came and went among the Bulleid Pacifics in their early years. A small batch (21C131-45) was similar to that originally fitted to the Merchant Navy class. These fifteen engines received fairings and the standard plain chimneys in 1953-4.

Though it will all be covered up by the overlays, the front end patching badly needs a touch or three of filler. I included this shot to show the comparative crudeness of the preliminary work — nothing needs to be overly neat and tidy unless it shows.

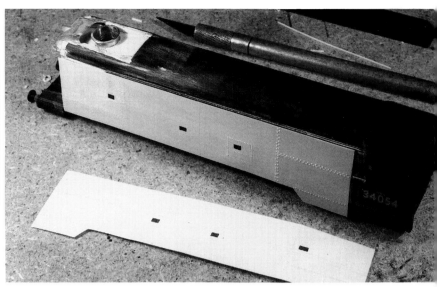

Having been drawn out and put through the riveting tool, the first of the side overlays goes on, using a strong solvent.

The top overlay is tricky — you can't pre-form thin plastic sheet as readily as you would a brass overlay. I flooded the issue with solvent and held it down with Sellotape.

A 'splint' (a length of square-section brass rod) may help the tightly curved sections to stay put.

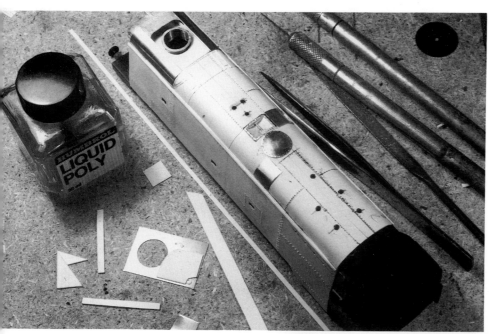

Amid a sea of offcuts, 'The Beast' visibly begins to take shape. The top of a Bulleid Pacific — rarely seen with any great clarity in prototype photographs — reveals all manner of hatches and openings, quite unlike any other class. I used 5-thou brass for a lot of this detail.

Below: *Hornby's V-fronted cab is cut away and smoothed off ready for the new cab overlays.*

opening up, rubbing down, coaxing into new shapes and generally being worked on until honour is satisfied.

Smoke deflectors are brass, from Albert Goodall. They have the correct flat profile but can be supplied curved if requested. The various covers along the top of the loco are 5-thou brass but the whistle in its little bird-bath trough is one of Albert's whitemetal castings, as are the unusual oval-shaped washout plugs. The cab is another of my Plastikard overlays, with the window openings cut out to accept Albert's etched frames — these are quite superb, with fold-up rain strips and windshields. The roof shutters are a Crownline etch, also of optimum quality and here modelled open to bring a little life to the scene. The cab rear came from another Crownline etch. This is designed to butt on to the moulded Hornby cab which is barely 8ft wide and slightly too short. Adding the overlays bulks it out to the correct 8ft 6ins and the etched cab rear now sits in a rebate behind the side sheets, which I made to the correct 5ft 10in length.

The addition of the cab really starts to define the character of the Light Pacific in its original form, but it also covers up the last of the visible part of the Hornby moulding. I found myself wondering whether, in the end, I really needed it and came to the fairly swift conclusion that I did; it has the correct profile and, more importantly, it forms a solid base for the conversion and detailing work, a safety net

The replacement cab is cut from a single sheet of 10-thou Plastikard. I made three before I got it right. The etched window frames are by Albert Goodall.

The front buffer beam is soldered directly to the frames – there wouldn't be much joint strength if it were glued to the body in the usual way. Note the unusual Southern Railway pattern of screw coupling with an extra swivelling link. This was found on many of the 4–4–0 and 2–6–0 classes as well as the Pacifics and also, surprisingly, on the BR 9Fs. Albert Goodall does an etch and this is what I used here.

in case anything starts to drift out of control. As I remarked in the Introduction, the proprietary moulding may be inadequate in itself but it can provide an excellent foundation or template around which we improvise better things. The only reason that I can see for making an upturned-bathtub shape of one's own out of Plastikard would be to have the satisfaction of having made everything from scratch.

Quite a bit of plumbing is visible around the cab of a Bulleid Pacific, which includes a Stone's steam generator very similar to that on the B1 and a set of Davies and Metcalfe injectors on the

Left: *There are some very unusual shapes at the front end which lend themselves admirably to modelling in plastic. Hornby, however, manage to get themselves in a real mess here and the whole thing really has to be rebuilt from scratch.* Right: *The front end of a Bulleid Pacific is unique. Care must be taken to get the details right.*

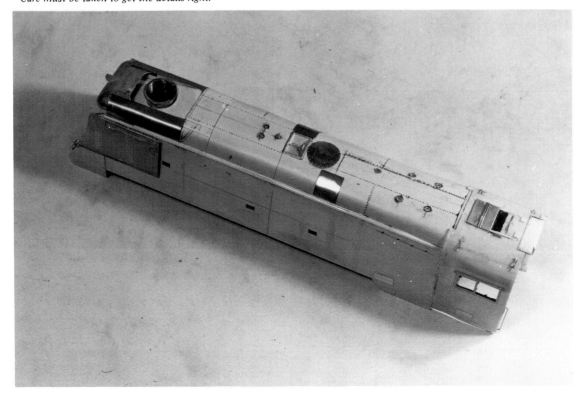

The top casing is an area of deep mystery, familiar only to initiates and rarely visible in photographs. It is frequently misinterpreted in drawings and was, in any case, subject to substantial detail changes over the years. I wouldn't say my rendition is perfect but it gives a reasonable impression of how things were with Combe Martin c.1952.

offside. This was all made from brass in the usual way and I hope the pictures will explain what is involved. Working out what goes where is basically a matter of looking hard at photographs, although close study of a preserved Bulleid Pacific will give some useful perspectives. Observation is 90% of the art of railway modelling and yet it never ceases to surprise me how far down the construction route I can go before I spot something — that an engine has this panel or fitting on one side but not on the other, that a handrail isn't straight but slightly curved to match the body profile, and so on. All the time I am building my models I am looking at pictures and, in the end, I think I manage to get most of it right.

TENDER BODY

I do like my models to be as accurate as I can reasonably make them, but I am not one to invent work for myself. I had originally felt that the tender ought to be a complete scratchbuild but then an old Kitmaster 'Battle of Britain' came my way and I had a rethink.

Over the years I have used one or two of these old Rosebud models as the basis of better things. In recent years the unbuilt kits have attracted fierce loyalty from the collectors although, as scale models, they fall into the curate's egg category — they are incredibly accurate in some respects but in other areas, often in the same kit, the dimensions are pure guesswork. This was certainly true of the Bulleid tender. After I'd pulled it apart (polystyrene cement degrades very quickly, which is one good reason why I rarely use it) I ditched most of the components but decided a few of them would come in handy. Reluctantly, I decided the sideframes had to go. They were a very brave attempt but the axlebox/spring assemblies were a shade overscale and the parts would have needed heavy thinning to get them to fit over P4 wheels (but there'd be no problem in OO or even EM, I'd have thought). I had intended to get the tricky shape of the tender side sheets by assembling thinnish Plastikard over formers but Kitmaster's moulded sides proved, by comparison with scale drawings, to have exactly the right profile, a tricky compound curve that invites error.

Having smoothed off the prominent lining, I cut the sides down to scale size; they are a couple of millimetres too long for the Light Pacifics but about right for

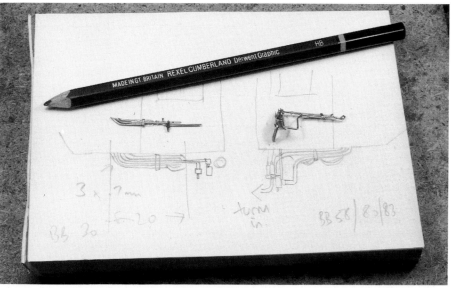

I do enjoy making injectors and suchlike. I find it helps, having studied the photographs, to make a little sketch of what I'm going to do. It is extraordinary how drawing helps me understand what goes where when I come to solder up the pipework.

An old Kitmaster tender, badly painted and cheaply acquired, was the source of the curved side panels — ancient polystyrene cement comes apart very easily. Checked against the measurements on Albert Goodall's drawing, the mouldings do quite well, though the dimensions of the bunker aren't right. The axleboxes and sideframes are very good indeed but they're much too thick to fit over P4 wheels.

H. F. WHEELLER

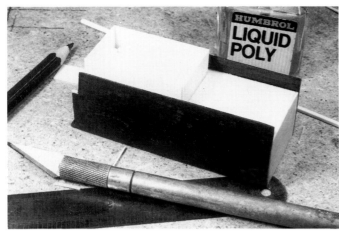

Left: *The tender body is basically a series of plain boxes, although the front coal plate is a little too far forward here and will need to come back a couple of millimetres. With a favourable wind, the shape goes together in less time than it takes for a cup of tea to go cold. How well Kitmaster have caught the curve of the sidesheets.* Right: *The Kitmaster tender front is largely fictitious so mine was fudged up from one murky photograph and recollections of the old Hornby-Dublo Barnstaple. Note the opening for the drive shaft and the minimalistic suggestion of a coal plate — even the educated eye can be deceived into seeing what it expects to see.*

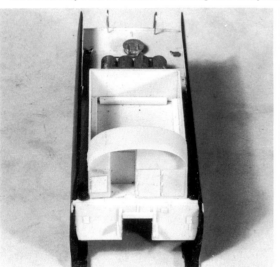
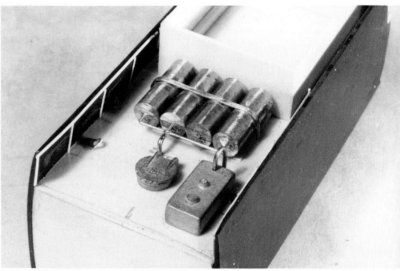

Left: *The tender front view emphasises the subtle curve of the side sheets.* Right: *The tender-top detail includes lifting lugs, water filler and vacuum tanks, which were uncovered on the high-sided tenders but plated over on the cut-down version. Although 34043 did not have water-softening apparatus until it acquired a cut-down tender in 1952, I have temporarily added a TIA doser for this picture to show where it would have gone. This feature, not always conspicuous in photographs, is rarely modelled on Bulleid Pacifics.*

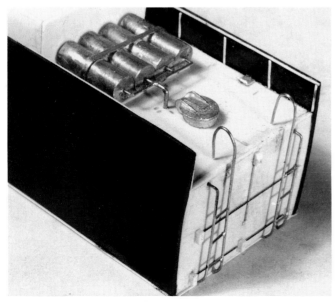

There is a lot of detail on the tender rear of a Bulleid Pacific. The ladders are soldered up from .45mm wire. They are shown here in their original configuration — a lot of things changed when the tenders were cut down. Note the bracing of the side raves.

The tender buffer beam is a prefabricated assembly in brass, again soldered to the inner frames. Note the prominent brake cylinders, a curious feature of the Bulleids. Combe Martin was one of a number of Light Pacifics that had LMS-pattern buffers — most of the Southern-built batch had buffers similar to the LNER group standard pattern.

the 5,000 gallon Merchant Navy tenders. I then thinned the top edge to get the inside face above the tank top almost vertical, a characteristic feature of these tenders in original form. The cut-out at the front also needed an extra couple of millimetres of Microstrip adding to bring its lower edge to five feet from the bottom of the sides. The sides were then united with scratch-built front and rear panels made from 20-thou Plastikard. Detailing was straight-forward — the tender brake stanchion was the usual confection from capillary tube, the steps and ladders were 0.45mm brass wire soldered up very quickly with a 1 mm bit, and the lighting conduits were 0.33mm brass wire. The lights themselves are cubes of 40-thou square Plastikard, countersunk with a 0.7mm bit and with a drop of Krystal Kleer run into the holes after painting to represent the lenses. These last are often red on models, as if they were

the tail-lights on an American car of the 1950s. They should, of course, be clear, since they function as headlamps in tender-first running.

I made new tender sideframes from 20-thou Plastikard, riveted in the Ganderton punch — the underframe embodies a

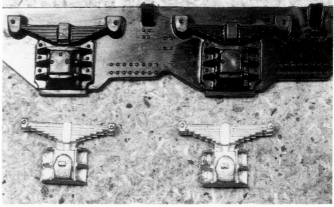

number of different rivet sizes which can be replicated using the choice of anvils supplied. The axleboxes came from the excellent Crownline castings. The Q1s share the same pattern — and indeed their whole tender underframe is remarkably similar to a Light Pacific's — but the

Crownline's whitemetal tender axlebox/spring casting is more faithful to the original than Kitmaster's, but the latter is still a fine piece of tooling.

I have marked out the new tender sideframes on a sheet of 20 thou and now I am putting in the lines of rivets, using the spacer bar of my 'Graskop' riveting tool.

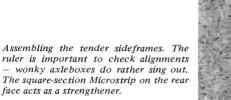

Assembling the tender sideframes. The ruler is important to check alignments — wonky axleboxes do rather sing out. The square-section Microstrip on the rear face acts as a strengthener.

Raw chassis, raw body — to many this might look like I've reached the point of no return but I find it all very exciting. This shot shows that the inside of the loco is pretty well filled with machinery. Actually Dyna-Drive will go into a far more compact area than this but, because I wasn't particularly pushed for space, I saw no need for compression.

The big Mashima 1833 motor is Araldited to a brass mounting plate which in turn screws onto the tender chassis. The cosmetic tender sideframes are in place, with Plastikard cross-members.

Merchant Navy class had heavier springs and different hornguides. I glued the castings with Evo-Stik contact adhesive.

The rest of the detail was straightforward and was effected predominantly in plastic strip and sheet, although I made the tender-top vacuum tanks from ⅙in brass rod. Anyone with any soldering experience will realise how much power was needed to join them together, using a length of brass shim to represent the prototype strapping — why I didn't simply glue the tanks is beyond me. The related pipework was formed from 0.45mm brass wire.

FINISHING TOUCHES

One of the effects that I find most difficult to pull off is of the engine in regular service that is well looked after. My interests focus on the last years of steam so I don't have to produce this kind of finish very often, but I still don't find it easy. What I try to avoid (it has happened in the past so I know what to expect) is to start off aiming for the cherished effect and then to lose my concentration and overdo things, so I end up with an engine that is just as weathered as the rest of my stock.

Everyday bulled-up cleanliness bears almost no relation to the kind of finish Swindon or Doncaster might have put on a locomotive destined for the Wembley Exhibition, and still less to the pristine semi-matt professional look. Rubbed down vigorously with the ubiquitous oily rag, the areas of the engine that are given a special paint treatment, such as a livery colour or lining out, tend to be pretty clean — although the paint might be bubbling here and there, and discoloured around the firebox, and chipped where the fitters' boots have repeatedly clipped it. Readily accessible bits such as the smokebox or the wheels, though normally painted black, may also be clean, although their colour is not blackberry black but more of a warm, gunmetal kind of colour. The motion may or may not have been given a wipe, but it will not look like chrome steel — it's more of an oily, tarnished ochre sort of shade. The less immediately visible (or cleanable) areas of the loco will, almost certainly, have received no attention at all — the lower firebox area, bogies and pony trucks, the bunker, tank or tender tops and cab roof.

Cleaning a steam engine was hard work and very time-consuming — the temptation to skimp, or to aim for a 'good-enough' finish, must have been difficult to resist. High-level photographs are, as we know, not easy to come by, but it is surprising how often they reveal that the top of the loco just hasn't been cleaned at all. On most engines, polishing the dome and other features of the upper parts of the boiler would have involved clambering up on to the running plate and then standing on the handrails. On the original Bulleid Pacifics, they used stepladders, and I don't think I've ever seen one with a clean lid, even an otherwise gleaming Stewarts Lane engine on the 'Golden Arrow'. The point is, I guess, that from normal viewing angles you rarely see the top of a loco whereas on the typical layout, everything is seen from two hundred feet up in the air. No wonder we get such strange perceptions of reality.

Anyway, to business. Armed with suitable photographs of the effect I had in mind, I gave the bodywork a coat of white acrylic primer and then sprayed it with BR Loco Green from the Railmatch range. Five or six thin coats were necessary to achieve the right intensity. Then I masked off those areas that were to stay this way and sprayed the waist panels satin black and the front end and top, plus most of the tender, with a darkish basic weathering mix. Masking tape doesn't often come into steam locomotive modelling but my experiences with painting the frequently complicated liveries of diesel traction has taught me to avoid plastic tapes, which tend to distort and sag, allowing paint to creep underneath, and go instead for a paper-based product known as Betto tape, which aeromodellers use. This wants to be removed by pulling it back over itself — sideways tugging is, for some reason, more likely to cause inadequately prepared brass to flake.

Once the basic painting was complete, I masked off those areas that would be matt and then sprayed the green and black areas with a gloss coating, prior to lining with a Bob Moore pen. This was to be a very clean engine but the orange still needs to be let down with some matt leather. If the lining on a real engine looked as loud and conspicuous as modellers make it, police cars would be decked out in British Railways passenger green.

The alignment of numbers and emblems varies between engines, as does the position of the 'West Country Class' scrolls; after 34043's overhaul in 1953, the latter were six inches higher on the side casing than they had been the previous summer. The graphics have a major impact on the appearance of these engines, and how well the big lion, so evocative of its period, looks on the tender sides. But it is surprising how important the black bands — and the lining, of course — are to the

Bulleids. Without them, they look quite squat. The bands serve to increase the apparent length of the loco and reduce its overall height, giving it a leaner, 'faster' look. The yellow-green stripe on the Deltics had the same function. The plain green that DP2 originally carried made it look chunky, low-slung and slow; the same deadening effect characterised the Deltics when they were repainted into corporate blue. Once the Bulleid tenders were cut down and lost their black panels, then the visual balance of the engine went haywire.

There is nothing much to say about the weathering of this engine — except that there is less of it than usual, concentrated on the ashpan area and the top of the casing. I went over the wheels and the smokebox front with a polishing mop in my mini-drill, which brought out the sparkle in the Humbrol Gunmetal. The glossy, wiped-clean finish of the casing and tender sides (but not the back) helps emphasise the subtle rippling in the bodywork, which was the principal effect I wished to capture. I used the excellent Protec Hydrocoating for this, brushed on with a No. 2 sable. Randomly painting some areas with gloss and others with satin helps break down the uniformity of the finish and, more importantly, gives a subtle emphasis to the different planes of individual sheets. Discreet streaking here and there suggests vertical ripples in the bodywork where the light catches it. I have a mind to try something similar on a Hornby A4, using panels of aluminium foil.

CONCLUSIONS

This is an unusual model in many ways — from its experimental transmission to the total revamping of its outward appearance — and, for all kinds of reasons, I can think of no more appropriate prototype than a

Bulleid Pacific on which such work could be carried out. I don't think I could ever find building any railway model to be boring and this was definitely one of the more interesting ones. It certainly stretched me, but that's all a part of the challenge. Some of the things that I did may not have been entirely necessary — the original plan was to keep the chassis simple, maybe even rigid OO with a D13 open-frame motor and Romford gears, but that soon went out of the window. What did surprise me, though, was how much work needed to be done to create a reasonable model of what is, after all, one of the most popular of prototypes. I would have thought that someone, by now, would have made a decent kit or RTR model but that doesn't seem to be the case — or am I just getting fussier than ever? Nevertheless, I think that with this locomotive we come as close to the true spirit of scratchbuilding as we can in the context of making models out of RTR mouldings.

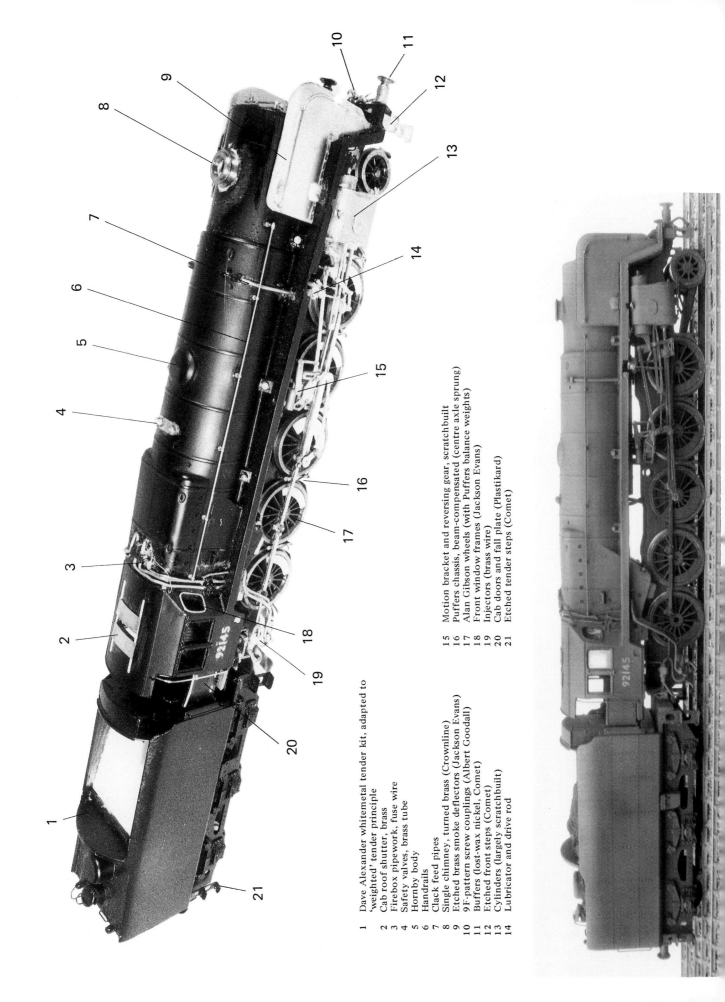

1 Dave Alexander whitemetal tender kit, adapted to 'weighted' tender principle
2 Cab roof shutter, brass
3 Firebox pipework, fuse wire
4 Safety valves, brass tube
5 Hornby body
6 Handrails
7 Clack feed pipes
8 Single chimney, turned brass (Crownline)
9 Etched brass smoke deflectors (Jackson Evans)
10 9F-pattern screw couplings (Albert Goodall)
11 Buffers (lost-wax nickel, Comet)
12 Etched front steps (Comet)
13 Cylinders (largely scratchbuilt)
14 Lubricator and drive rod
15 Motion bracket and reversing gear, scratchbuilt
16 Puffers chassis, beam-compensated (centre axle sprung)
17 Alan Gibson wheels (with Puffers balance weights)
18 Front window frames (Jackson Evans)
19 Injectors (brass wire)
20 Cab doors and fall plate (Plastikard)
21 Etched tender steps (Comet)

CHAPTER SEVEN
HIGH, WIDE AND HANDSOME
A 9F USING A HORNBY BODY, A PUFFERS CHASSIS AND
A DAVE ALEXANDER TENDER KIT

I'M not sure why we're ending with the 9F — perhaps it's because it's the highest-numbered engine that I've ever built, although the other projects in this book are not in numerical sequence. The choice is more, I think, to do with the fact that in many ways this model is a summation of the approaches and attitudes that have been described earlier: the major reworking of a useful, but ultimately flawed, plastic moulding by means of scratchbuilding and the adaptation of commercially manufactured detailing parts; the modification of a chassis kit and other mechanical components to suit personal whims; the integration of different materials to produce a consistent whole; the modelling of a specific prototype locomotive at a particular period of its life; above all, perhaps, the realisation that seemingly complicated assembly sequences are rarely more than a progression of simple steps followed through sequentially. These five issues, I think, are what this book has been about, and they reach their clearest expression in this project.

And what a marvellous machine with which to finish. The 9Fs were always such a favourite with me and, judging by the response to the earlier model that I described in *MRJ* 90 and 91, with many other modellers as well. In those articles I've already said about as much as I want to say about my feelings for these locomotives. Muscular, heroically capable, possessed of a special kind of dignity, the 9Fs have a timeless quality about them. They share this property with other classic pieces of industrial design that are elegant without being conventionally beautiful — I think of JCB excavators, the Bic pen, the wartime pillbox. Of course I love the Stirling singles and the Eurostar trains too, but effective design, in its purest sense, has nothing to do with cosmetic styling. It is entirely concerned with fitness for purpose and in the near-perfect marriage of form and function, the reduction to simple essentials, the avoidance of the unnecessary; the 9F illustrates everything that I find most exciting about the disciplines and processes of design.

No. 92145, the subject of my model, blasts up the East Coast main line at Chaloner's Whin in April 1961 – a treasured snap from junior school days.

PROTOTYPE MATTERS
How much as modellers, do we really need to know about the 9Fs? They were the last of the BR Standard classes to appear and the engineers were beginning to get their act together. As a result, in-service modifications and minor detail differences between locomotives are comparatively few by comparison with, say, the Britannias. Fortunately, most of us will know the main story already, but there are still quite a few deviations from the well-trodden path. Until the relevant volume of the RCTS history of BR Standard classes comes out, we don't really have a standard text on the subject, so the following paragraphs may have to suffice.

In days of steam the old Ian Allan *ABCs* were my prime source of published information, shaping many of my ideas of locomotive history, but it amazes me now to see how many factual errors and inaccuracies they perpetrated. Mercifully they got the major variations among the 9Fs more or less right — the Crosti-boilered versions, the ones with air pumps for the Consett iron ore trains and so on. Nos 92165–7 were indeed built with US-manufactured Berkeley mechanical stokers but the *ABC* doesn't record their conversion to hand firing in 1962. After experiments

with a double chimney on No. 92178 (which ran without smoke deflectors on trials in 1958), Nos 92183–92202 of the Eastern Region and 92203–50 of the Western were built with double chimneys; No. 92250 acquired its famous Giesl ejector only after several months in traffic with a double chimney. In 1960 the WR made a start on fitting its single-chimney 9Fs with double chimneys, but the work halted after only five had been converted — Nos 92000–2/5/6 (the *ABC* records only three of these conversions but, confusingly, also includes 92079, the Lickey banker). The stoker-fitted 9Fs had double chimneys from new (the only Crewe-built engines so fitted) but they were alone among their kind on the London Midland until ex-Western Region engines were drafted in during the mid-1960s. However, the Eastern Region's allocation of double-chimney 9Fs (all delivered as recently as 1958) went with the mass withdrawals of ER steam locomotives in 1964–5 and none was transferred to the LMR.

Five different kinds of tender were fitted to the 9Fs and these were designed to regional specifications. Original allocations were as per the official lists reprinted in the *ABCs* but, just to keep us alert, some minor swapping around took place in the final years, when the engines were concentrated on the London Midland Region. All of the LMR's original allocation of 85 9Fs — Nos 92015–19/45–59/77–86/100–39/50–64 — had the high-sided BR1C design, which was not found on other regions' 9Fs. The twenty BR1B tenders were attached to the Crostis and also to the Tyne Dock-Consett 9Fs. They were identical to the BR1C apart from the position of the central coal plate. The BR1K (for the three stoker-fitted engines) belonged to the same family; it didn't have a coal plate at all. The BR1F was another high-sided design, 85 of which were produced to Eastern Region requirements and attached to Nos 92010–4/30–44/67–76/87–96/140–9/68–92202; they looked even bigger and squarer than the others because they had a larger water capacity (5,625 gallons) than any other BR Standard tender. Twenty BR1F 9Fs were allocated to Annesley shed for work on the

Great Central main line and when its administration was transferred to the LMR in 1958, the regional allocation of its 9Fs changed accordingly; in time these engines (92067–76/87–96) moved to other areas of the London Midland where latterly they were joined by a handful of other ex-Eastern Region engines (92010–14/30/1/2/3/43), all with single chimneys and still with their BR1F tenders.

With the exception of Nos 92008–9, built for the Western (complete with WR lamp brackets) but immediately diverted to the LMR, where they were to stay for the rest of their careers, the low-sided BR1G was exclusively a Western Region tender, fitted to Nos 92000–9 and 92203–50. It was, in all but minor detail, identical to the BR1 and BR1A tenders attached to many Standard Pacifics and class 5 4–6–0s. As the WR steam allocation was cleared out, BR1G 9Fs were moved to the London

Midland and the North Eastern. This was the first time 9Fs had been allocated to the latter region, apart from those used (primarily but not exclusively) on the Tyne Dock–Consett ore trains. By 1965 double-chimney rebuild No. 92001 (ex-WR BR1G) had further distinguished itself by acquiring an Eastern Region BR1F tender and two years later 92218, 92233 and 92249 had the BR1C pattern; I'm sure there were other swaps. A few BR1G tenders were, in turn, reallocated to other locos: No. 92079, built with a BR1C tender, received a BR1G when it moved from Toton to Bromsgrove in 1956 to take up work as the Lickey banker and received the large headlight formerly carried by 0–10–0 No. 58100 (this fitting was removed in 1959). In addition, No. 92118 (ex-BR1C) had a BR1G tender from 1964 onwards, following a move to Banbury. At

Quite apart from the prominent air pumps on the running plate, the Tyne Dock–Consett 9Fs differed in a number of ways from the main production run. They had AWS gear, the cab roof was more heavily riveted and this picture of No. 92065 shows a number of additional pipe runs in the already congested vicinity of the injectors. Although these engines were, on occasion, let loose on the East Coast main line, I would love to know what this one was doing at Chester on 5th March 1967.

least two ex-Crosti 9Fs, Nos 92023–4, latterly ran with BR1G tenders, which I think suited these ungainly engines rather better than the BR1B design.

Now on to the minor differences. By comparing photographs of early and late-model 9Fs you will see changes in the pattern of return crank — from a circular to a four-bolt fixing — and the addition of ashpan doors on the lower firebox. Uniquely among BR Standard engines, the 9Fs originally had screw couplings with an extra top swing link, as on the Bulleid Pacifics and other Southern classes; some later acquired the conventional pattern. None ever had a speedometer and photographic evidence suggests that far fewer members of the class than might be imagined had BR AWS equipment — the

cylinder and battery box, if fitted, were on the left-hand framing, beneath the cab and there is a wiring conduit along the lower left-hand running plate; examples are Nos 92049, 92150, 92168, 92211, 92231 and 92239, plus the ten Tyne Dock 9Fs. However on Western Region 9Fs with their own pattern of ATC, the battery box appears on the drag beam on the left-hand side, directly beneath the cab handrail. On these engines, the clips securing the wiring conduit are less prominent than on those fitted with BR AWS. A rather shadowy area, literally, concerns the rear frames: on some engines there is a lightening hole directly behind the rear wheelset but on others it is about a foot forward of the drag

beam, between the two triangular bracing plates. This area is clearly visible in so few photographs that it is impossible to infer any pattern.

The cab roof is different on the Tyne Dock air-pump engines; the most visible manifestation is a heavy line of rivets around the cab roof shutter, a feature which I have occasionally registered on Eastern Region 9Fs, such as Nos 92035/8/40. As built, all the 9Fs had two small steps under the smokebox door but around 1962 a start was made on fitting a single large step in their place; by 1965 it was rare to see a 9F still with the original pattern but one or two — Nos 92002, 92218/23 for instance — went right

A lot of 9Fs were pretty well identical but – as the text relates – odd locos had minor and seemingly random variations. This picture shows No. 92239, at Barrow Hill on 14th March 1965, bearing the marks of an itinerant career – Western and Southern styles of lamp irons and BR-pattern AWS gear (note the reservoir behind the rear coupled wheels). This last was a real rarity, being found only on the handful of 9Fs that were allocated to the Southern and the North Eastern. No. 92239 was one of five ex-Western Region 9Fs transferred to Eastleigh for the Fawley oil traffic before being move to Feltham and from there on to York.

through to scrapping in 1968 in this form. Many WR 9Fs — most as built but including, inevitably, the charismatic No. 92001 as subsequently modified — had a flat fashion plate over the reversing rod cover on the left-hand footplate. *Evening Star* was of course painted in lined green and some Eastern Region 9Fs overhauled at Darlington received 10in cabside numbers instead of the standard 8in pattern. Western Region engines had blue route availability discs on the cabsides and their own pattern of lamp iron, not always replaced on transfer to other regions. In the mid-1960s the top lamp iron on most (but not all) London Midland engines was repositioned between the smokebox door hinges; this modification is found on some ex-WR engines. At the same time, the central lamp iron on the front platform was moved to the right. Apart from the chimney and tender variations, these are, as far as I can tell, the only significant differences among the 251 engines of this class at any stage of their careers. They may be slight but, once again, I feel it is advisable to check against dated photographs before proceeding with a model of a 9F.

My own model is of No. 92145, a single chimney 9F with BR1F tender that remained on Eastern Region until withdrawn from Immingham in 1966. It was inspired by one of the first action pictures I ever took (with a Kodak Brownie!) showing the engine pounding through Chaloner's Whin Junction, York, with a northbound rake of brand-new Palbricks. These days, I would probably be more interested in the wagons, but at the age of ten and probably still in short trousers, I was a stranger to such arcane pleasures.

MODELLING OPTIONS

Kitmaster released quite a creditable attempt at a 9F as far back as 1961 and there can be few modellers who haven't built one. Airfix subsequently reissued it and latterly it's been available from Dapol. For a plastic kit aimed at the popular end of the market it's not too bad — the BR1G tender is good and I quite like the cab, but the boiler looks a bit undersized and there are some nasty moulded-on handrails and three-inch thick boiler bands to get rid of. As the basis of a finescale modelling project, it appears to offer more than it can actually deliver.

DJH do a composite whitemetal/etched brass kit for a 9F with various tender options — BR1C, BR1F and BR1G. I have reservations about the tenders but the loco body is excellent — as it ought to be, at the price. The chassis, however, is undistinguished. Hornby's RTR *Evening Star* dates back to the last years of the old Triang regime. The chassis is not suitable for our purpose but the body is fundamentally accurate and has lots of promise for better things. It can readily be bought as a spare for a few quid. I think it will be obvious which route I chose.

CHASSIS

There are some very unusual things about the chassis of a real 9F, mostly concerned with getting it round curves. For a start, it has driving wheels of three different types. The centre wheels are not flangeless, as is commonly believed, but do indeed have a small flange, though it is barely visible at normal viewing distances. The inner and outer pairs of wheels have different tyre profiles and one of the most amusing things I have ever heard in my modelling career was someone telling me, without a hint of a leg-pull, that he was going to replicate this by using OO and P4 wheels on the same model, which was to be in EM gauge. I should imagine he's still trying to get it to stay on the track, let alone negotiate a 4ft radius curve.

I wanted to do the decent thing by this 9F's chassis but I wasn't going to go quite so far. I have never been one for doing the same thing twice and so, having already described building a single-chimney 9F using a hacked-about Hornby body, tender drive and a rigid chassis, I decided to try something different. The original thinking was to put a big can motor in the tender and build a beam-compensated chassis. Puffers had been promising a 9F chassis for years and while it had certainly been test-etched, it had never publicly gone on sale. My intention was to use the same Comet chassis that I'd used previously, with the chunky and reliable Sharman gearbox on the rear axle, driven by cardan shaft. But then Porter's Cap Productions brought out their 'Contorto' gearbox, specifically designed to fit into awkward prototypes such as the high-boilered 9F. Since I'd already done the tender-motor thing in the Bulleid and the B1, I decided to use one of these — the self-same gearbox, of course, that I used on the diminutive Terrier — and mount the motor in the loco in the usual way.

The tender-driven, rigid chassis of my first 9F had run very well and I began to wonder if compensating the new one would offer all that many advantages. An 0–4–0 is one thing but a 9F has a lot of wheels and under normal circumstances a few of them, at least, will be in contact with the track at the same time. For a while, then, the prevailing orthodoxy turned once more towards a rigid chassis, with the same Comet components that I'd used before. Apart from having to rectify some funny business with the cylinder mountings, this chassis is wholly satisfactory although I am aware that the wheelbase has been stretched slightly to accommodate coarse-scale Romford drivers.

The variety of forces that compel us to make decisions never cease to amaze me, as does their timing. I happened to be watching a TV programme about tourism when a 9F suddenly hove into view, filmed almost head-on down the track through a powerful telephoto lens. I was struck by how visible was the movement of the wheels in the hornblocks, literally hugging the track as the engine thundered along. That was enough for me — compensation was back on the agenda and at this point Puffers suddenly and at long last released their 9F chassis kit, which had been announced as far back as 1988.

I was so surprised that I ordered one on the spot. It's a typical Perseverance 'curate's egg' effort; it looks good, the wheelbase is correct but the coupling rods are parallel, not tapered as they are on the prototype (and the Comet kit) and the pony truck and the motion brackets did not impress me at all. There are one or two decorative bits whose purpose will probably remain a mystery to me always — I certainly could not find them on a real 9F. The kit lacks refinements such as instructions of any kind, as well as the various items that are normally done as castings, such as valve chests and cylinder covers. Unlike the usual Puffers/Perseverance chassis kit, it doesn't have hornblocks or any other compensation components, apart from a pair of etched beams on the main chassis fret. This is not, I would have thought, the kind of thing any modeller facing a crisis of confidence would want to tackle, but it was a start.

The Puffers chassis appears to be designed for multiple-beam compensation but, in the absence of instructions and most of the relevant components, I found it difficult to divine exactly what the designer had in mind. Out of curiosity I spent some time trying to figure out what might be involved — and in particular how it was meant to be motorised — but in the end I settled on twin beams on the rearmost axles (with drive on the fifth), a sprung centre axle to keep it happy on peaks and troughs, and a single central beam on the front pair of axles. I don't know if this was as intended but, playing with only half a deck, it was the most effective game plan I could devise. The hornblocks were MJT and the sprung bearings were some rather swish milled brass efforts from Brimalm of Sweden, available from Formil Model Engineering.

MOTOR MATTERS

Getting a motor into a 9F is not easy. The chassis is very open and exposed, making it difficult to conceal the working parts, while the firebox is perched up high, immediately above the rear wheels. For an engine of this size to be capable of hauling a decent load, a big prime mover is mandatory. The smart money is usually on an RG4 with either a layshaft or one of Mike Trice's adapter gearboxes, but we used the remarkable 'Contorto' gearbox in the 'Terrier' and I decided to do the same here — not least because designer Chris Gibbon's preliminary thoughts were very much angled towards the 9F as the 'worst case' scenario for potential applications. The fact that the same design can be used in such widely varied prototypes as a tiny 0–6–0 and a hefty 2–10–0 says much for the soundness of the concept.

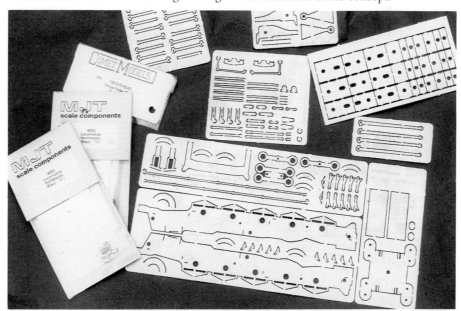

The Puffers 9F chassis kit, with extras.

Brimalm sprung bearings for the centre axle.

I have a North Eastern Railway class TI 4–8–0T with a Mashima 1630 motor driving the 108:1 version of the 'Contorto'. Like the prototype, this large, heavy hump shunter has awesome power and its slow-speed running is flawless (a steady 1 or 2mph, mile after mile, with the controller well notched up). However I wanted the 9F to be capable of making reasonable headway and so I chose a faster-running but still powerful motor (the rarely used Mashima 1626) and the 80:1 reduction option on the 'Contorto'. A test-bench mock-up suggested a top speed in the region of 25mph (the latter being the statutory maximum for the unfitted freights and mineral turns which I envisaged this loco working). I also tried the smaller Mashima 1624 which gave very similar results but at the expense, I would imagine, of a slight loss of power. The 1620 doesn't have the wallop for a big heavy loco like this, whilst I would imagine the 1630 would be hard pressed to achieve more than about 15mph, flat out, with such a gearbox. This is fine in a shunting engine like my TI but I build drive trains to meet specific needs and applications — in this case, a steady plod rather than a slow crawl.

The etched gearbox for the 'Contorto' can be simply adapted to suit an almost infinite number of configurations and here I designed things so that the motor sits high up in the firebox with the linear three-stage reduction dropping straight down. The articulated final drive swings round under the ashpan to drive the rear axle, the whole thing tucking neatly between the compensation beams.

CHASSIS ASSEMBLY

The sideframes — once the openings have been made for the hornguides — went together pretty easily. Instead of the OO spacers supplied which were, as usual, unnecessarily narrow, I thinned down the EM set to 12mm excluding the locating tabs. I calculated this on the basis of the 15mm back-to-back of the Alan Gibson wheels, less the 0.5mm moulded bosses on the rear of each, and 1mm for the overall thickness of the frames, to give a maximum 1mm of sideplay/running clearance on alternate axles, the first, third and rear axles being washered to control lateral movement.

With a long chassis such as this we don't want anything bending in the wind and so I was liberal with the spacers, fitting seven in all. Using the simple wooden jig ensured everything was straight and true and I soldered the spacers alternately, first one on this side and then one on that, to prevent the kinking that may be caused by unequal heating.

The datum point for the axles was the centre wheelset. This was sprung using Brimalm's milled brass bearings and, prior to assembly, I carefully cut out the openings for these, one exactly to size and the

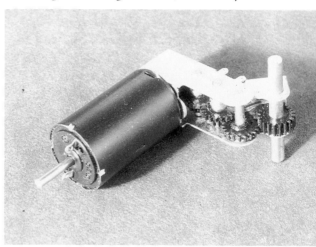

The 80:1 'Contorto' gearbox, with Mashima can motor. Designer Chris Gibbon has subsequently introduced new configurations of this remarkable gearbox, known as the LoadHauler and sold by his own company, High Level Kits. The LoadHauler + version is ideal for a 9F.

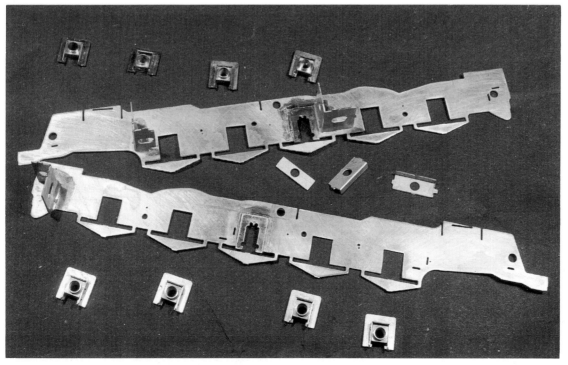

The frames have been prepared and the main spacers are in position. These were cut down from EM gauge components. The milled brass guides for the centre (sprung) axle have already been soldered in place. At this stage I was going to use hornblocks on the other four axles but then realised that simple brass top hats would suffice for the twin beams on the rear pair.

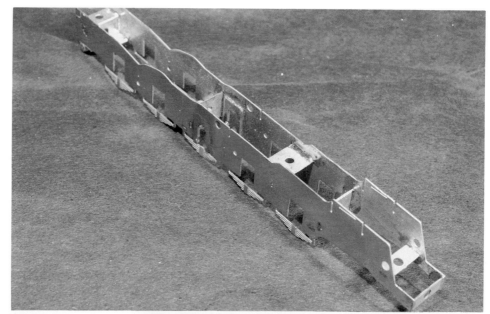

We need plenty of spacers — there are seven in all here — to brace that long chassis. They need to be sited carefully, not merely to clear things like motors and motion brackets, but also so they don't intrude on the 9F's distinctively open-framed look.

Left: *The moulded body has some fake 'front frame extensions' which need to be got rid of.* Right: *The result is a very good fit of body to chassis, with daylight in all the right places. The frames are pretty well to scale length so a little under 2mm will now need to be taken off the front to allow for Hornby's thickly moulded front running plate — otherwise the cylinders, steam pipes and chimney won't align properly.*

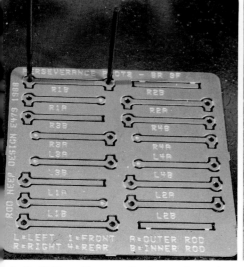

Left: *Making a jig to enable the coupling rods to be soldered to length accurately. The drill bits act as positioning guides for the crankpin holes. The 145° solder won't take to blackened steel.*

other just very slightly undersize. I fitted
the first bearing in place and then, with the
two sideframes exactly aligned, used it as a
jig for the other. I opened out the second
cut-out until I was able to slot this second
sideframe precisely over the first. Each
bearing is exactly double the thickness of
the frame material and is soldered flush on
the outside.

The hornblocks for beam compensation
are soldered in place in the standard
fashion using the coupling rods as jigs.
These are the usual double-thickness
efforts and the left-hand side is a mirror
image of the right, so we have, in effect,
two identical sets, which is more forgiving
if things become muddled. In my system
the two rearmost axles do not have hornblocks but instead use plain bearings in the
twin compensating beams supplied with
the kit. The holes in the latter are etched
$\frac{5}{32}$in diameter, presumably to fit over the
boss on a Perseverance hornblock.
Standard $\frac{1}{8}$in bearings have an (approximately) $\frac{9}{64}$in outside diameter and whilst
$\frac{5}{32}$in OD top hat bearings do exist (I know
because I found one in the stores department) I was unable to locate a trade supplier and so I had some turned for me.

*It's not every day that
most of us have to jig
up a ten-coupled chassis.
This sequence shows
how it's done, by
treating the 2–10–0 as
two 0–6–0s back to
back. The sprung centre
axle – with bearings
temporarily in place –
is the reference point.*

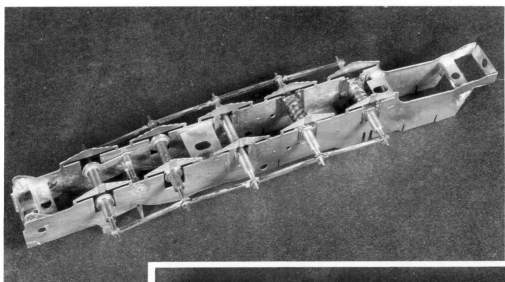

*This is the end result. Note the
twin beams on the rear axles and
the single beam on the front pair.
The sprung bearings on the
centre axle will not be fitted until
the chassis is painted.*

I wasn't greatly smitten by the second-rearmost rods. Had there been some instructions, no doubt a foolproof method of forming them would have been explained. They need to overlap with their neighbour's front face at one end but with the rear face at the other. One might have thought that all that was needed was two identical layers, each with a boss at either end. They could be soldered together with the crankpin holes in alignment and then the bosses could be filed down, the front face on one side and the rear face on the other. This way, the correct distance between crankpins would be automatically arrived at.

Instead, we get a rod that comes in two separate halves, with a boss at one end only. They join in the middle but how do you get them the correct length? Once again the solution lay in creating a simple jig. Each rod on a 9F is exactly the same length — all the more reason to align this set precisely — and so I took the coupling rod etch, laid it flat on a piece of chipboard and drilled ¹⁄₁₆in through each crankpin hole. With the same size of bit, drilling down into the chipboard through the holes at either end of a rod gave me the correct spacing. I jammed two brand-new ¹⁄₁₆in bits tightly into these two holes and used them as the jig for assembling the rods.

I allowed only the most niggardly amount of clearance in the rods for the crankpin bushes. I didn't open out any of the holes and instead relied on the fundamental accuracy of the chassis to ensure the wheels went round without tight spots. Oversize (or worn) holes make rods incline themselves at strange angles and whilst the loco will undoubtedly run after a fashion, it looks absolutely terrible, even on an 0–4–0. On a ten-coupled chassis, the accumulated slop would lead to rods that, instead of lying dead straight, take on the appearance of a gradient profile. I preferred to keep everything as tight as a bank manager.

CYLINDERS

I wasn't at all happy with these — Comet's are much better, if a mite underscale to my eye. The Puffers version have the right dimensions but the etch is rudimentary — a frame, an outer wrapper with the riveted cover plates (rather nice, actually) and that's it. We have to source or make our own piston glands, valve guides and cylinder covers. The valve guide centres on a real 9F

Alan Gibson does the flangeless centre driving wheels as a stock item and I'm sure Steve Hodgson (Sharman Wheels) could be persuaded. Because of its scale wheelbase, the Puffers chassis won't take Romford wheels although the non-scale Comet and DJH ones will. The point is academic, since Romford 20mm wheels have plain rather than bevelled rims and the wrong number of spokes. This long-established make looks just about passable on a Gresley loco, but on anything else, forget it.

Clearance on flanges is minimal and we still need to get the brake hangers in.

Brimalm bearings in place on the centre axle.

are not in vertical alignment with the piston rod, but they are arranged thus here — or at least the holes for them have been etched as if they were. To gain clearance for the two leading pairs of wheels, the piston rod centres appear to have been pushed out from true scale dimensions by approximately 0.75mm on either side. I do dislike this habit among kit designers but I know from past experience that the 9F is about as difficult as they come in terms of clearance. Perhaps it's justified in this instance, perhaps it isn't.

The missing bits, however, were fairly easy to put together. All my modelling leftovers are recycled and I have a little box specifically devoted to flat discs in various sizes and materials. Here I found sufficient etched kit salvage to make up a reasonably

matched set of cylinder covers. Everything else came from brass tube — it is surprising just how much can be made using commonly available diameters from the K&S metal centres. I am hopeless at sawing these things straight so I cut oversize and then file down. At one stage I think there was a scheme to have working valve spindles but this fell by the wayside.

The slidebars in the kit are made by soldering up four layers of nickel. Some pinning arrangements à la Bradwell might be advisable but I got by doing it freehand. I like a scale-thickness slidebar — it really does give the impression of hefty metal forgings and contrasts with the delicacy of valve gear components. In so many kits the whole thing — from connecting rods to slidebars to union links — is done in one

thickness of 15-thou and it's hardly surprising it doesn't look right. The crossheads, by the way, are the excellent Comet lost-wax brass castings, the kit providing some oddly one-dimensional etchings to which (in the wake of my experience with the Bulleid) I gave a wide berth.

In the absence of any locating holes, the designer's inclination appears to be towards butt-jointing the slidebars against the rear face of the cylinders, which is never good form. I made a little excavation to secure a more positive seating for them. The slidebars are a mite over-length anyway and the extra can pass through to the inside of the cylinders, secured by a good blob of solder. The slidebar brackets on a 9F also support the mechanical lubricators and the kit pro-

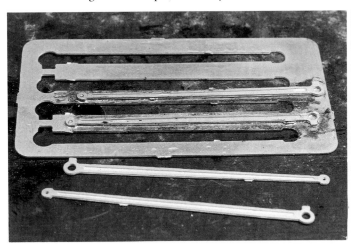
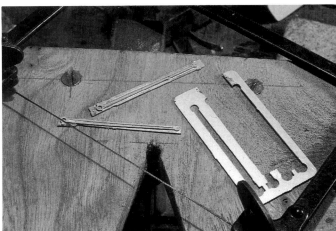

Left: *The connecting rods of any steam engine are massive forgings, especially when viewed from the big end. Double-thickness rods don't do them justice and I make mine triple-thickness, using fret waste. First of all, the outer rods are soldered to the filler piece.* Right: *This is then roughly sawn out with the piercing saw.*

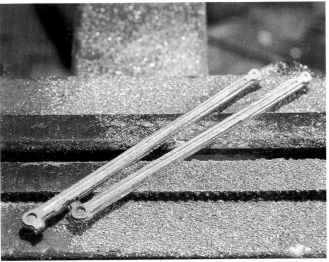

Left: *Careful filing starts to create an accurate profile.* Right: *The rods are drilled through and then the rear section (from the original fret) is sweated in place, once again using drill bits as jigs. Here we see finished and part-finished rods. Note the notch at the little end where the rod will slot into the crosshead.*

vides a couple of etches that are intended to represent these fabrications, but I discarded these and made my own, with a backward glance at the way Comet had done it. Though described as an 'advanced kit', I have to say that I was uncomfortable at the amount of improvisation and/or rectification required during the assembly sequence. I have come to regard building some etched kits as a form of scratchbuilding with prepared parts, a concept coined by Dave Bradwell in a characteristically well-argued letter in *MRJ* No. 52. Dave's B1 chassis kit, I would imagine, conforms to most people's definition of 'advanced kit'. This 9F doesn't.

Cylinder framework folded up, with brass tube for the piston rods in standard Perseverance fashion. Cylinder covers aren't provided with the kit — which seems a bit niggardly, since there's oodles of space on the etches in which some could have been drawn — so I trawled some up from my collection of offcuts and chuck-outs.

The basic form of the cylinder/slidebar assembly emerges.

The slidebar support is cut from two pieces of fret waste sweated together. After filing to shape, the halves are separated and soldered to a spacer piece. Slots are cut in the sideframes and the assembly is jigged up and soldered on site.

No smoke deflectors, valve gear or pony truck as yet, but the raw essence of a 9F is unmistakeable. I built the body and chassis concurrently, but usually the latter is completed before any cosmetic work begins.

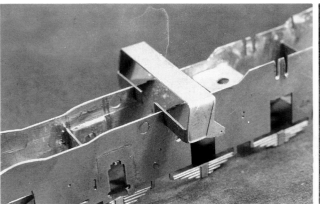

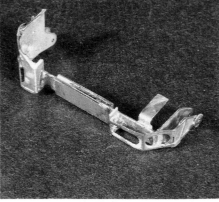

I thought everyone knew the centres of the return crank match the crank throw — evidently not. The Puffers kit (left) is 50% out; the crank at right shows how it should be. Without modification, the valve gear will tie itself in knots. Does no one ever check these things?

Left: Puffers' motion bracket is a dismal effort, bearing very little resemblance to the prototype. Hornby Dublo, even, would have made a better fist of it. My interpretation of the 9F motion bracket is a composite of the Puffers item and the equally dubious Crownline etching, but mostly made out of fret waste. Note, on the right, the seating for the cylinder that operates the reversing gear. Still to come — the massive cross-shaft for the reversing gear, plainly visible in photographs.

The cylinders and valve gear are in place. Note the importance of the cross-pieces that keep the sub-assemblies aligned with one another, especially the motion bracket, the reverser cross-shaft and the slidebar support bracket, which carries a pair of mechanical lubricators (Jackson Evans castings). I made a forked joint for the radius rod/combination lever because it's surprisingly prominent — the radius rod in the kit is too short so you need to make a new one anyway. I wish, with hindsight, that I'd made it oscillate in proto-typical fashion but there were already complications enough.

FITTING THE GEARBOX

The unique articulation feature of the Contorto soaks up a measure of displacement of the wheels on the track but the gearbox itself plainly needed to move up and down in sync with the movement of the twin beams on the rear axles (there is no space between the frames for conventional hornblocks). The motor also needed to be deterred from any urges towards rotary motion but, because it hangs in space directly above the void between the frames and the boiler, there was no way of securing it directly to the chassis. My solution, practical if far from elegant, was to solder a plate between the frames and butting against the rear of the gearbox to stop it tipping forwards. To prevent it falling over backwards, a wire runs across the front face of the gearbox and slides against the vertical edges of two flat guide pieces soldered to the frames. On the inside faces of these guides are L-shaped brackets which slide against the front face of the gearbox. The photographs should make this plainer than my convoluted prose; for added amusement while trying (or not) to fathom this, remember that the front of the gearbox faces the back of the loco.

PICK-UPS

Most things militate against making the wiring-up of a 9F a simple operation. It has deep frames, comparatively small wheels, prominent springs and brake-gear clearances measured in thousandths of an inch. The only bonus point is that, on a real 9F, there are a couple of hefty feed pipes right where our motor leads need to be, so we needn't bother about concealing them.

The thing that immediately struck me, while weighing up the options, was that there were precious few gaps where a pick-up wire could dart out from its place of concealment to make contact with a passing wheel. My 'wide' chassis makes backscratcher pick-ups unlikely, whilst top-acting wipers are obviously impossible on such an open-framed design. With beams and springs in some abundance, there are enough forces shifting about the place without plunger pick-ups weighing in with the odd gramme or two of pressure in the wrong place. Split frame construction would probably be the engineer's answer but not, I wouldn't have thought, where a Contorto gearbox is used.

Cracking the pick-up conundrum is, however, one of the things I enjoy most about building locomotives. The plan of

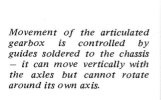

Movement of the articulated gearbox is controlled by guides soldered to the chassis – it can move vertically with the axles but cannot rotate around its own axis.

'Contorto' gearbox driven rear axle.

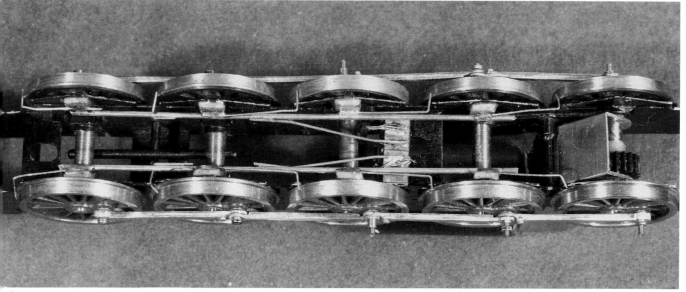

Careful thought is needed in siting and shaping the pick-ups. They don't want to be too flexible or they will quickly find something on which to short out.

Left: Pony truck from hacked-about kit components. The flat triangular plate isn't prototypical but hides the lead weight underneath. The springs are 8BA bolts. Right: Simplified dragbeam fretted out of 15-thou brass. The drawhook mates with a pin under the tender.

action ultimately decided on was to glue small pads of copperclad to the centre of each dummy spring (except the rearmost pair, where the gearbox gets in the way). I then ran a length of 0.9mm hard brass wire along each side to act as a busbar. These are tucked up between the frames — the depth of the Brimalm bearing on the centre axle dictates the highest point. The pick-ups themselves are L-shaped lengths of 0.33mm wire, soldered to the busbars and dipping round the edges of the spring to make contact with the wheelrims. The clearances are very fine but the × 2.5 magnification of my Optivisor enabled me to

Of course, there is an element of bravura in this shot but it does demonstrate that, for all the seeming complexity of the 9F chassis, each element is actually quite simple when considered in isolation.

The chassis complete. In an age dominated by easy solutions, where craftsmanship is seen as bought-in folkiness rather than a range of skills that can be practised by almost anyone, I find quiet satisfaction in the sheer effort and initiative demanded by such a project.

I could — just — have had full-width brake cross-shafts all round but didn't want the extra risk of a short from the pick-ups. Problems would have been even more likely had I used the prototypical flat pattern of cross-shaft, with its greater surface area. Cutting the middle three short really doesn't show and it also gives a little extra room for any tweaking that may be necessary. The central pull rod is double-thickness for extra structural strength.

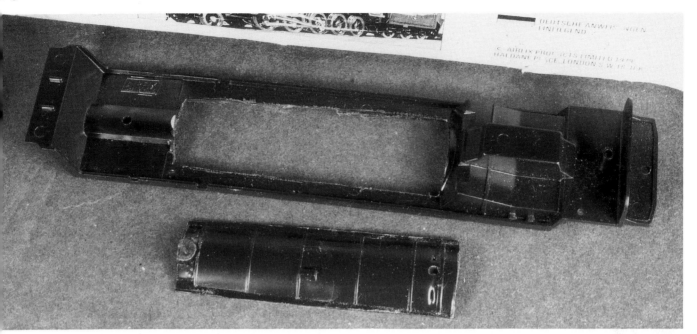

The false bottom of the boiler, clearly visible beneath the running plate, came from an obliging Airfix Evening Star *kit. The inside of the boiler is packed with lead.*

get all but a couple right first time, without any tweaking. Once I was happy with the electricals, I could proceed with the brake gear — which was a piece of cake — and the motion. Here, I am afraid, the toolkit had to come out to put right some mistakes: radius rod too short, eccentric crank too long, and a very poor motion bracket. The pictures show my remedies.

BODYWORK

Not for the first time, I may be imagining things but the current Hornby version of the 9F seems to be substantially the same moulding as the ancient Triang model that I used as the basis for my BR1C conversion in *MRJ*. It's still a damn fine piece of work, all the same. I bought mine as a spare for £3.50 and that to me is value.

Stripping down consisted mostly of deft scalpel work to lose the cab doors and handrails, the firebox piping, the reverser rod and the clack feeds (although the clacks themselves can stay, ready for a little extra detailing with brass rod). Later versions of this body have separate handrails, which is good because removing the moulded-on ones on the first 9F conversion I did was a bit of a pain. At the front end, the double chimney can go — it looks a bit underscale to me — as well as the smokebox lamp iron, door handles, the step between the front frames and the various lugs for the smoke deflectors.

With that lot out of the way, we can make a start on detailing the body. I tend

Slow, patient work with a new blade gets rid of unwanted detail such as the moulded firebox pipework, which looks one-dimensional and far too tidy.

The cab sides on Hornby's 9F are pretty good but the front spectacle windows are a nonsense.

Left: *The spectacles opened out to their correct dimensions.* Right: *Etched window surrounds from Jackson Evans capture a difficult shape superbly – the cab windows are one of the key features of the 9Fs. Note, in the bottom corner of the cab, the representation of the hatches that give access to the boiler washout plugs. I drilled a hole, filed it square and added a little square of Plastikard at a slight angle.*

Above left: *Double chimney removed and filled, along with the recesses into which the plastic smoke deflectors were plugged.* Above right: *The safety valves are made of telescopic tubing and pins. The mounting plate is cut from 5-thou brass. There may be an awful long way to go yet but I always get the feeling, once the handrails are on, that the end is in sight.*

to begin at one end and work my way forward, rather than adding details here, there and everywhere. This model has the usual freewheeling mix of bought-in and scratchbuilt details — buffers and steps are by Comet, couplings, smoke deflectors and cab spectacles came from Jackson Evans, turned chimney by Crownline, underside of boiler from an Airfix 9F kit. Everything else is improvised. Tender details are mentioned separately.

Much of what needed to be done is routine and I hope that the pictures and their related captions cover anything that is noteworthy. Of more than particular interest, however, is the pipework that is such a

The cab roof shutter is from 5-thou brass with runners of Microstrip. The raised lip on the front section is from the useful Scale Link fret of riveted strips (ref SLF 16).

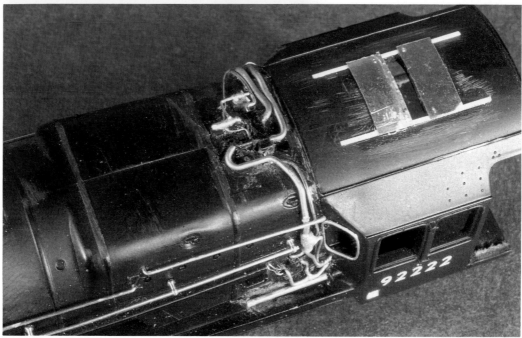

The firebox pipework was built up on site in 5, 15 and 30 amp fuse wire, soldered where practicable and, where not, glued into holes drilled into the plastic bodywork. I made my own boiler fittings, although excellent lost-wax castings for the BR Standard locos are available from Steamline of Sheffield.

distinctive feature of this locomotive, and I might say a word or two here, since I always go to considerable trouble with it on my models. Features such as injectors and firebox piping play a large part in creating the character of BR Standard locomotives, just as the subtle curves of a splasher or the profile of a dome or chimney do for an older generation of engines, and we need to model them as accurately as we can if we are to capture the special flavour of our prototype. I use a mixture of soft brass wire (not Alan Gibson's hard stuff, which isn't so amenable to curving) and fuse wire in various ratings, as well as small nuts and

washers (14 and 16BA mostly) and brass capillary tube sawn into little collars and suchlike.

Before starting work, I have a good long look at the relevant photographs and any drawings that look as though they might be trustworthy, and try and figure out what goes where (I haven't a clue what job these things do on the real thing) and how the fabrication of the different bits might best be effected. I might, for instance, need to decide if I can butt-joint two different thicknesses of wire together, or whether tube might be better. The telescopic brass tubing from the K&S metal centres is very good and if it's a bit overscale for a partic-

ular application, it can be skimmed in the chuck of a mini-drill to reduce the wall thickness.

After this, it's just a matter of bending and forming and trimming, then offering up and maybe bending some more until everything goes where it should. It may not be possible to match scale diameters exactly and if there is a discrepancy I err on the side of underscale — over-chunky pipework looks bad. Real-life injector pipework tended to suffer a few unexpected knocks and, like bent handrails, twisted running plates and wonky buffer beams, the effects are often quite spectacular. Unless executed with consummate skill,

Left: *Grinding down the domed head of a cast buffer (nickel silver in this case) with a carborundum disc.* Right: *What a fine job the Margate pattern-maker made of the buffer beam, with all the rivets as per prototype. Additional detailing is simple but subtle.*

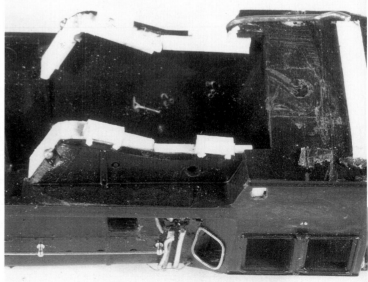

Left: *You can see very little of the cab interior, so I left it alone apart from adding a new chequer plate floor. The cab rear and doors are from black Plastikard, with beadings in .33 wire.* Right: *Ashpan detail from Microstrip.*

however, this kind of feature in 4mm scale just looks like crummy workmanship and I think it's best to be as neat as possible. For most modellers, myself included, neat probably means slightly bent anyway, no matter how hard we try.

As far as is practicable, I will solder up my injectors, manifolds and their related feeds as a separate assembly. A resistance soldering unit, of course, is the bee's knees for this kind of work, but for some years now I've also been using, quite interchangeably, a 1mm bit on my 25w Antex XS. This gives pretty good control over where the silver stuff goes and the degree of precision it facilitates is only marginally less than that of the RSU.

Some prefabrication work on the piping can be carried out on the bench but a lot of it is best done on-site. If you're fast, the 1mm bit isn't going to melt anything; it may be tempting to use a smaller iron, say 15w or so, but in my experience these tiddlers take so long to heat up the copper fuse wire that is one of the main ingredients of my pipework that the plastic starts to take umbrage.

If you have good photographs it should be obvious where most of the pipes go and it's as well to use these vanishing points for anchorage. The bodywork can be discreetly drilled and the wires or pipes bent around and tucked in neatly with a small blob of epoxy or cyano. Black plasticine seems to be quite hard to find but it's a good material for filling any holes that may survive, especially after painting. Split pins are also useful for holding pipework to the body and can represent pipe unions quite

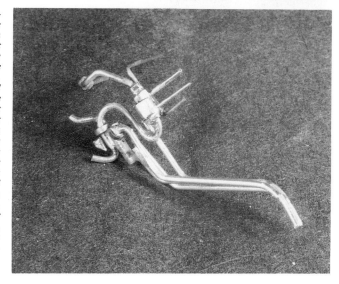

The fearsome complexities of the injectors are represented in softish brass wire – most 0.9mm – and capillary tube, with a few washers and nuts here and there. There are twenty-odd soldered joints in this little lot, which meant I had to move very fast with a 1mm bit on a 25w iron – the assembly only fell apart on me once. Most of the tricky stuff was done with the work clamped up in a vice, which doubled as a heat sink. I soldered the injector pipework to the chassis, using the pipes themselves as anchor points.

effectively — elsewhere, a little twist of 5 amp fuse wire serves very well.

THE TENDER

To model a BR1G-fitted 9F I would probably go for Hornby's 9F tender moulding, which also does for their Britannia. It's quite a reasonable approximation of the standard design, though the nomenclature is different. This one-size-fits-all philosophy is OK here, since the BR1/1A and 1G tender bodies are outwardly the same apart from the filler dome. The Hornby chassis moulding needs a lot of work — I'd ditch it and use Comet's sideframe etch and

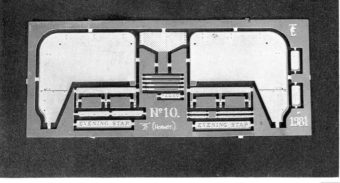

The Jackson Evans smoke deflectors are very well detailed and come complete with all the inner bracing.

The superb Jackson Evans smoke deflectors were the last thing to go on, to avoid damage. The front end of a 9F is very characteristic. Every detail has a part to play in creating the overall effect.

axlebox castings — but the basic bodyshell is sound and is available cheaply as a spare. Kitmaster's *Evening Star* tender — latterly available through Dapol — is another possibility but again some remedial attention is needed.

As the basis of one of the high-sided tenders there is also, of course, the BR1B design which Bachmann produce for the BR Standard class 4 they inherited from Mainline. This is a much better moulding and needs only cosmetic reworking to create a BR1C or BR1K tender for a 9F. I already have a BR1C 9F so I chose the BR1F tender instead! This design was unique to the Eastern Region 9Fs apart from ten supplied to the Southern for a batch of BR Standard class 5s, Nos 73110–19. DJH do this tender — a composite brass and whitemetal affair — as an option with their kits for these two classes but it's not available separately. This is no bad thing, as I don't think it's very good at all — the side profiles and the tender rear are wrong.

Infinitely better is Dave Alexander's whitemetal kit for this tender (he does the BR1C version too) which is also sold under the Crownline name. The castings are crisp, detailed, accurate and clean-fitting — they don't come much better than this. Even the cast tender steps look pretty good but I happened to have some etched Comet steps to hand — an *MRJ* review sample, I think — and so I used these instead. I also had a set of Comet's BR-pattern buffers in lost-wax nickel and these got the nod instead of the whitemetal ones provided.

I was glad to be using a whitemetal tender because, other than a few detailing components, we haven't really seen much of this popular material in these pages. Some modellers are terribly sniffy about whitemetal but I have no problem with it. In the right hands it can have surprising delicacy and it is the best material I know for suggesting heavy, solid objects like springs and axleboxes — it also possesses weight and bulk. This was important, because I was going to build this as a weighted tender with floating front axles, to ballast the back end of my 9F.

Except where very small components are involved, I always solder-assemble whitemetal kits. I use a temperature-controlled Litesold 50w iron specially balanced for whitemetal work — Hubert Carr sells them; they're expensive but you'll never

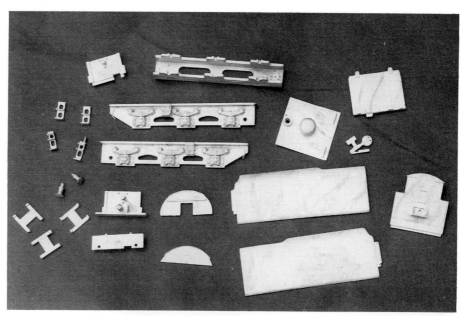

Dave Alexander's cast whitemetal kit for the BR1F tender.

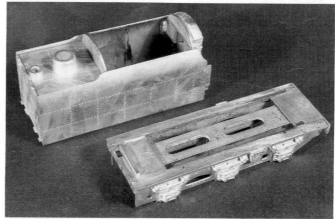

Basic tender body and chassis assembled. Comet do an etched BR tender chassis which fits the Alexander bodywork perfectly, but I wanted the extra weight of the whitemetal castings.

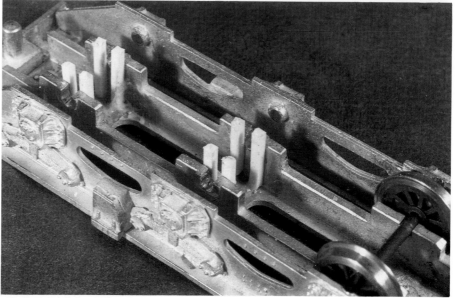

Tender chassis modified to allow for floating axles. Approximately 2mm needs to be taken off the front frames — the extra length being, presumably, to allow the tender to couple with a Hornby 9F.

melt a casting. The same gentleman's Red Label flux is the one for me, every time, though I'm promiscuous in my choice of solders.

Being snug-fitting and practically flash-free, the tender went together pretty quickly. I found it necessary, however, to modify the chassis, which is designed for 14mm diameter Romford wheels rigidly mounted, to allow for scale 3ft 3in diameter wheels with the front two axles floating. The fixed rear axle locates in holes on the inside of the axleboxes; if the scale diameter wheels were carried, as designed, in the dummy inner frames, the ride

Tender water filler drilled away.

The assembled tender body, clearly showing the additional details in brass. Just the lamp irons to go on now.

Bereft of its smokebox numberplate, No. 92121 is seen in typically workaday condition at Stoke on 24th July 1966.

height would be wrong. I made slots for the front two axles by gluing strips of 60-thou square Microstrip 2mm apart on the inner frames. If they wear, they wear, but they're easily replaced.

Detailing of the tender was routine — wire handrails, brass ladder, scoop/brake handles and so on — but, rather late in the day, I decided to model the water filler open. Like open cab roof shutters or the fireman's gas-mask bag hung over the brake standard, this is one of those little details that breathes life into a model. I put the tender body in the vice, protected by strips of softwood, and then drilled away the cast filler. I made a new one out of thin-walled ¼in brass tube, soldered to the whitemetal body by lightly smearing the inside with solder paint, tinning the body with low-melt, then adding a drop or two of flux and applying the tip of my RSU probe to the brass. A hiss, a sizzle, and the solders fuse together. This is how all the other brass and nickel silver parts were fitted to the whitemetal body — it's so much easier and quicker than other methods. The lid is the casting from the kit, suitably thinned to remove its locating

plug. Attaching the lid to the edge of the filler alone probably isn't enough and a little support inside the body of the tank filler provides an additional fixing point for extra security.

WEIGHTING

With two sets of beams, a sprung centre axle and half the weight of the tender pressing down on the dragbeam, it was obvious that there would be a fair bit of science involved in balancing this engine. Instead, I simply shoved in lead until it ran well. There's about 6oz in the boiler and another 3oz between the frames, aft of the gearbox. The finished loco weighs 1lb 3oz and I am pleased to note that this does not seem to place any undue mechanical strain on the Delrin gears, although I took the precaution of Aralditing the final drive in place on the axle.

SURFACE FINISH

With the exception of the celebrated *Evening Star*, I doubt if 9Fs were ever cleaned between works visits. Even when fresh from the paint shop, they looked as if they'd been coated with bitumen, applied

with a clapped-out six-inch brush. Anything further than the 'exhibition finish' beloved of professional model-painters is difficult to imagine and even this tartily glossy look lasted a matter of hours. I have a photograph of *Evening Star* less than a week after its release to traffic and already it is heavily streaked and stained, with the boiler top blackened and the motion tarnished. This is not at all the kind of light dusting that many modellers use to represent the weathering of an engine when still recently ex-works, a period that is usually interpreted as meaning anything up to five years.

I never make up the weatheirng of a loco. OK, I may know a bit about it but I always use — at least as my starting point — some good colour photographs of the kind of thing I have in mind. During the 1960s more and more people began using colour transparency film and as a result we have plenty of pictures of 9Fs to confirm what those of us of mature years saw with our own eyes. I think I would find it quite difficult to model the railways of the pre-nationalisation era, not so much on account of the scarcity of colour images

but because my perception of this period is drawn almost exclusively from black-and-white pictures. I have never felt very comfortable with colour photographs in the model railway magazines because they introduce an entirely unknown dimension to the way I think about these things.

I may see the Lancashire & Yorkshire and the Great Eastern in black and white but the 9Fs are definitely in wide-screen Technicolor. To my way of thinking, colour is every bit as important as finescale wheels and correctly spaced lettering in establishing the visual character of any model locomotive (we might, for a moment, tactfully ignore the fact that this one was built to oo gauge!). Having primed the various brass bits with brushed-on Protec, I sprayed the entire loco with two or three variegated shades of Gunmetal and Matt Leather and left it to harden overnight. Airbrushing leaves a wonderfully consistent finish, but for weathering this needs to be broken up. My methods centre on a little localised rubbing and texturing — in this case, a stiffish, flat brush lightly moistened with lighter fuel and then, when almost dry, stroked vertically down the boiler and firebox. Most of the background colour still remains but it is not quite so uniform as before.

The main weathering is done as usual with Carr's powders, mostly dark greys and browns. This is brushed on much as one would apply paint and then flicked away, but I also find a stabbing or stippling motion creates interesting effects. Gently brushing on the powders serves to tickle up the metallic particles in the Gunmetal part of the base coat, bringing lustre and body to the underlying colour. I do not subscribe to the orthodoxy that everything

should be matt, which I find has a deadening effect on models because too much light is absorbed.

After the first application of powders, I go away for a while and then take another look. Usually this appraisal calls for a little more airbrushing and then a little more powder, and so on and so on until I feel I can safely leave it alone. The key words, always, are observation and restraint. As a case in point, prototype photographs may reveal a lot of lime-streaking on 9Fs. This is a feature so often seen on weathered models that it has become a cliché, but it should be treated circumspectly. Long white trails running down the boiler from clacks and safety valves were evidence of an exceptionally hard water supply at the home depot, so much so that chemical treatment was necessary. Toton, Annesley, Wellingborough and Langwith were sheds with notoriously bad water and their engines showed all the tell-tell signs. A measure of leakage around the regulator valve is almost universal on 9Fs but you will not find anything like so much lime-

streaking on engines from soft-water distructs.

IN RETROSPECT

This was a very satisfying project — but then all of the ones in this book have been. It was good to have the experience of my earlier 9F to go on and it was also pleasing to ring the changes. I think particularly of the chassis which, for me, was very much a step into the unknown. And yet, at the same time, it wasn't, because it involved putting existing methods and technologies to fresh uses. The only element that was entirely new to me was the Brimalm bearings, which I look forward to using again on a fully sprung chassis.

I know that bouncy 4mm scale 9Fs exist but, for whatever reason, I didn't want to use springs alone. Over the years I've given a lot of thought to how a compensated chassis for a ten-coupled engine might be designed. I have asked quite a few modellers of high renown — no names, no pack drill — how they would go about it and the answer, universally, has been

"Dunno, I've never tried." Nor, in the finescale modelling press, have I read anything specifically related to 2–10–0s, though I'm sure if I looked harder I might have found something. I guess I had to wait until I felt confident enough of my own abilities to go it alone.

I certainly never thought that I'd be the one to write the article I never found. And yet, less than an hour after the almost-complete locomotive ran under power on the track for the first time (in other words, when it was far too late for a rethink on anything but the most minor points of detail), I remembered a locomotive that had always been an inspiration for me — Jack Newton's magnificent scratchbuilt 9F in the September 1963 *Model Railway News*. I rummaged through my back numbers and there it was. I don't know why I'd forgotten it — even when I was still into three-rail, this awesomely powerful, twin-motored model made a huge impression on me and I have re-read the article many times since.

I'd always thought this was the kind of grand spectacular that I'd like to attempt one day and thirty-odd years on, I got my chance. It is strange that it should have slipped my memory and yet the message seems clear enough now — I was meant to do it my way, and not to rely on precedent.

The fact that the *MRN* 9F was 92245 and mine was 92145 was just coincidence (or was it?). In almost every respect, though, the models were totally different, and this diversity is something I welcome. Anyway, now it's built and I can't change anything, although I wonder about adding a working lubricator drive. I'm sufficiently pleased with my version, though, to apply the same principles to yet another 9F — a rebuilt Crosti, this time. But that, as we say, will have to be another story . . .

CONCLUSIONS

At irregular intervals during the eighteen months or so that it took me to build, photograph and describe the locomotives that are featured in this book, I found time — when I thought Paul Karau wasn't looking — to assemble a kit or two and even to do a little scratchbuilding. I'm glad I did, because it helped me to understand and put into context the modelling philosophies whose exposition has occupied these past few pages.

Through building some top-of-the-range kits (and the odd stinker) side-by-side with these six projects, I became aware of how eclectic and individual, if far from unique, my methods had become. At their heart is a spirit of improvisation, not through any conscious decision but because it simply happens this way. As a creative process, it's more like collage or patchwork than model engineering — a bit from here, a bit from there, some recycled junk, some found objects, some things bought or made specifically, all put together with a common goal in mind. Bob Barlow, who knows about these things, calls it 'découpage', but I'll go for 'pick 'n' mix'.

Whatever name we might care to put on it, I came to realise that what this approach offers me, more than anything, is an abundance of choice. Scratchbuilding provides an even greater, indeed almost infinite range of options but not all of us want to go this route. The kitbuilder, however, is very much tied by other people's logic — the decision of the designer or manufacturer to build in compensation or to ignore it completely, to provide this kind of tender but not that, to use this motor/gearbox configuration rather than any other. Of course, the modeller is quite at liberty to go his own way, though this may involve wholesale modification and the junking of many bought-in components. This is not the most economical or inspiring approach and yet it is one that I repeatedly follow with kits, because I can't see any other way of getting what I want.

My magpie approach to building locos pays scant regard to convention (standardisation, as Nigel Gresley once said, is a form of stagnation) but at the same time, I doubt if there has been anything startlingly new in these pages. My manual skills are quite poor by comparison with many modellers, so perhaps I have to compensate by being a bit more imaginative, and learning how to steal ideas and use them in new applications. Also, one needs to know the

field and how to play it — what articles there have been that might be relevant, who makes what and where to get it, the difference between this product and that, the things to avoid. In the end, it all comes down to experience — and experience, it should be said, is only gained through a willingness to experiment. There is, as far as I know, no fast-track access to modelling expertise, no software solution that will do the job in a fraction of the time. It's all down to rehearsing the old hand-eye coordination, over and over and over again. And because I value old-fashioned craftsmanship, I'm glad it's this way.

This brings me to something else that, with the benefit of hindsight, I'd like to add. Maybe some people make models where everything goes swimmingly from start to finish, but I'm not one of them. Some maddening cock-up or accident befalls everything I make, and the locos built for this book are no exception — the newly completed tender top of the 4F being all but crushed flat, the fun and games with the B1 transmission (and once I'd finally got the loco running nicely, I promptly dropped it on a marble worktop), the weathering of the Terrier going, at one stage, almost totally out of control. Every such episode causes distress but each, in its way, is also an opportunity to learn. Whilst I do occasionally throw things at the workroom wall, it's more usually the case, when things go wrong, that I find myself genuinely intrigued to know why this or that isn't doing what I thought it would. If a model is really giving me grief, then I just down tools and do something else — it's amazing how problems diminish after being left to settle for a couple of days. It all comes right in the end, if we want it to.

That's the psychology. The two practical questions that I imagine would be uppermost in most readers' minds will be, is it any quicker doing it my way, or any cheaper? This invites a comparison, but I'm not sure with what. My County didn't take anywhere near as long as an equivalent Mitchell or Finney kit, because of the not inconsiderable amount of time saved by not having to roll the boiler, form the footplate, build the tender and so on and so on. However, I still had to make the firebox, do the backhead, get the chassis running and many other things that were directly comparable. As a result, the model took much longer than, say, a whitemetal kit built straight out the box, without any modification to or refinement of the parts supplied and assembled with a simple rigid

chassis. But then it isn't a race, and it's perhaps more reasonable to say that each build occupied about the same length of time that it would take me to produce a souped-up version of a halfway-reasonable kit for a similar type of engine.

Although my composite models are more expensive than a complete, off-the-shelf RTR loco — but not all that much dearer — the cost factor, surprisingly, is quite difficult to assess. The 9F, all in, worked out at slightly less than the DJH kit for the same loco. The kit has Romford wheels but no motor or gears, and various other features which the individual modeller may or may not want to stick with — but which he has to pay for nevertheless (and to which should be added the cost of the drive train and any replacement fittings and parts that may be required). I reckon I got much more for less — head to head, at least 30–35% cheaper than a finescale upgrade of the DJH kit. As a rule of thumb, then, I would reckon that these models cost about as much as a basic kit for the same class of loco but — and it's a big but — for similar money I'm getting a posh chassis, good wheels, a high-quality drive system and many cosmetic refinements. All of these are plus points that, to me, suggest I'm getting excellent value for money.

So how do we leave things? I think the key issue to be addressed is not whether one method or material or modelling technique is faster or cheaper or has more validity than any other, but rather that we should simply enjoy building locomotives and get fulfilment and satisfaction out of what we do. If this kind of scissors-and-paste modelling doesn't appeal, don't do it — buy a kit instead, or scratchbuild. We don't 'have to' do anything, if we don't want to, whether it's sawing up proprietary mouldings, applying individually riveted overlays or producing fancy drive trains. But something impels me to do these things and it has nothing whatever to do with convenience or profit or self-aggrandisement or material progress or any of the allegedly desirable tenets foisted on us — and, in my case, immediately shrugged off again — by consumer society. Model-making, in whatever form best suits us, allows us to be ourselves for a little while. And if our approach is in some way peculiar to us, and maybe even a little eccentric, then it's quite a nice way of discovering who we are and what we stand for. This, I'm given to understand, is what life is all about.